# THE FACTS THAT BOWLED ME OVER



## REKHA SINGH

**BLUEROSE PUBLISHERS**

India | U.K.

Copyright ©Rekha Singh2023

For permissions requests or inquiries regarding this publication,
please contact:

BLUEROSE PUBLISHERS
www.BlueRoseONE.com
info@bluerosepublishers.com
+91 8882 898 898
+4407342408967

ISBN: 978-93-5741-061-8

Printed in INDIA

Cover design: [Muskan Sachdeva]
Typesetting: [Rohit]

First Edition: June 2023

*But for the ever inquisitive boys -Arjun, Siddharth, Atman, Shaurya, Aryan and Shaan, who want to know everything under the sky and beyond.. my Mom and Dad, who raised us with this gargantuan appetite to know the unknown..my sister, brothers and sisters-in-law and needless to say the husband, this book wouldn't have been possible!*

*Interestingly none, but one knows I am writing this book...*

*'Facts That Bowled Me Over' is dedicated to all similarly curious and 'craving for more' hungry minds..*

# PREFACE

Storytelling is an art and like any art form, it needs two participants conjugated through a medium. So here we are - ME the Teller, YOU the Listener and the Book, the Medium!

The stories I am sharing are no yarns, they are hard Facts- facts that are literally unknown, collected from all around- they are interesting, elating, intriguing, bizarre, occasionally disturbing, even outlandish and sometimes enraging, whatever emotion they prompt, trust me each one of them is exceedingly fascinating. The book has four sections, each unravelling incredible facts from diverse realms- some needed just a couple of lines to tell, while the others required much more than that to convey their case - in short the book is a collection of big and small unheard stories, each one gripping, compelling and pulling us in. For instance few would know that in 1938, the TIME magazine put Hitler on its cover page as the Man of the Year and the following year they proposed his name for the Nobel Peace Prize. After facing a backlash, it was clarified that the suggestion was a sarcastic one. Even Swedish MP Erik Gottfrid Christian Brandt nominated Hitler, but on being questioned, he said that shouldn't be taken seriously. No Nobel Prize for Peace was awarded in the year 1939. Or this one, that Japan has specially constructed Turtle Tunnels to save them from being run over by trains. Then there's yet another really interesting fact, one about the Olympics- The Olympics held between 1912 and 1948, apart from the sporting disciplines, also had competitions in Literature, Music, Sculpting, Painting and Architecture.

I had a great time compiling similarly engrossing stories, 1313 in all. Hope you too relish them as much as I did during my journey through these engaging pieces.

Go Ahead! Have Fun !!!!

# CONTENTS


**THE INTRIGUING WORLD OF NATURE & SCIENCE**

Plantae ....1

Animal Kingdom ....13

Human Body & Mind ....26

The Corporeal Environment ....36

Space & Technology ....42

Tidbits ....51

**FROM THE PAGES OF HISTORY**

The Ancients ....63

The World Of The Royals ....70

The Victorian Era ....81

Customs & Traditions ....90

Christmas Trivia ....95

Olios From The Past ....102

**THE WORLD OF ENTERTAINMENT & RECREATION**

The Arts ....128

Language & Literature ....139

Games & Sports ....150

Olympics ....161

The Show Business ....166

**THE POTPOURRI**

Innovations ....182

Record Makers ....199

Food Facts ....210

What The Heck…!!! ....222

Miscellany ....236

*Acknowledgment* ....253

# THE INTRIGUING WORLD OF NATURE & SCIENCE

## Plantae

*I go to Nature to be soothed, healed and have my Senses put in order.*
-John Burroughs

1. Vanilla, the second most expensive spice after saffron, belongs to the family of orchid and is the only variety out of 25,000 species to produce it. With more than 200 flavour compounds, the flower was introduced to Europe by the Spanish in the 16th century after their conquest of the Aztecs. Since it could be pollinated only by an indigenous bee 'Melipona', efforts to grow it commercially outside its native environment of Mexico failed. It wasn't until 1841, Edmond Albius, a 12-year-old enslaved boy in the French island of Réunion invented a method to pollinate it by hand. This hand pollination revolutionized the production of vanilla, which is used even to this day.

2. Banana, one of the world's oldest fruits, has its origin in India and South East Asia. Known by its Sanskrit name kadalikā, it is believed to have been taken by Alexander in 4th BCE to the Middle East where it was christened 'banana' ("finger"in Arabic). From there the fruit travelled to Africa, Latin America and by the 15th century landed in the Caribbeans. The 17th and 18th century saw the import of the exotic fruit which had made its way into the English palate. In 1835 Sir Joseph Paxton, the head gardener at Chatsworth Estate, cultivated them at the greenhouse. He gave it the botanical name "musa cavendishii", after his employer, William Cavendish, the 6th Duke of Devonshire. Although there are around 300 varieties of bananas grown around the world, the Cavendish variety tops the chart, where almost all bananas available in North America and Europe are of the cavendish variety. In India, however, 15-20 varieties of bananas including dwarf cavendish, are commercially cultivated.

3.  The giant water lily was first spotted in 1801 in Bolivia but its description was published only in 1837 by John Lindley, with the botanical name Victoria Regia, after the British monarch Queen Victoria. Victoria Regia aka Victoria amazonica is the world's largest water lily plant. With its stalk about 26 feet long, and the floating leaves acquiring a diameter of up to 10 feet, other life forms such as algae or the organisms that feed on it, cannot survive beneath its enormous sunlight blocking expanse. The pollination process of the flower, which lasts just about 48 hours- one night female and the other male, is quite interesting. On the first night of its bloom, the sweet smelling white lily allures beetles. Once trapped, the flower snaps shut and remains closed until the following evening. During this period the plant produces pollen and changes from female to male. By the next day it has lost both, its scent and colour. Now it is a red purple fully mature flower, with its purpose fulfilled, it closes up descending deep into the water. Meanwhile, coated with pollen, the released beetle flies off to the next white flower. Joseph Paxton was inspired by the pattern of these lily leaves when he designed Crystal Palace in London in 1851.

*(Victoria amazonica, lives in sluggish waters in the Amazon Valley of South America : Getty Images )*

4. Scientists maintain that, for coffee plants to acquire the biochemical defence mechanism against insects, took a couple of million years. A high dose of caffeine can be toxic to insects. Consequently insects too, evolved taste receptors that keep them warned of such plants. It's not just insects, but other plants too are affected. When the dead coffee leaves fall on the ground, they infect the soil with caffeine there, thus killing the competition from other plants. Caffeine has almost similar effect on humans- a moderate consumption acts as a stimulant but toxic if consumed in high doses.

5. The tropical fungus Ophiocordyceps creates zombies out of insects by infecting their central nervous systems. According to National Geographic, once it stays in an insect's body for a period of nine days, it takes complete control of the host's movements. It can then make it climb trees, then convulse and fall into the cool, moist soil underneath, where the fungi thrive. The fungus then waits until the sun is high at noon, and then forces the host to bite a leaf. Once it nibbles into it, all that's waiting for it is- it's death.

6. Traditional winemaking allowed the pressed grape juice to go through all the natural processes needed for maturing the wine therefore it did not necessitate any filtering or refining during its bottling. Unlike the modern times, where wine styles and consumer pressure demand a faster processing, often compels the manufacturers to use "processing aids". It's during fining, that animal products such as gelatin, egg whites, milk protein, crustaceans shell, and fish bladder protein are used. Since they get filtered out before packaging, 'fining' agents are not labelled as ingredients on the final bottle of wine. So yes, your wine might have animal derivatives, it all depends on how it was clarified during the 'fining' process.

7. Cellulose, which is essentially sawdust, is digestive wood pulp. It is used in various shredded cheese products and cereals to prevent them from clumping and is FDA approved.

8. The beautiful orchids your florist sells as 'fresh' are actually decades old. Once germinated, the Orchid takes about five to seven years to bloom. An orchid, which has a lifespan of a hundred years, is sturdy enough to stay fresh for a long period of time.

9. The baobab, called the 'Tree of Life', has been around for 200 million years. In all, there are 9 species of baobab found in the world. Six of these grow only in Madagascar, 2 in Africa and one, not clear how, but has made it to Australia. This succulent tree may grow as tall as 12 metres and live up to 3,000 years. To withstand long periods of droughts, the life giver can store some hundred thousand litres of water in its trunk. Baobab products include textiles, rubber, soap, medicine, fresh leaves, and fruits. Some of the trunks are so huge, measuring more than 40 metres in circumference, are being used for different purposes, such as a jail, post offices, bush pubs etcetera. In fact the Sunland baobab tree houses a wine cellar and bar. It sure is a unique creation of Nature!

*( Madagascar:Fony baobab (L),estimated to be more than 1,000 years old, Grandidier's baobab (R ) an endangered species :. Encyclopedia Britannica)*

10. A 2020 study led by Clemson University scientists determined that the UV pigmentation in flowers has increased over a period of time, which has led to the degradation of their pollen. Although human eyes may not detect the loss of bright hues, it poses a serious problem for pollinators like bees, who are majorly attracted to bright colourful flowers. Thus the deteriorating quality of pollen and not enough pollination activities are impacting the ecological survival of plants and in turn humans.

11. An Oak tree can live up to a thousand years. Unlike other trees, this one starts fruiting only after they are at least 50 years old and can produce about 10 million acorns during its lifetime.

12. The titan arum is the largest unbranched flower in the world. It is also known as the 'corpse' or 'carrion' flower, because of the smell it produces, which is that of rotting meat. The largest scientifically documented inflorescence of the titan arum is 306 cm from the tuber and 274 cm from the surface of the soil.

13. The Bristlecone pines are almost prehistoric trees. The oldest among these Methuselah (nicknamed after the longest-lived Biblical character Methuselah), is located in the Inyo National Forest, California. To protect the oldest of all living things from vandalism, Methuselah, its precise location remains undisclosed for the public by the US Forest Service. Methuselah's age, which is over 4,789 years, was determined by the core samples taken in 1957.

14. Chilli pepper is a berry fruit of plants from the genus Capsicum. It is believed to have originated in Bolivia and first cultivated in Mexico. The heat in a chilli is caused by its active ingredient Capsaicin and its hotness is measured in Scoville Heating Unit (SHU), a method which was developed by American pharmacologist Wilbur Scoville in 1912. It involved testing the level of pungency or heat of a pepper by a panel of specially trained tasters, who sampled a diluted version of pepper and gave a value. With the development of technology, more accurate computerised testing methods which indicate parts per million of capsaicin, have evolved. Chilli, which has been a part of human diets since about BCE 7,500, comes in 400 varieties. With 2,200,000 SHU, Carolina Reaper, created by American breeder Ed Currie is the hottest, but the most expensive is the Peruvian one, 'Aji Charapita', which would cost you a staggering $25000 for a kilogram. Although chilli pepper is grown across the globe, India is its largest producer, consumer and exporter and also dominates the international chilli market.

15. The banana, a berry, is the tallest herbaceous plant, known to man. With an annual consumption of more than a 100 million world over, it's the fourth most consumed agricultural product after rice, corn, and wheat.

16. Even though the bell peppers may appear the same- the green, yellow, orange, red or the rare purple are all different. The green colour of the pepper isn't its unripe stage nor is the red colour indicative of it being ripe. The large furrowed fruits are technically berries and come from genetically different varieties of plants.

17. Russian scientists from the Institute of Cell Biophysics revived the oldest ever, a 32,000-year-old seed cache of "silene stenophylla", a white flowered native plant, in 2012. The seeds unearthed from 38 metres beneath the permafrost in Siberia, are believed to have been buried by some Ice Age squirrels.

18. The seeds of the Alsomitra macrocarpa tree have paper-thin wings, which are produced by a football sized pod. These wings, which make them look like giant gliders, help them disperse hundreds of metres across the forests before they settle down.

19. One of Australia's oldest and most distinctive trees is the Idiot fruit. Also known as Ribbonwood and the Green Dinosaur because of its ancient lineage, it is found nowhere in the world other than the rainforests of North Queensland, particularly in the Daintree. It bears unusually large seeds, which may be something around 80mm in size. The oldest known fossils of this highly toxic fruit date back 120 million years.

20. The largest organism in the world is a fungus. Also known as honey mushrooms, Armillaria ostoyae, was first discovered in 1998 in Oregon's Blue Mountain region. The enormous fungal mat that covers an area of 2,384 acres, is not visible on the surface because it is composed of underground filaments that connect the honey mushrooms we see blooming overground in autumn. One of the major reasons for its spreading so massively is lack of competition for land and the other is its dependence on both live and dead wood for nutrients, which is available to it in abundance.

21. Ears of corn generally have an even number of rows, which is usually sixteen.

22. Most of the orchids do not produce nectar, therefore the professional growers lure pollinators by creating flowers that resemble a female wasp and even produce scent that attracts male wasps. In the process of mating with these, the wasps pollinate the plant.

23. Apple seeds produce apple trees, but they aren't the same as their parents. Seeds from a Melntosh or Honey Crunch apple won't produce the same fruit. To achieve that, they are grafted. A portion of one plant bud or scion is placed into the other plant's stem, root or branch to make it grow as one and that's how you enjoy the fruit-same tree, just split apart.

24. Orchid seeds are the tiniest in the world and can only be seen under a microscope. A single pod may have some 3 million seeds

25. Lithops, a genus of succulent plants in the ice plant family, Aizoaceae, are native to southern parts of Africa. Known as pebble plants or living stones, they camouflage themselves by blending in with the surrounding rocks and pebbles and become one with them. Although lithops grow mostly underground, their translucent top layer allows sunlight in, which gets turned into energy by the plant. Researchers hope that studying the plant and its ability to harness both bright light above ground and low light below it, would help develop more efficient crops in the future.

*(Lithops:Living Stones" whose rocklike camouflage protects them from herbivores.*
*Image Credit: Pinterest)*

26. The Yoruba people in the southwest part of Nigeria are known to give birth
to more twins, than anywhere else in the world. The possible explanation
offered is that the yam variety they regularly consume could have a
stimulating effect on ovaries, resulting in twins.

27. The cavendish variety of bananas do not reproduce naturally, instead they
are cultivated via identical cloning as a monoculture crop for commercial
purposes. Large areas of land have been brought under banana plantations,
leading to not just massive deforestation and biodiversity degeneration in
the region but even affecting the fruit itself. The agricultural scientists have
raised concerns that the lack of genetic diversity, excessive use of pesticides
and chemicals could endanger the fruit and push it closer to its extinction.

28. One among many reasons why some trees are able to live for hundreds or
even thousands of years, is a condition called "negligible senescence", which
means that instead of declining in health with age, these trees actually
become healthier.

29. Bananas, almost identically curve upwards, it's because of the phenomena
of negative geotropism, meaning instead of growing towards the gravity, as
the roots do, bananas turn back towards the sun, thereby becoming slightly
curved in shape.

30. Phytoremediation is a plant-based, cost effective sustainable technology for
environmental cleanup. It uses the hyperaccumulators to detox the soil.
There are about 721 species of hyperaccumulator plants, which are adept
at extracting radioactive metals from a particular place in a period of 3 to
4 years. The common sunflower, Indian mustard, Chinese Brake Fern,
duckweed, sweet asylum are some of them. Hyperaccumulators are tolerant
to aluminium, silver, arsenic, copper, mercury, manganese, lead, zinc,
naphthalene and similar other metals and toxins.

31. When attacked by insects, a lot of plants release a distress chemical to
attract the predators such as birds or wasps, who in turn save the plant by
eating up these insects.

32. One of the most striking sights of the Peruvian side of Lake Titicaca, are the floating Uros Islands. Of 2,000 Uros people in Peru, about 1,200 live on this archipelago. Believed to be the descendants of the earliest inhabitant groups of South America, the Uros have been building mobile islands to protect themselves from the invaders and calamities. When faced with a threat, all they would, was to just move islands to another part of the lake. The island, their homes on it and their boats, everything is made from the endemic totora plant that grows in abundance in the lake. They stack layers upon layers of totora reed to make a strong base. Naturally buoyant totora keeps the island afloat. The islands are anchored at one place by tying ropes to the eucalyptus stakes driven into the bottom of the lake. The islanders can maintain an island for up to 30 years and keep adding layers as and when required.

*(Lake Titicaca: Uros floating islands: photo by Peru for Less)*

33. Studies in plant behaviour show that the plants exhibit competitive behaviour in terms of access to water and nutrients among strangers of the same species, but they are more accepting and accommodating to their siblings.

34. When you eat fruit, you are eating the plant's ovaries.

35. Often called the 'tree of life', or 'goat tree', the argan trees in Morocco can be seen swarmed by goats, perched upon their shaky and stabby branches, feasting on its fruits, these days, majorly for the tourist attraction. However, the goats have been a major contributory helping in seed dispersal. The goat herders collect the seeds either regurgitated and spat out by the goats or from their excrement. Seeds gathered at this stage helped in reducing the efforts of an otherwise tedious and rather long oil extraction process. Traditionally, Amazigh women had been extracting oil in their homes that would sell on the roadsides at $3 per litre. It was in 1956, when the women no longer required the man's permission to leave their homes, were gradually brought under cooperatives and collectively began to produce oil commercially using large oil pressers and extraction machines. And from being virtually unknown 'oil' until a couple of decades ago became the most expensive edible oil in the world. Moroccan women have transformed Argan oil into a billion-dollar industry. Today this oil, which is used both for culinary purposes and in the high end cosmetic products, would cost you $300 per litre.

36. Cobra Lily has the unique ability to change gender. When young the plant produces male flowers with pollen. When they are ready to fruit, the plant produces female flowers, and that's how the pollination takes place.

37. The ghost flower (also called Indian pipe) is a very unusual type of plant called a myco-heterotroph. These types parasitize certain types of fungi, getting their food from them instead of through photosynthesis. Their outlandish pale appearance, entirely lacking in any green pigments is due to lack of chlorophyll.

38. There are more than 600 carnivorous plant species, where carnivory is six times higher in the flowering plants than the non flowering ones. Carnivory actually helps the plants to survive in poor soil conditions. Although Carnivorous plants seem to prey upon small insects and arachnids, they are photosynthetic and do not fulfill their energy needs from these insects. In fact these organisms act as nitrogen supplement and also provide other nutrients that are not available to their roots due to harsh environments.

39. A study by the American Meteorological Society states that oak trees are struck by lightning more often than any other tree. This is because of its height and the particular structure of its roots that are hollow and run deep into the earth. The water filled cells run up the tree trunks, making them excellent conductors for lightning. Therefore avoid taking cover under an oak tree during a heavy storm.

40. Although a sunflower may look like one large flower, it actually is a cluster of hundreds of tiny flowers, called florets, which when ripen become seeds. All plants in the family of sunflower, including asters, bachelor's buttons, coreopsis, daisies, goldenrod, or yarrow, flower in a similar fashion.

41. If the weather is favourable, Burmese bamboo, (Bambusa burmanica) the fastest growing grass in the world, can pick about 3 feet in height in just one day. You could actually watch it grow. Bamboo produces 30% more oxygen and absorbs more carbon dioxide in comparison to any other plant.

42. Many kinds of plants can tell what season it is, even if the temperatures are unstable. The winter might have warm days, but many plants will not start growing, because they are sensitive to the amount of sunlight and day length.

43. The largest tree in the world is the Hyperion, which is coastal redwood. It is located somewhere in California's Redwood National Park and is a massive 380 feet tall. In order to protect it, its exact location is kept a secret from the public.

44. Deep beneath our feet, lies the world of fungi and plant-roots. Spread like the underground cable wires, these plants have developed their own communication networks. For instance mycorrhizal fungi that live on the roots of the trees or the fly agaric, a mushroom species, which have a network of long, thin threads called mycelium, which reach miles down in the soil and attach themselves to the end of tree roots where they help the tree absorb more water and nutrients from the soil, and in turn receive sugars from their photosynthesis process. In their symbiotic relationship when a plant is threatened by a leaf-eater or any such 'enemy', it sends out an SOS signal through the fungi network to warn its neighbours. And as soon as the message is received, the trees start with releasing chemical repellents to fend off hungry bugs.

45. Figs are syconia, which means it is a cluster of hundreds of flowers enclosed in the fig 'fruit' (infructescence) and are pollinated by fig wasps. A female fig wasp enters the fig through its narrow opening, the struggle makes her lose her wings. Once inside, she lays eggs and eventually dies. Meanwhile the larvae hatch and pupate into matured wasps. These wasps mate with the female ones. Now fertile, the female wasp, which has both wings and antennas, will exit through the tunnels created by the male wasps. Laden with pollen, which she has collected from inside the fig, the female flies off to lay its eggs in a new fig. The male, which is wingless and antenna-less, will die there, if it hasn't been able to crawl out. Thus the cycle of pollination goes on. Because figs are the result of wasp's death inside the fruit, it's suggested that figs are not vegan.

# Animal Kingdom

*Animals Are Not Brethren, They Are Not Underlinings; They Are Other Nations, Caught With Ourselves In The Net Of Life And Time.*   - Henry Beston

1.  Otters have a pouch in their fur to store their favourite rock.

2.  The Nine-banded armadillo is a unique creature. It always gives birth to 4 identical quadruplets and they are all born with the same gender. What makes it possible is their coming out of a single egg after it has split in four. If stressed, they can even delay implantation of the fertilized egg for as long as 20 months to two years.

3.  Owning a single guinea pig is illegal in Switzerland. The guinea pigs are habituated to living in groups and crave social interaction, depriving them of that is a crime. In case one of the guinea pigs passes away and you are not in an immediate hurry to buy another, the Swiss government allows you to rent a guinea pig as a companion to your remaining pet.

4.  All whales, dolphins, and porpoises belong to the animal group called Cetacea (derived from the Ancient Greek word for "sea monster" ). Cetaceans are bifurcated into two groups: the Toothed Whales and the Baleen Whales (do not have teeth). An orca is a toothed whale belonging to the oceanic dolphin family, of which it is the largest member. The presence of melon, a fatty deposit that exists only in dolphins, makes it a dolphin, although its size technically makes it a whale. Orcas are extremely fast swimmers with exceptionally sophisticated echolocation abilities. Being highly intelligent, they are able to communicate and coordinate hunting tactics. Although called 'killer whales', they are not known to have hunted or intentionally harmed a human.

5.  Squirrels carry their food in their cheeks which can hold up to about 10 hazelnuts in one go.

6. The deer are herbivores generally, however Muntjacs are the species of deer with fangs and they occasionally hunt and eat small animals and birds.

7. Although very thick, a rhino's skin is still susceptible to sunburn. Its excessively sensitive skin makes it wallow in the muddy waters to keep it cool. Once dried, the coat of this dry mud on its skin, forms a layer of protection both from sunlight and insect bites.

8. The male yellowhead jawfish is a mouthbrooder, after the female has laid eggs, it gathers them in its jaw and incubates them until they hatch.

9. It's generally believed that Chameleons use camouflage as a defence tactic. But this is not entirely true, even a blind chameleon can adjust to the colours of its surrounding environment. The colour change, which is possible because of its special cells (called chromatophores), is required for regulating their body temperatures and also to communicate with other chameleons. Since they can't generate their own body heat, a cold chameleon may become dark to absorb more heat, and a hotter one may turn pale to reflect the sun's heat. When it comes to communication, a male chameleon might become bright to signal its dominance and turn dark in aggressive encounters. Similarly a female may switch to a different colour to let a male know, it's willing to mate.

10. Native to Australia, the superb male Lyrebird is one of the world's largest songbirds. It is renowned for its ornate tail and courtship displays, and exhibits most 'sophisticated voice skills'. It can imitate the calls of as many as twenty other birds and even other sounds such as a car alarm, camera clicking, whistling and many others.

11. Cheetahs are naturally reserved creatures and in captivity tend to be very stressed and too reluctant to mate. Keeping this in mind zoos, with cheetahs keep dogs in their enclosures for their socialization and to give them emotional support.

12. Squirrels will adopt abandoned babies of other creatures if the parents cannot be found.

13. As a courtship gesture male Gentoo and Adele penguins are said to gift pebbles to their mates. These stones are used by them in their nest building, particularly to keep the eggs safe. If the female accepts the pebble, the pair bonds and mates for life.

14. It is estimated that about 500 species of tropical plants are pollinated by bats, including some 80 medicinal plants that solely depend on the nocturnal creature. Chiropterophilous plants (plants pollinated by bats) even produce such substances that may be of no use to itself but are of great benefit to the bats. In fact as they travel, the migratory bats pollinate a variety of plants, which can be seen blooming across the migratory routes that the bats take. This "nectar corridor" helps scientists to study bat behaviour.

15. The giraffe has the highest blood pressure in the animal kingdom because its heart pumps hard against gravity to reach its head.

16. Just as their fur, a tigers' skin too is striped-black and orange, derived from pigments eumelanin and pheomelanin, respectively. And much like human fingerprints, they are never the same. The stripe patterns are unique to each wild cat which is how surveyors prepare population census of the tiger.

17. If a goldfish is kept in a dark room for a long duration, it will eventually lose its colour. Its chromatophores won't produce more pigment. In the absence of new cells, which aren't stimulating to produce pigment and the existing ones are naturally dying, the colour will start to fade off. And the goldfish will look dull and pale, losing all its bright colours.

18. Even though the Hippos may seem to spend the majority of their lives in water, the fact is they can't swim well. Actually it's their extremely sensitive skin which needs to be protected, hence the water body shelter.

19. Bats, which eat insects, save U.S. farmers an estimated $3.7 billion a year on pesticides.

20. Baby koalas are fed poop by their parents after they are born which helps them digest Eucalyptus leaves later in life.

21. Polar bears which look snow white, actually have black skin underneath. This helps them to absorb heat from the sun and keep warm despite the harsh Arctic climate. Their fur, which is see-through, appears white as it reflects light and protects them from harmful UV rays.

22. For humans, facial hair like a moustache may be just for an ornamental purpose but a cat's whiskers have very important biological functions. Their whiskers, which are loaded with nerves and act as sensory tools, are deeply embedded in their body and are connected to their muscular and nervous system. A cat's whiskers are not just confined to their nose region, they're also above their eyes, ears, jaw and forelegs! The whiskers on their forelegs called carpal whiskers, work as a built-in ruler to help them gauge the spaces and to determine movement of the prey. The multifunctional whiskers act as night vision aids and give an insight into a cat's behaviour too. Snipping them off can get a cat very disorientated.

23. So deafeningly loud is a tiger's roar that it can cause an instinctive paralysis in the other animals. Its vocal chord is built in the shape of a square, which allows it to be really loud. It can go up to 114 decibels which is almost as loud as a jet engine's sound.

24. The Poison dart frogs are poisonous only because they eat poisonous ants and insects. In zoos, where their diet is controlled, they do not produce any poison.

25. The sloths are one of the slowest creatures of the animal kingdom. So slow a sloth is that in their native environment, even algae may grow up on their fur. In this symbiotic relationship, while the sloth provides the algae with shelter and water, the algae helps the sloth camouflage itself and at the same time absorb extra nutrients from the algae. Its physical slowness reflects in its metabolic system, which is the slowest of any mammal. In fact a sloth takes about two to four weeks to digest its food.

26. After sucking in nectar from the flowers, the bees keep it in their "stomach." Once they're back at the hive, they regurgitate this into the hive. In short, honey is bee vomit. Eww!

27. Oysters can change genders! They start their lives as males, but as they grow they may swap to the other gender and this, they can do throughout their lives, multiple times. In fact they can have both sex organs at the same time. Scientists are still not sure about the mechanism behind the gender change. The possible factors that prompt the gender change could be environmental- climate, waterbody temperature and the health of the oyster reef.

28. Often referred to as "sheep pigs," Mangalitsa pigs with long, woolly coats have a strong resemblance to sheep. Geneticist, Peter Toth, saved the species from becoming extinct. These Austro-Hungarian origin sheep-pigs behave like dogs. They have become pets and are raised for their meat. Though hard, its wool is also spun by farmers.

29. A study by Ohio State University has found that alcohol has similar effects on bees' behaviour as it does on humans. It claims that a honeybee can consume the human equivalent of 10 litres of wine in one sitting. They can even drink pure ethanol, which no other known organism can.

30. The bulls used for Spanish bullfighting can fight only once. It's because the scarred memories of the previous fight impacts its behaviour, which makes it unfit for another fight.

31. Lobsters pee out of their faces to turn each other on.

32. 90% of all the wildlife on Madagascar is found nowhere else in the world.

33. Approximately 78% of marine life is at risk of accidental deaths due to human negligence and indifference. This includes pollutants like oil spills, plastic bottles, polythene bags, rubber slippers, metals, even shipwrecks, all of which end up in oceans, and this is apart from the sea animals hunted for meat, which kill over 1,000,000 sea animals every year.

34. A study of the hydrodynamics of defecation states that all mammals with faeces like humans, regardless of their body size, take 12 seconds on average to relieve themselves..

35. Armadillos have shells so hard they can deflect a bullet.

36. An octopus will eat its own arms if it gets really hungry.

37. Unlike humans, dogs can breathe and smell simultaneously. Their 300 million olfactory receptors equip them with a forty times more powerful sense of smell than us humans. Another characteristic that the dogs have is their being neophiliac, which is to be attracted to new and interesting smells and things.

38. The bellowing sounds that male fin whales make are used to attract mates. These are the loudest of all marine life and can be heard up to 1,000 kilometres and reach depths of 2.5 kilometres under the water and its bounce back can provide researchers with accurate measurements thus sonically map out the ocean floor.

39. The only known marine birds which have their bills that reflect ultraviolet (UV) light, are the Emperor and King male Penguins. UV light may be invisible to the human eye, but can be detected by most birds. During courtship, king penguin males flaunt their bills to find and select a possible mate. The sexually immature king juveniles' bills do not reflect UV light.

40. Although ambergris, "Treasure of the sea" had been in use for over a thousand years, its source was a mystery. It wasn't until large scale whaling in the 1800s, that uncovered the fact that sperm whales are its sole producer. Theories differ, some call it 'whale vomit', however the most common and accepted one is, it is 'whale poop', because of the place it is found on a whale. The indigestible elements of its prey are vomited out by the whale, but when that doesn't happen, these clumps of squid beaks and fatty secretions get stuck in its intestines and stay there as a solid mass. This 'rock' like stuff, released by the sperm whale in the oceans is ambergris, out of which an odourless liquid ambrein is extracted. Even though they may not mention it because of environmental issues, most high end perfumers use ambrein in the manufacturing of perfume. The only perfume to openly claim its usage is "Fleurs de Bulgarie" by Creed. It was originally created in 1845 for Queen Victoria and apparently she always wore it.

41. A research at Stockholm University on "Sperm dumping", which is practiced by some animal species including birds and insects, found that when hens ejected a larger proportion of inseminations by socially subordinate males, they preferred strong mates. Thus they reject the sperm of the mates they do not find eligible for them.

42. Unlike other animals who have iron-based blood, octopuses have copper-based blood, which is why instead of red, their blood is blue. There is no link that correlates it with any other marine life species.

43. All clownfish are born male and have the natural ability to change their sex later on. Usually the dominant male of a group turns female when the female of that group dies.

44. Honeybees are some of nature's most efficient architectural designers and their beehive, one of the finest examples of most methodically created structures. They not only know the earth is round but even determine angles too. Once a bee has found a flower patch, she informs the other bees in the colony. She does this by waggle dancing- a series of figure-eight movements, that are indicative of the direction and distance of the food source from the hive. She even encourages the other bees to sample the nectar she had collected earlier. Motivated, the bees fly towards the location of the nectar, using the same angle, as the bee had displayed.

45. In one of its raids by Australian police on a crystal methamphetamine lab, instead of drugs they found a 6ft-long jungle python with visible signs of addiction, evidently the drug fumes and particles got through its skin. It was sent for a period of seven months for rehabilitation under the care of 14 prisoners of a Sydney prison in 2016, where these men helped it to become normal. This particular prison with the Wildlife Care Program has been taking care of hundreds of animals including kangaroos, wallabies, possums, wombats and a number of native birds.

46. Musth is a natural phenomenon in bull elephants which is characterised by increased reproduction hormones. During this period, elephants tend to be very aggressive and dangerous and the annual deaths because of elephant attacks is as many as 500 people a year.

47. Zebras have a completely black skin underneath the striped coat. They have white stripes on the black skin.

48. According to scientists sharks have been around for 450 million years- pre-dating the dinosaurs, the mammals, the grass, even the formation of Saturn's rings took place when sharks were already in existence. They are great survivors and have endured several mass extinction events. Such a tough creature this marine predator is, that the K-T extinction event responsible for eliminating about 80 percent of all animal life, including the dinosaurs, could wipe out only 30 percent of the sharks.

49. Ravens and crows remember faces well and connect them to certain experiences, which is why they are capable of holding a grudge against people who did something wrong to them or express their gratitude for a good turn. They've also been known to leave gifts for humans.

50. Ilha da Queimada Grande, popularly known as the Snake Island, situated off the coast of Brazil in the Atlantic Ocean, is the only natural habitat to the critically endangered, but deadly snakes- the Golden Lancehead Pit Viper. Thousands of years ago, subsequent to the end of the last ice age, when the rising levels of the ocean isolated the island, the snakes became trapped there. Their increasing population has made the island extremely dangerous for public visitations. The Brazil Navy, which controls the region, oversees the research teams, the only people permitted, to collect data. The prohibition is to protect the lives of both- the snakes and humans.

51. A bee's life span is just a little more than a month. During its lifetime it visits at least a thousand flowers, and despite the drudgery, it's not able to produce even a teaspoonful of honey. In fact a teaspoon of honey is actually the lifework of 12 bees.

52. Tiger, the apex predator, has an advantage when it's on a hunt. It can imitate calls of other animals, thus lulling them into a false state of security and then attack them when they least expect it.

53. In Australia sheep outnumber humans by three times.

54. Giraffes' purple colored tongue protects them from sunburns when eating.

55. Owls don't have eyeballs. Instead, they have fixed "eye tubes" that require them to move their entire head to look in different directions.

56. Declawing a cat is anatomically equivalent to removing the entire last bone in a human finger at the joint.

57. With a ring-shaped brain and oesophagus running through the hole in it, squids need to eat very small pieces of food lest it should damage their brains.

58. Sharks and humans share a common ancestor, and some of our genes are still similar.

59. The longest living koi fish ever recorded was Hanako (flower child in Japanese). She was born in 1751 and died at the age of 226 in 1977. In her life span of over two hundred years she had many owners, the last being Dr. Komei Koshihara. In 1966, two of her scales were removed to make an extensive research that would determine her real age. In July 1974, the study of the growth rings of one of the koi's scales confirmed that she was over two and a quarter century old.

60. According to the U.S. Geological Survey, there is evidence that proves that some sea animals such as sea turtles and salmon, are equipped with the ability to sense the Earth's magnetic field which they use for navigation.

61. There are some 60 known species of sea snakes, which have evolved from two independent groups - the true sea snakes (Australian terrestrial elapids), and the sea kraits (Asian cobras) and almost all are poisonous, with several of them capable of severe envenomation. The highly potent venom is a mixture of neurotoxins and myotoxins, which is even more toxic than that of King Cobra's. There are almost no reported human casualties from sea snake bites, but even when they do, the snakes rarely deliver venom. They are found throughout the coastal waters of the Indian and Pacific oceans but do not occur in the Red Sea, Atlantic Ocean, or Caribbean Sea.

62. Cows, sheep, and goats are ruminants. Ruminants do not have upper front teeth but they do have molars on top, in the back of their mouths. And in place of upper incisors they grow a hard fleshy layer of tissue called a dental pad. They use that with their bottom teeth to pull out grass.

63. For tiger sharks, the fight for the 'survival of the fittest' begins in the womb itself. The unborn babies eat each other in the womb until only the strongest is left to be born.

64. Although the Flamingos are born with greyish white feathers, they become pink as they grow older, only because of the carotenoid, a chemical that is present in the algae and fish they eat.

65. The octopus has no bones, so it can fit even in the tiniest holes and enclosures, regardless of its size. This is how many of them managed to escape zoos which were not built with them in mind.

66. Rhinos can be extremely aggressive in the wild because they are nearly blind and incapable of telling the difference between a predator and an inanimate object, but in zoos they are reported to be very affectionate with people.

67. Panther is not a separate species of big cats. It is a genus comprising the tiger, lion, leopard, jaguar and snow leopard. Any of these big cats with a mutation that causes melanism are called "black panthers".

68. A misconception is that camels store water in their hump which allows them to survive in the hot deserts with water scarcity. Studies however, reject that claim. According to the findings, camels can dehydrate without changing their blood viscosity, allowing them to function normally in high heat- no water storage in the hump!

69. Orcas are at the top of the food chain in the ocean and are capable of hunting and killing whales and sharks. They have been known to murder sea animals for no reason other than enjoyment.

70. According to VOX media, pandas, wherever they are, in whatever zoos around the world, are on a loan from China- they are technically the property of the government of China.

71. Once exposed to oxygen, a lobster's colourless blood turns blue.

72. It's from their skin, not mouths, that the frogs drink water.

73. A tree's age is calculated by its rings, a whale's by studying its earwax, called earplugs. The hardened earwax forms a pattern of alternate light and dark coloured bands. With the whale's annual cycle- abundance of food in summers and migratory in winters, the band changes from light to dark colour. These bands do not just tell the age but also give important information of the oceans too- the contaminants, diverge temperatures, hunting, availability of food and many more facts of the time when the creature was alive. Not surprising then, that scientists call the earplugs a 'chemical biography' of the whale.

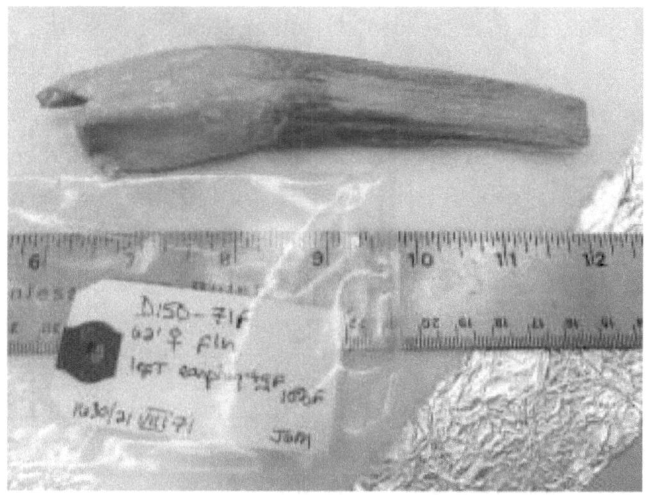

*(Image Credit: Fin whale earwax by Stephen Trumble)*

74. It is said that the zebras are the most unpredictable and aggressive creatures. They may seem as docile as horses which can be ridden but that's not true. In fact the Zoo workers consider zebras to be one of the most dangerous animals in the zoo.

75. Within ten minutes after it's born, a duckling starts treating anything that it comes in contact with, as its parent.

76. There's a species of jellyfish that never dies, literally! Turritopsis dohrnii or the Immortal Jellyfish achieves this by ageing backwards after sexual maturity, going through reverse-puberty so it can start the cycle again. It can repeat the cycle indefinitely, making it biologically immortal.

77. Qizai, the only specimen of a brown panda in captivity in the world, was abandoned by his mother when he was just two months old. The weak and neglected baby was bullied by other pandas for being different. Qizai was rescued and taken to Shaanxi Rare Wildlife Rescue, Breeding and Research Centre where he was given medical treatment and since then has a personal caretaker. Qizai, scientists believe, has a rare genetic mutation, which gave him a brown and white coat.

78. Cuckoos are ruthless birds but contrary to the popular belief that all cuckoos plant their eggs into the other birds' nests, the majority of species raise their own young, it's only some species which are brood parasites. While the non-parasitic cuckoos lay white eggs, many of the parasitic species lay coloured eggs to match those of their passerine hosts. If the host bird rejects the cuckoo's egg, the cuckoo destroys the host's clutch. In such a situation raising a cuckoo baby is less catastrophic. Also the cuckoo eggs hatch earlier than the host's and grow faster, they knock down all the other eggs in the nest. Pushing their competitors over the edge of the nest guarantees their own survival. This behaviour of a cuckoo chick is an instinct passed on genetically. Thus adaptations and counter-adaptations are important to survival, where any species would lose the race to the other if they didn't adapt to the situations.

79. 'Urohydrosis' is a cooling mechanism, where a creature urinates and defecates on its own legs to keep cool on hot days. A vulture uses this mechanism not just to cool it off but the chemicals in its urine kill bacteria it had picked up from the dead carcass it preyed upon.

80. A Koala's fingerprints are so strikingly similar to that of a human that even under a microscope it isn't easy to tell. There have been reported cases where the presence of a koala fingerprints on a crime scene have confused forensics.

81. Stone fish, common to Australia, is a 30 cm long creature with 13 sharp fin spines on its back, each equipped with two venom glands. The sting of this most poisonous fish, if untreated, can kill a person within 2 hours. Since it resembles a stone, and is almost impossible to tell apart among rocks at the bottom of the ocean, it gets often stepped on by humans, which is where the sting happens.

82. A seahorse is the only animal species on earth where the male and not female goes through pregnancy and gives birth to babies. The male seahorse has a pouch on its stomach which has the capacity to carry as many as 2,000 babies at a time.

# Human Body & Mind



1. The Japanese word 'Kuchizamishi' literally translates into 'lonely mouth'. So you eat not because you are hungry but to give the mouth some company. It can be explained as mindless eating or cravings, kuchizamishi, however, is treating binge eating as natural and non guilty eating.

2. A baby is born with 300 different bones, to give it extra flexibility to pass through the birth canal. With age, many of the bones fuse to create the skeleton and by the time it grows up to be an adult, only 206 bones are left in the human bone frame.

3. Contrary to the prevailing myth, having high total cholesterol is not bad for the brain. In fact 60% of the human brain is made of fat and about 25% of the body's cholesterol resides within the brain. In the absence of adequate cholesterol not only would the brain cell die, but even increase the risk of dementia. These fatty acids are crucial for the brain's overall performance. The modern diet is low in omega-3 essential fatty acids, which leads to brain shrinkage equivalent to two years of structural brain aging.

4. An Imperial College study claims that humans shed around 200 million dead skin cells each hour, which become one of the main ingredients in household dust.

5. According to a study, as we age and evolve, our memories may change. And in certain cases, possibility is we might unintentionally 'create' memories that actually never occurred. Such 'made-up' memories are a part of everybody's life, however, the austerity of such creations vary among people.

6.  Tears have a way of telling- the first tear drops from your right eye are the tears of happiness whereas the first tears from the left are indicative of sorrow and pain inside you.

7.  Scientists at Bangor University UK, theorise that speaking out loud to yourself is a "trait of higher cognitive function". Dr. Paloma Mari-Beffa, psychologist and co-author of the study, states that talking to oneself is more effective simply because hearing one's own auditory commands holds better control on the mind than a written text. People who are in a regular habit of 'talking' to themselves, achieve a higher IQ and a better analytical approach.

8.  Research says that taking a short nap after learning something new can actually help your memory.

9.  People around you hear a higher version of your voice than you do, because you're hearing it resonate through your bones and they hear it directly from your mouth.

10. Genetic comparisons place fungi such as mushrooms closer to human beings than to plants. Our genome consists of as many as 145 genes that have jumped from bacteria, fungi, and viruses.

11. The human eye has a 576-megapixel resolution. However, we only see at about 150 dpi, since that is more than enough visual stimuli for us to see objects.

12. Research scientists at University of Southern California claim that an average human brain generates some 70,000 thoughts per day. And of these about 70% are random thoughts, majorly of negative nature- self-critical, defeatist and stress giving. That is one of the reasons Dhyan (meditation) and Yog (yog) are recommended to create a positive internal and external environment.

13. Grey matter forms early in fetal development and its volume keeps on increasing until around 8 years of age and then until 20, only the density increases. This increase in density allows for high processing and further mental development. Although neurons do not renew or regenerate, when we learn something new, the brain forms new connections between neurons, this then increases visible gray matter in the brain.

14. Brown eyes beneath the layer of melanin are blue in colour. A laser procedure can get the browns turned into blue by removing the melanin.

15. The brain size in men and women differs. While the average weight of the brain in an adult male is 1336 grams, it's 1198 grams in an adult female. After 50 years of age the brain volume goes on a progressive decrease, with 2.7 in males and 2.2 in females per decade- before 50, the decrease is observed predominantly in the grey matter of the cerebral cortex and afterwards the decrease in white matter is greater. Although men may have slightly bigger brains than women, it's the women who use their brains more efficiently.

16. According to psychologists the duration of our emotional pain is not more than 20 minutes, anything longer is actually self inflicted by over thinking and thus making it seem much longer than it actually is.

17. When our brains are low on glucose, it becomes difficult for us to control our emotions and we start feeling hungry.

18. A healthy adult sleep cycle has four distinct stages- the first two 'light' and the third 'deep' Non-REM stages and the fourth one the REM ( Rapid Eye Movement) stage. During the NREM stage while the body repairs and regrows tissues, builds bone and muscle, strengthens the immune system, the brain sorts and filters out important memories, including the emotional ones, from the previous day and eliminates other information. With deep NREM, these selected memories become more concrete and continue until REM sleep. Getting sufficient sleep helps in processing new information but lack of it lowers one's learning abilities by as much as 40%. Sleep deprivation shuts down the production of essential brain proteins vital to neurons for effective communication, decision making skills, emotional and behavioural control, and ability to learn and focus. Quality sleep, therefore affects the way memories are consolidated and eventually in the long run one's performance.

19. Research claims that over one third of the population of Europe suffers from depression, with France topping the list.

20. Human brain remembers the information which required efforts to obtain as against the information that was easily accessible.

21. If you thought those stomach rumblings you feel are an 'indication of hunger', then you are mistaken. It's actually the air moving through your digestive tract which causes that, which need not necessarily be due to craving for food.

22. Earwax is often referred to as a type of sweat, actually Earwax ('cerumen'), is a combination of dead skin cells, sebum and various waxes that the ceruminous (sweat) glands produce. There are two kinds of earwax - Wet and Dry! While the wet ear wax is most common in people with European and African roots, the Asians have mostly dry wax, the other parts of the world have a mix of the two kinds.

23. A study says, curvy women generally have a higher IQ than the skinny ones because of the omega-3 fatty acids stored in the extra fat cells on their hips and thighs. These fatty acids result in higher intelligence levels, longer life expectancy and brainier kids.

24. It takes about 20 minutes for a human body to realise it is full. That is because your gut requires twenty minutes to suppress a hormone called ghrelin, and release anti-hunger hormones, signalling your brain, you are done with the eating.

25. Your tongue is covered with about 8,000 taste-buds, each containing up to 100 cells helping you taste your food.

26. The only living cells in the human body that do not get any direct blood supply are the corneas in the eye. A cornea needs to be transparent for the light to pass through, presence of a blood vessel would obstruct the light. It therefore takes oxygen directly from the air. Oxygen and nutrients diffuse directly from the tear fluid all through the cornea layers and carbon dioxide is released via the same process back into the atmosphere. One of the reasons why doctors do not recommend wearing contact lenses for long duration- it curtails the only source of oxygen to the eyes.

27. There exists a bond between your brain and digestive system known as the gut-brain axis. When you are under stress or suffer some kind of a brain disorder, your digestive system gets affected by that.

28. A research paper published in the medical journal Laryngoscope, claimed that wearing headphones for an hour can lead to an alarming increase of bacteria in the ear. The researchers studied the bacterial flora of 20 headsets. A typical headset which had 60 microorganisms before it was worn, escalated to 650 in an hour's usage. Scientists maintain that unless it's absolutely necessary, one should avoid wearing headsets for longer periods.

29. There is a popular myth about people being left or right brained personality/ skill types. Debunking this theory, scientists say humans are not left-brained or right-brained; they are all "whole-brained" people.

30. Recent neurological studies state that the human nose can detect and recognize at least a trillion different odours and is capable of remembering at least 50,000 of them. Our nose has about 12 million receptors to which the odour molecules attach and thus we are able to know different smells.

31. You don't 'forget' things under the influence of alcohol. It's just that an intoxicated brain does not have the capability to form memories, so you do not remember things that happened when you were drunk.

32. According to a study published in Behavioral Neuroscience, fathers' brains respond to sons and daughters differently. A daughter's happy face led to "higher activation in brain areas involved in reward, emotional regulation, and face processing". While fathers' faces had lit up at their daughters' being about- became more open and expressive, attentive and responsive, the same wasn't found with the sons around.

33. The human brain can store around 2.5 PETABYTES of data – that's 2,500,000 Gigabytes and the human brain takes just eighty milliseconds to process information.

34. Eyebrows and eyelashes in humans renew themselves every fifty days.

35. Your immune system destroys cells on a daily basis that would have become cancer if allowed to live.

36. Men cry less than women not only because of social or psychological reasons but physiological too- they have larger tear ducts, prohibiting their eyes from leaking easily.

37. The colour yellow decreases the production of Melatonin, a hormone which makes you sleepy, hence advisable to keep yourself surrounded by yellow light to stay alert and focused.

38. According to the Scientists our brain purposely forgets certain memories to avoid both, information overload and emotional hangovers.

39. Research reveals that in the last 20,000 years, the human brain has lost a significant volume, which is roughly about the size of a tennis ball. The average size of the Paleolithic male used to be 1,500 cubic centimetres, which now is 1,350 ccm.

40. Brain development in humans is a protracted process, starting with the two week old embryo it continues well into adulthood, which is until 25 years of age. The process of development begins from the back of the brain and works its way to the prefrontal cortex. This is why, however much 'brainy' you are, the sense of planning and reasoning, ability to differentiate among conflicting concepts and orchestration of thoughts and actions, come to you only when you have attained that biological maturity.

41. If the colour blindness is an inherited one, then it's passed on to you from your mother, not Dad.

42. People who are early risers and expose themselves to bright morning light tend to be more alert throughout the day.

43. Every step you take uses 200 different muscles in the body.

44. Scientists claim that our dreaming in colour is indicative of a higher IQ as against those who have black and white dreams.

45. A study reveals that the average IQ has gone down 1.6 points per decade, since the last century and a half, making it about 13.35 points lower than it was in the 19th century.

46. Some people do not need an alarm clock to wake up when they want. That is because of the natural stress hormone which is produced in the body making the person wake up.

47. Antibiotics work only on bacterial infections, that's why they do absolutely nothing when you suffer from a cold, cough or flu as these are viral infections.

48. Experts have come to conclude that the human body is composed of some 30 trillion human cells and 39 trillion bacteria which is roughly a ratio of 1:1.3. In the past, the researchers however believed that we were ten times more bacteria than human.

49. Unlike women, men don't experience a monthly cyclical hormone shift. Instead, they experience a daily rise and fall of testosterone, which is believed to have evolved five million years ago.

50. As much as twenty percent of all oxygen that we take in, is used by our brain. Even five minutes without oxygen can cause severe damage to the brain.

51. A protein in human saliva called Histatin has antimicrobial and antifungal properties, and can help wounds heal faster.

52. Almost every atom in the human body was made from an exploding star, which means our body is billions of years old.

53. The white dots you see while looking at a bright blue sky are actually your white blood cells (WBC), bouncing around and moving across your retina.

54. The brain produces about 4 fluid ounces of cerebrospinal every day. This fluid in which the brain floats, acts as a shock absorber and protects the brain from being crushed by its own weight.

55. A study revealed that as many as 22% of teenagers in the US experience depression even before they have reached adulthood.

56. Researchers from Stockholm University and the University of Manchester Trust have debunked the theory that the sperm that arrives first, fertilises an egg. According to them, it is the one which gets selected by the female reproductive cell through chemoattractants. In short, the fittest and not the fastest one that gets to fertilise.

57. Our tongue can feel the taste of the food only after its chemicals have dissolved with our saliva, where they get detected by the receptors on the taste buds. During this process, some salivary constituents chemically interact with taste substances. Since saliva acts as a solvent for taste substances it's absence can be one of the factors for the loss of 'taste'.

58. According to the scientists the genes responsible for the most common type of colorblindness are found on the X chromosome. If men inherit the gene on their only X chromosome, they will be colour blind. With a similar gene defect, a woman's proper functioning X chromosome makes up for that loss, which does not happen in the case of a man.

59. Brain fingerprinting technology or Brain Electrical Oscillation Signature Profiling (BEOSP) is a method of interrogation where the suspect's brain wave pattern, which is unique to him, is studied. The first use of BEOSP was done on James Grinder, a murder accused, who kept retracting and contradicting his own statements. In 1999 Dr. Lawrence Farwell, the sheriff put him to test by using certain short phrases related to the crime, which only the perpetrator could have known. A computer analysis revealed that some of the details of the crime were recorded in his brain as 'information present'. Grinder not only confessed to raping and murdering Julie Helton 15 years ago but also of murdering 3 other young women. Although legitimate, the test results alone cannot be produced as evidence unless the information or material discovered during the tests is a part of the other evidence collected. It was a Supreme Court ruling in Selvi versus State of Karnataka case in 2010.

60. As you exercise, the burned fat metabolises to become carbon dioxide, water, and energy. You exhale the fat that you lose.

61. Thanks to the increase in junk food consumption and commercialization, obesity is now a bigger killer than malnutrition.

62. The stapes (stirrup), is the smallest and lightest bone in the human body. It is located in the middle ear along with malleus and incus, the other two bones of the auditory ossicles. Together they are responsible for transmitting sound waves from the air outside to the cochlea. The auditory ossicles are the first bones to harden and mature at the time of birth, after which they never grow.

63. With the fast paced lifestyle and technological advancements, multitasking has become inevitable, however the human brain is not naturally meant to focus on two distinctive things at a single time. When you try to juggle between your tasks, the brain becomes an oscillator, toggling back and forth between multiple assignments. In the process it affects your short term memory (STM), reduces your attention span, incapacitates learning, in fact it debilitates your overall mental performance impacting your IQ, lowering it as much as by 15 points.

64. Nose is one of the most remarkable parts of the human body. It has two major functions- respiration and olfaction. It is also a filter, heater and a humidifier. Our nose is lined with bone-like shelves known as turbinates, which contain blood vessels that can heat the air and goblet cells that help humidify the air. The nose takes in about 20,000 litres of air in a day, which it filters before allowing it to reach the lungs.

65. The burning sensation you feel on consuming spicy peppers is a mental reaction, not a physical one. Chilly peppers contain capsaicin, a chemical that naturally binds to the pain receptors on your nerves, making the brain think you are ingesting something hot. So your face turning red and your starting to sweat is your body's way of trying to cool you down, even though there is no real rise in temperature, just a perceived threat.

66. Just like our fingerprints, our tongue too has unique identifying marks. According to researcher David Zhang, the tip of our tongue has a distinctive physiological texture and geometric shape that can possibly be used for verification purposes sometime in future .

67. Children who breathe from their mouth more frequently than their nose are at risk of developing a lisp when they talk.

68. Scientists believe that about 95 percent of the decisions we make in our day-to-day lives are taken in the subconscious mind and not the conscious one.

69. Intense workouts make you sweat, which is a biological function of the body to keep it cool. Even swimmers perspire in the pool, but being in water, that gets barely noticed.

70. Your sitting posture impacts your memory too- while sitting upright and looking upward helps recall positive and empowering memories, sitting and looking downward makes it easier to recall negative memories,

71. Human sense of smell is closely linked with their memories. Certain smells may trigger very strong emotions and memories almost instantaneously. Women have a stronger sense of smell and equally stronger memories.

72. Apart from the five senses that of sight, smell, touch, taste, and hearing, humans also have other senses. The sense of balance -EQUILIBRIOCEPTION, sense of temperature THERMOCEPTION, sense of time, TEMPORAL PERCEPTION, sense of space PROPRIOCEPTION and sense of pain NOCICEPTION.

73. A team of researchers at King's College London have found that a 90 minute workout can temporarily shrink the brain, if losing fluids through sweating is not replenished immediately. It also causes deterioration equivalent to 75 days of Alzheimer's disease. Reduced intake of water forces the grey matter to work harder to process the same information. Studies show that human brain, which is 73% water, even 1% of dehydration can decrease as much as 5% of cognitive functions such as thinking power, aptitude for learning, logical reasoning, attentiveness and reading ability. And a 2% of dehydration can result in short term memory loss, trouble in maths computation and slow reactions.

# The Corporeal Environment

*We Don't Inherit The Earth From Our Ancestors, We Borrow It From Our Children.*
- Native American Proverb

1.  Natural Mineral Water and Spring Water are types of underground water that contain naturally-occurring minerals. Carbon dioxide is added to Sparkling Water to make it fizzy. If this occurs naturally, it is often removed and replaced to ensure that it is always at the same level.

2.  If you go deeper than 30 feet underwater, the blood will appear green to you, because of the absence of red light there.

3.  Hawaii is steadily moving closer to Alaska by 7.5 cm every year. It is due to the tectonic plates underneath in the Pacific, which are in constant motion, pushing it to the North American platform.

4.  Lake Natron in Tanzania is red in colour. According to the geologists, it is due to halo archaea microorganisms that live in the lake.

5.  Scientists estimate that 50-80% of the oxygen production on Earth comes from the ocean. Plankton, seaweed, and other photosynthesizers produce more than half of the world's oxygen, which is more than the largest redwoods.

6.  Liquids exhibit thermal expansion in volume, therefore while filling a liquid in a container, a little space is left. This space with air is called its "ullage", meaning "the amount that a container lacks in being full."

7.  Apart from the commonly known three states of matter- solid, liquid and gas, there exists a fourth one too-plasma, a hot ionised gas. But beyond these known states, scientists have discovered diverse exotic states of matter that occur under special conditions. One of them is the Bose- Einstein condensate, where atoms chilled to only 0.000001 degrees above absolute zero, start behaving like one super atom and act in unison.

8.  What we see as 'white' colour in nature is actually the absence of pigment.

9.  Acid cannot dissolve a diamond but intense heat can definitely damage it.

10. Known to the First Nations of the Okanagan Valley, as Kliluk / Ktlil'k, the Spotted Lake in British Columbia, Canada, is one of the most remarkable natural wonders of the world. This saline endorheic lake, fed by rains, snow and groundwater, looks like an ordinary lake, come summers, and it completely transforms. With most of its water evaporated, some 400 big and small multicoloured pools appear, giving the kidney-shaped lake a leopard skin pattern. These spots look the colour of the minerals they have the concentration of. The lake contains 8 different minerals with the crystallised Magnesium sulphate, calcium and sodium sulphates in abundance and low amounts of silver and titanium- all of which, collected in the water, give spots their colour. The other minerals harden and form pathways around these pools. The lake has been held sacred by the natives for its therapeutic properties. But during WWI, as much as one tonne of minerals were extracted everyday from the lake to use for the manufacture of war ammunition. The ownership of the lake has changed hands since. In 2001, about 22 hectares of the land was acquired by the First Nations from Ernest Smith Family who were trying to make a spa there. It's now a culturally and ecologically sensitive area, where tourists are not allowed inside the erected fence.

*(Image Credit: My Best Place The Lake & the Gateway to Ktlil'x (Spotted Lake), a traditional medicine lake for the Syilx people)*

11. If we were to speak in a place with Helium all around, our voice would change. It is because helium is less dense than oxygen, our voice would travel over two times faster than usual and will make us sound weird.

12. The mysterious sailing stones near Death Valley National Park in California move completely on their own. The source of their peculiar movement is shifting ice layers.

13. The oceans contain almost two hundred thousand different viruses.

14. The fastest gust of wind ever recorded on Earth was 253 miles per hour. In 1996, a tropical cyclone named Olivia hit off the coast of Barrow Island, Australia.

15. The town of Churchill in Manitoba, west of Hudson Bay province has less gravity than the rest of the world.

16. It's estimated that less than 1% of all the species on Earth have been fossilised, so 99% of life that used to exist on this planet will forever remain unknown by us.

17. People who are currently alive represent about seven percent of the total number of people who have ever lived.

18. According to a study, Americans dispose off some 25 trillion styrofoam containers including cups and boxes annually, which adds an alarmingly high percentage of non-biodegradable matter to the environment.

19. Lake Balkhash, which is one of the largest lakes in Asia, has two types of water. While its western side enjoys fresh water, its eastern half is saline. It is because of a land separation that doesn't allow the water to mix properly.

20. Sound travels about four times faster in water than in the air.

21. Atacama Desert is the driest place on Earth if we exclude the two poles. Some of its parts have not seen a drop of rain in over 500 years.

22. Around 80 percent of the forest that dominated the Earth 8,000 years ago is gone today due to human intervention. We are left with one-fifth of the forests that used to exist.

23. The Pacific Ocean has certain points where, if a hole is dug to the opposite point on Earth, you would still be in the Pacific Ocean. It has the world's deepest location- Mariana Trench, which is 11,034 metres deep. If Mount Everest, the world's highest mountain, is placed at the bottom of the Mariana Trench, its peak would still be 2,133 metres below sea level.

24. According to an estimate Australia has over 750 different species of reptiles, highest in the world.

25. Among one of the driest regions of Antarctica, north of the Taylor Glacier lies a waterfall, fed by an underground lake. The infinite white stretch of frozen desert is broken by this deep red colour water of the 'Blood Falls'. First discovered by Australian geologist Griffith Taylor in 1911, the mysterious red colour of the fall was attributed to the presence of algae. However, research by University of Alaska Fairbanks have found that the colour is due to oxidized iron in brine water.

26. Fluorescence is the phenomenon where a material absorbs light of a certain color and then emits light of a different color with a longer wavelength.

27. Hot water freezes faster than cold water. It's called the Mpemba effect. This is because the velocities of water particles have a specific disposition while they're hot that allows them to freeze more readily.

28. Oxygen is odourless and colourless as a gas but when it is liquified or solidified it appears pale blue.

29. There are Dry Valleys in Antarctica, which have not seen a single drop of rain or snow in the past 2 million years, which according to the scientists, is due to the Earth's gravitational pull.

30. Alaska is both the Westernmost as well as the Easternmost State of the U.S.

31. Blue zones are regions in the world where people tend to live longer and healthier than any other places. Identified by Gianni Pes, Michel Poulain and Dan Buettner, the five "blue zones" postulated are: Okinawa (Japan); Sardinia (Italy); Nicoya (Costa Rica); Icaria (Greece); and Loma Linda California (US).

32. That typical fresh, salty whiff that you get of beach air is actually the smell of rotting seaweed.

33. The Great Barrier Reef in Australia is the planet's largest living structure made by marine animals covering an area of about 3,44,400 sq km, has another distinction too- it has its own post office box on the Agincourt reef, 72 km offshore at the coral sea. One of the requisites for sending a letter here is to use the special Great Barrier Reef stamp.

34. If you keep going North, you will eventually go South, but if you keep going East, you will never go West.

35. Lonar Lake, a saltwater lake in Buldhana, Maharashtra, India, was created by a meteorite collision impact during the Pleistocene Epoch. It is one of the four known, hyper-velocity, impact craters in basaltic rock anywhere on Earth.

36. Minus 40 degrees Celsius is exactly the same as minus 40 degrees Fahrenheit. Celsius and Fahrenheit are two different temperature scales, but they intersect at one point when they equal each other, which is at -40 °C and -40 °F.

37. If you cool liquid helium just a few degrees below its boiling point of -452°F, it will turn into superfluid. It can trickle through molecule-thin cracks, climb up and over the sides of a container, and remain motionless when whirled. Physicist John Beamish points out that any other liquid, if stirred and then set aside for a few minutes, would stop moving because the collision of the atoms in the liquid slows them down and finally they become still. "But if you did that with helium at low temperature and came back a million years later," he says, "it would still be moving." Such is a peculiarity of this element!

38. That liquids expand on being frozen can be seen from an ice cube which takes up about 9% more volume than the water used to make it.

39. Time goes faster at the top of the tall buildings than at the bottom. According to Einstein's Theory of Relativity, the farther an object is from the Earth's surface, the faster time passes. This effect is known as "gravitational time dilation".

40. Under the 8.7 miles of ice in Greenland, there exist fossilised plants.

41. Thioacetone is the world's smelliest chemical. It's so bad that, after a lab technician dropped a vial of it, it induced instant vomiting even from people in buildings almost half a mile away.

42. Located in the middle of the Bering Strait, Diomede Islands are shared by both the USA and Russia. While the smaller one is with America, the bigger one (called Gvozdev island in Russian), lies with Russia. Geographically they are just 2.4 miles apart, but have a 20 hour time difference because of the Date Line. Which is why they are nicknamed-Tomorrow Island (Big Diomede) and Yesterday Island (Little Diomede).

43. When being poured, you can actually tell the difference between hot and cold water just by listening to it. That's because water makes different pouring sounds at different temperatures. Heat changes the thickness or viscosity of the water, giving it a different pitch. And when cold, the water is more viscous, and so makes a higher- pitched sound.

44. The pH scale indicates the acidity or alkalinity of a solution. The scale's values range from zero (most acidic) to 14 (most basic). While pure water has a pH value of 7, the acid in the human stomach is typically between 1.0 and 2.0, which means it's incredibly strong. A study on Human stomach acid, published in the journal 'Gastrointestinal Endoscopy', stated that the "thickened back of a single blade", which was immersed for 2 hours in the gastric acid, dissolved completely.

# Space & Technology

*The Earth Is The Cradle Of Humanity, But Mankind Cannot Stay In The Cradle Forever.*   - Konstantin Tsiolkovsky

1.  The vastness of the universe is literally unfathomable. Despite billions of galaxies and a considerable amount of galactic dust, there are huge tracts of space-time not just between any two stars but also among galaxies. If the stars were shrunk to the size of tennis balls, they'd be lying no less than 4,800 km apart from each other, that's the kind of "empty space" that exists in the Universe.

2.  In 2001, Dennis Tito, an American businessman became the first space tourist to be launched into orbit aboard a Russian supply mission to the International Space Station. For a six-day space trip he is said to have paid twenty million American dollars.

3.  Our weight is the combination of all the large-scale and long-term forces on our body. The four dominant ones are- the gravities of the Earth, Sun and Moon and the centrifugal force of the earth. That is the reason we weigh less at the equator than the poles, though our body itself does not change.

4.  Clouds are not weightless. The average cumulus cloud can weigh up to a million pounds. That's about as heavy as the world's largest jet when it's completely full of cargo and passengers.

5.  The atmospheres in Neptune, Uranus, and Saturn have such extreme pressure that they can crystallize carbon atoms and turn them into diamonds.

6.  Neutron stars are massive stellar objects with a mass about 1.4 times that of the sun. Born from the explosive death of another supergiant star, these tiny objects are extremely dense. If a teaspoon of mass is dug from a neutron star, the mass will weigh around 6 billion tons, such a high density it has.

7.  In 2015, Canadian astronaut Chris Hadfield released his first album in space, which was entirely recorded while he was in orbit.

8.  Nothing can ever exceed the speed of light and nothing with mass can ever reach this level, but assuming it could, it would still take about 10 million years to reach the edge of the Milky Way.

9.  The spacesuits that are in current use were originally designed for the Space Shuttle program in the 1970s and had cost an eye-popping $12 million each, of which 70% cost is only for backpack and control module. At today's pricing, a space suit would be something like $150 million. Lack of funds has made NASA continue with the use of the repaired aging spacesuits. Recently the agency awarded contracts to two private companies to build and maintain the new generation spacesuits. Axiom Space and Collins Aerospace will be using the technology NASA was using. However, designing, development, qualification certification, and production of spacesuits with the support equipment to enable space station and Artemis missions, will be sole responsibility of the two companies. The contract for all of the task orders has a ceiling of $3.5 billion, from now (2023) until 2034.

10. For tens and thousand years, photons will remain trapped inside the Sun.

11. Big Freeze is the expected end of the Universe. Since the Universe is expanding at an accelerated speed and simultaneously cooling, once all the usable heat is denuded from the Universe, it will go cold and ultimately die.

12. The sun doesn't change colour during sunset. We only see it that way because the sun's wavelengths react to the different substances in the atmosphere.

13. Although astronauts drink recycled water that comes from their showers, sweat and even urine, their water is much cleaner than the majority of water people drink on Earth.

14. Moon might seem to be a barren land but it actually has ice on its poles, much like the Earth, and water in the interior.

15. Venus has no varied seasons as such. Its circular orbit helps maintain an almost same temperature throughout its revolution.

16. Some scientists believe that Neptune is not the last planet of the Solar System and that there is the so- called Planet Nine, five to ten times larger than the Earth, that has thus far remained undetected.

17. Jupiter has 79 known moons revolving around it.

18. Mars is the only planet known to mankind that is populated by robots, which were sent there from the Earth.

19. Planet J1407b's ring system is two hundred times larger than that of Saturn. It has around 30 rings and each of those rings are tens of millions of kilometres in diameter.

20. A gigantic cloud was discovered in 1995 near the constellation of Aquila, which is a thousand times larger than the diameter of our Solar System. According to the scientists it contains 400 quintillion litres of alcohol, which is enough to last for a billion years even if 300 thousand litres of alcohol is consumed daily.

21. The Universe is expanding at an accelerated speed, possibly due to the fact that the repulsive gravitation of dark energy is overpowering the attractive gravitation of matter.

22. The Sun's magnetic field and the energy that constantly explodes there, makes its atmosphere a million degrees hotter than its surface.

23. The moon rotates at 10 miles per hour compared to the earth's rotation of 1000 miles per hour.

24. Buzz Aldrin is said to have claimed $33.31 in NASA travel expenses on his return trip from the Moon.

25. Since the moon attracts you in the same way as it does the water bodies on earth, you weigh slightly less when it is directly overhead.

26. Pluto is only half as wide as the United States from the West Coast to the East, and its entire surface is smaller than the territory of Russia.

27. The Chinese started documenting the appearance of Halley's Comet as early as in BCE 613.

28. Russian scientists expect mankind to encounter alien civilizations within the next couple of decades.

29. After the discovery of ethyl formate in the Milky Way, one may say that the centre of our galaxy smells like rum and tastes like raspberries.

30. Neutron stars rotate extremely fast- up to a hundred times per second.

31. Astronauts wear specific colour spacesuits based on the nature of their job. The Advanced Crew Escape Suit (ACES), which is of "International Orange" shade, is the space shuttle ascent and entry suit. It is equipped with a parachute, life raft, radio set, strobe lights, flare kits, motion sickness pills and other similarly important stuff. The ACES' orange colour is highly visible against any kind of landscape, particularly in the seas, which makes the astronauts' landing safe. The Extravehicular Activity (EVA) suits, which are bulkier, are worn when space-walking. Its white colour best reflects sunlight and is easily distinguishable against the black expanse of space. The EVA is designed with a life support system in an essentially vacuum-space, and thus has a tough shell to prevent astronauts from small pieces of space hence equipped with an in-built drink bag, an adequate supply of oxygen, battery power, a radio a tether,that keeps the astronaut connected to the space station and a temperature control system, which recycles body sweat and keeps the astronauts cool despite extreme conditions. The backpack weighs 45 kilos. The Intra-Vehicular Activity (IVA) suit is much more comfortable and flexible than the EVA. It's built to provide both more mobility and protection in the event of an accident, say for example depressurization of the spacecraft. When not performing any specific duties, the royal blue jumpsuit is the standard NASA attire for astronauts. They can be seen in blue when making public appearances or during their training sessions.

32. In about 4.5 billion years, the Milky Way will collide with the rapidly approaching Andromeda Galaxy, and this collision will be the end of these two galaxies.

33. Olympus Mons on Mars is the tallest mountain in the Solar System.

34. Saturn is mostly made of gas and has a very low density.

35. Sunsets on Mars are blue because the light is reflected from the dust particles in its atmosphere.

36. Stephenson 2-18 is the largest known star for now.

37. Jupiter has such a strong gravitational pull that it attracts most of the asteroids in the solar system, thus being the primary reason the majority of potentially harmful asteroids do not reach the Earth.

38. The atmosphere of planet K2-141b basically comprises rock material, so pebbles condense out of the air, and it rains stones into the oceans of molten lava.

39. Composed majorly of frozen ammonia, methane or water, comets can be easily called giant space snowballs.

40. Jupiter doesn't orbit the sun's centre, it orbits a spot in empty space between it and the sun called the barycenter.

41. The reflective panels installed by NASA's Apollo missions in 1969, have shown that the moon is currently drifting little by little away from the earth by about 1.5 inches every year.

42. The most distant photograph of the Earth is called 'Pale Blue Dot'. It was taken from an incredible distance of about 6 billion kilometres.

43. Almost all hydrogen atoms were formed during the Big Bang 13.787 billion years ago, and as we carry hydrogen atoms in our bodies, at least some part of us dates back to the beginning of time.

44. Since some parts of space would never have come into contact, it's surprising then that the temperature of the Universe is uniform everywhere.

45. After the explosion of a gigantic star, the core that gets formed into a neutron planet becomes so dense that a teaspoon of its material might weigh more than Mount Everest.

46. The Great Red Spot on Jupiter has shrunk by 40% in the last one and half century. What looks like a spot is a huge storm, the strongest in the Solar System, and it's been going on ever since Jupiter was first observed.

47. Assuming that every star has at least one planet rotating around it, the Milky Way galaxy would contain a minimum of 100 billion planets.

48. The footprints of the Apollo astronauts left on the surface of the Moon will remain there for millions of years to come, because the Moon has no atmosphere and therefore no winds or other factors to undo them.

49. The sun, including our whole solar system, orbits around the centre of the Milky Way Galaxy at an average speed of 828,000 kilometre an hour and completes a galactic or cosmic year in about 230 million years, meaning, the last time the sun was in this exact location was during the time when the dinosaurs roamed the Earth.

50. A NASA study concludes that a bolt of lightning is four times hotter than the sun.

51. Venus takes 243 Earth days to complete one rotation on its axis and 224.7 Earth days to orbit around the sun, which makes its one day longer by 17.16 to one year.

52. Pluto didn't even complete one revolution around the sun between its discovery in 1930 and its declassification as a planet in 2006.

53. 95% of the Universe is made of dark matter and dark energy, and mostly impenetrable.

54. Neptune, the blue planet, has the strongest winds of the entire Solar System. With the speed of 1,100 mph, the winds are 1.5 times faster than the speed of sound.

55. Active stars are primarily made of plasma, which is a neutral ionised matter.

56. Not the Great Wall of China, but China's pollution that's visible from space. Although during Covid-19 the nitrogen-dioxide emissions over China dropped, post pandemic the situation, as the satellite visuals capture, are going up again.

57. Swathed in thick layers of clouds, the mountains on Venus are covered with snow, but unlike the Earth, the Venusian snow is mostly made from heavy metals : galena (lead sulphide) and bismuthinite, which gives the 'snow' a light grey metallic lustre. About 96 % of the atmosphere on Venus is composed of carbon dioxide, and it has nearly 100 times as much atmospheric gas as Earth does.

58. Every atom in existence is about 99.99% empty space, which means everything in the entire universe is made up of mostly nothing.

59. Astronauts in space lose significant bone and muscle mass because of zero gravity.

60. The word 'Astronaut' was first used in 1880 by the British writer Percy Greg. It was the name he used for a spaceship in his novel "ACROSS THE ZODIAC". By the 1950s it has become the commonly used word for a space traveller.

61. Ceres, Pluto, Haumea, Makemake, and Eris are five officially recognized dwarf planets as of now, with more discoveries, new ones will get added to the list. Pluto became the ninth planet of the solar system after being discovered in 1930, but by the 1990s its status as a full fledged planet began to be challenged. In 2005, when Eris was discovered, it was considered to be a large asteroid. Further studies on it revealed that it was a dwarf planet, giving rise to the debate on Pluto's status- if a larger and denser Eris could be a dwarf planet, why was Pluto still a planet? Finally in 2006, the International Astronomical Union's (IAU) sealed Pluto's fate, demoting it from the status of a planet. Dwarf planets are celestial objects that are smaller in size than a full fledged planet and lack the gravitational forces needed to pull in and accumulate all of the material found in their orbits. None of the known dwarf planets in our solar system is bigger than the Earth's Moon.

62. "Veggie" is the Vegetable Production System on the Space Station. The NASA astronauts study plant growth in microgravity while adding fresh vegetables to their diet. These lab-plants are grown in a "pillow" filled with a clay-based growth media, water and fertilizer. The absence of gravity makes plants use other environmental factors, such as light, which they receive from the LEDs put above them. The first plant grown in Space was Thale Cress in 1982. While Russian cosmonauts have been eating some space-grown veggies since the early 2000s, the NASA astronauts ate their first space crop on August 10, 2015, when they sampled red romaine lettuce.

63. In 1998, the perfume industry giant International Flavors & Fragrances (IFF) teamed with the Wisconsin Center for Space Automation and Robotics (WCSAR) to take aboard the Space Shuttle (STS-95) a miniature rose "Overnight Scentsation", cultivated by IFF researcher Dr. Braja Mookherjee for 9 days. It was to examine the effect on the production of essential oils in the rose plant in microgravity. The fragrance of a rose is made up of nearly 200 different compounds, and a slight shift would open up hundreds of more possibilities and so it did. The results were literally 'out of the world'. The Space Rose had a critically altered fragrance. Once commercialised by IFF, the Space Rose note was incorporated by Shiseido Cosmetics Ltd. (US), in creating a perfume called 'Zen', which according to the company combines three notes for the fragrance- floral, woody, and spiritual.

64. Clouds are not water vapour. Water vapour is the gas state of $H2O$ and is invisible. Clouds are collections of liquid water droplets or ice that are small enough to float.

65. The Murchison Meteorite, is the oldest rock on Earth, which landed in Murchison, Australia in 1969. It is believed to be 4,600,000,000 years old and existed even before the earth was completely formed.

66. The first food item to be eaten in space was applesauce. It was aboard Friendship 7 that American astronaut John Glenn had it through a packaged tube, along with sugar tablets with water. This was to prove people could eat, swallow, and digest in a zero-gravity environment.

67. In 1781, during a telescopic survey of the zodiac, English astronomer William Herschel noticed a new planet and promptly named it the Georgium Sidus (the Georgian planet) after King George III. In 1850 on the proposal of the German astronomer Johann Elert Bode, the name was switched from Georgium Sidus to Uranus, the Greek god of sky.

68. The Japan Aerospace Exploration Agency spacecraft Hayabusa2 (launched in December 2014), became the first mission to complete a successful landing on a fast-moving asteroid body (Rygyu) on 27 June 2018. In its report in March 2023, the research team's analysis of samples of asteroid Rygyu confirm that life came to Earth from deep space, it did not emerge on its own on the planet. Two organic compounds essential for living organisms- Uracil and Niacin were detected in the asteroid rocks. This validates scientists' theory that bodies like comets, asteroids and meteorites that hit Earth billions of years ago seeded it with the primordial ingredients that were crucial for the advent of life on the planet.

69. In 1977, NASA launched 2 Voyager probes with phonograph records on a 12-inch gold-plated copper disk containing 116 images and sound recordings, should some intelligent extraterrestrial life be encountered. A committee chaired by Carl Sagan made the selection. The compilation has interesting pieces such as- human sounds like heartbeats, footsteps, laughter, child-mother kiss, the animal sounds of whale, chimpanzee, elephant, frog, dog, sounds of train, bus, rain, wind. Then there is music from different cultures including Indian classical music (Raag Bhairavi: Jaat Kahan Ho), compositions by Johann Bach, Beethoven, Mozart, greetings from Earth people in 59 languages, of which 10 are Indian. Apart from the sounds from earth there are images as varied as could be imagined- sun, planets, human body organs, hand X-ray, DNA structure, Indonesian flowers, a Japanese Schoolroom, a dancer from Bali, a Turkish old man, a gymnast, a Street scene of Pakistan, Golden Gate Bridge, Great Wall of China, Taj Mahal, UN Building, Sydney's Opera House and so on. There are printed messages from the then US President Jimmy Carter and U.N. Secretary-General Kurt Waldheim. In August 2012, robotic Voyager 1 probe entered interstellar space, creating history. Although no bumping into any extraterrestrial lives has been reported so far, the Voyager, which is currently zipping through space at around 17 kilometres per second, has definitely raised hopes of catching up with some 'deep-explorers' in the future.

# Tidbits

*Aerodynamically, The Bumblebee Shouldn't Be Able To Fly, But The Bumblebee Doesn't Know It So It Goes On Flying Anyway !* - Mary Kay Ash

1. The first "around-the-world" telegram was sent on August 20, 1911 to test how fast it could travel to different countries before returning. The message travelled almost 28,000 miles in 16.5 minutes.

2. '2520' is the smallest Number that can be exactly Divided by all the Numbers from 1 to 10. It was discovered by the intuitive mathematical genius Srinivas Ramanujan. He made substantial contributions to the analytical theory of numbers and worked on elliptic functions, continued fractions, and infinite series.

3. Firefighters use 'wetting' agents to make water wetter.

4. Cans of diet soda will float in water but regular soda cans will sink.

5. Prior to the use of mercury, thermometers would have brandy filled into them.

6. According to an American magazine, before the invention of colour TV, 75 % of people said they dreamed in black and white. Now only 12% do.

7. The Metric System, which emerged in the nineteenth century, got a formal sanction by the US Congress in 1866. More than a century and a half later, the US remains the only nation in the world to still stick to the Imperial system. A periodical in defence of the traditional system published in Ohio in the 1880s will tell you why. It read that the imperial system of measurement is "a just weight and a just measure, which alone are acceptable to the Lord."

8. In its issue of Nature, in August 2011, scientists claimed that Earth once had 2 moons. This second moon may have orbited Earth before it banged into the other one. This explains why the two sides of the surviving lunar satellite are so different from each other.

9.  Scientists have concluded that the chicken came first not the egg, because the protein which makes egg shells is only produced by hens.

10. Situated in Plantage Kerklaan Amsterdam, Micropia is a unique museum. It aims at generating interest of the general public in Microbes. The exhibits are grouped majorly under three categories- Fermentation, Viruses, and Vaccines. One of the popular corners here is the exhibit called "Mouth to Mouth". The Kiss-O-Meter measures the number of microbes that get transferred when people kiss. It was opened in 2014 and has already earned quite a name for itself.

11. In April 1995, a NASA tech briefing "Using Spider-Web Patterns To Determine Toxicity" was published. The experiment was to demonstrate how psychoactive drugs such as amphetamine, mescaline, marijuana, chloral hydrate, theophylline, IBMX, caffeine, benzedrine, LSD, and others incapacitated the mind and body of the spider resulting in erratic and abnormal web patterns.

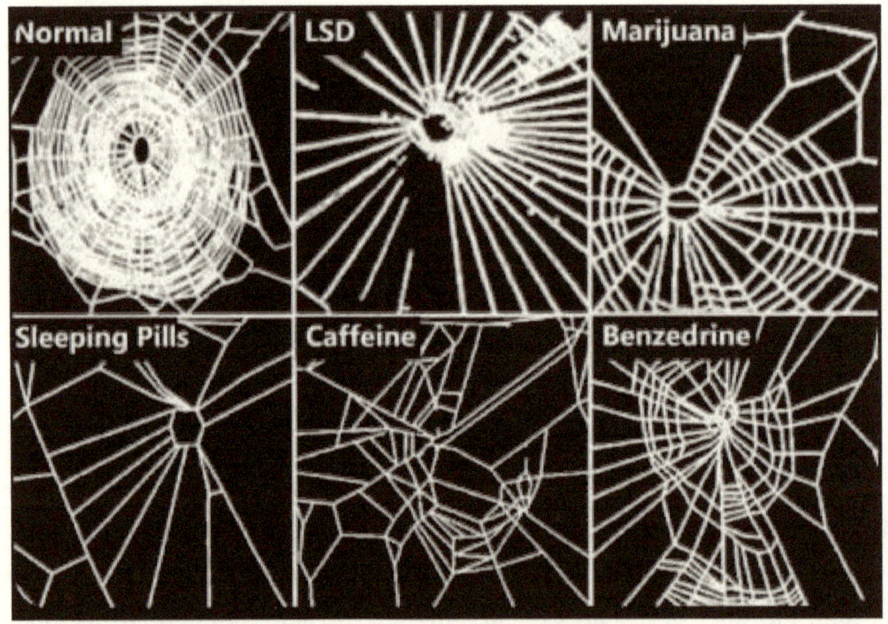


*(Web-Spider pattern under intoxicated state: NASA/Wiki Commons)*

12. There is an interesting story behind the introduction of the word "Spam". It was in 1993, when software developer Richard Depew accidentally posted the same message some 200 times, essentially "spamming" the chat board. Later in 1998, the word was added to the Oxford English Dictionary to describe junk email.

13. The Internet was called "The Galactic Network" when it was first created.

14. A 1995 study shows that the birds like a pigeon can tell the difference between the two artists- Picasso and Monet.

15. We have come a rather long way indeed! In 1973 the entire Internet had only 45 connected computers, the boxes in the image are the nodes which were the first-generation routers on ARPANET, the predecessor of the internet we know today. The ARPANET project was originally funded by a branch of the U.S. Military. Today there are about 5 billion active users of the internet.

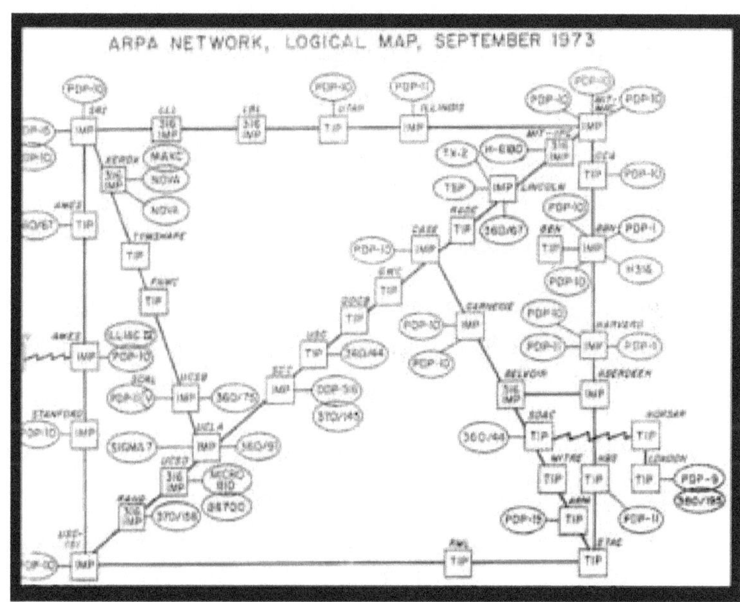


*(Image : ARPA/ARPAnet Completion Report)*

16. Conservationists in South Africa are infusing a special red dye into the horns of live rhinos. The mixture renders the horn completely useless to poachers trying to sell it commercially, and is also toxic for human consumption.

17. One of the reliable pregnancy tests before the 60s was to inject a woman's urine into a female African clawed frog, if the frog ovulated in 12 hours, the woman was pregnant.

18. Studies show that Flip-flops add about 25% to the ocean plastic and rubber accumulations.

19. Water slide testers check to see if the water slides in resorts, theme parks and hotels are both fun and safe.

20. The silk of spider web is the strongest natural material. It is five times stronger than steel.

21. Surtsey in Iceland is one of the world's youngest islands. No visitors are allowed to visit this spot, because human intrusion will upset the ecological sequence that is currently ongoing on the island.

22. During winters when the temperatures are really low, Chicago is said to set its railway tracks on fire to ensure the smooth running, departures and arrivals of the trains on time.

23. The introduction of the smartphone has increased mental disorders multi fold. As per a report, while depression rates among teens have increased by more than 60%, suicide cases have gone up by 56%.

24. Due to overfishing and disease, the oyster population in Maryland's Chesapeake Bay seriously suffered. But with dedicated efforts by the scientists, the Army Corps, the NOAA, and the Nature Conservancy, the state is now home to the world's largest man-made oyster reef. Home to more than one billion oysters, the area is a no-fishing zone, which is expected to give the population a chance to recover.

25. Clara Lazen, a 5th grader in Kansas City, Missouri, is credited with conceiving the structure of a molecule 'Tetranitratoxycarbon' in 2012. It was during her Chemistry class that she assembled a ball-and-stick model and presented it before her Science teacher Kenneth Boehr. Boehr, not sure, sent a picture of the model to his chemist friend Zoellner at Humboldt State University. Lazen had created a new molecule. In his paper on the molecule, published in Computational and Theoretical Chemistry, Zoellner credited both Clara Lazen and Boehr as co-authors.

26. Bhutan is the only carbon-negative country in the world.

27. According to studies, Twitter causes insomnia and it has become the most common sleep distraction in the world.

28. Toilet paper is bleached to make it softer and extend its life. The whiteness of toilet paper is just a by-product.

29. Laser tattoo removal doesn't actually erase a tattoo; it just helps break it down so white blood cells can carry it away.

30. The loudest noise ever recorded was the eruption of the volcano Krakatoa, Indonesia in 1883. The sound travelled around the world multiple times.

31. Svalbard Global Seed Vault in Norway stores 100 million seeds from across the world to restore the plant kingdom in case anything bad happens to our planet's vegetation. The vault is closed to the public.

32. There is a compound called geosmin which gives rain its distinct smell. Humans are very sensitive to it and are capable of detecting it at very low levels, similar to how sharks are able to detect blood.

33. A study on the plastic usage in our daily lives, conducted in the United States, revealed that humans ingest about 2,000 tiny pieces of plastic every week. Microplastics accumulating in human blood and organs, flags the concern for increase in the usage of environment friendly materials.

34. Longview in Washington has small treetop bridges called Nutty Narrows, made specifically to help squirrels cross the street. The bridge was proposed after some locals noticed squirrels, while crossing the street in search of nuts, would often get crushed under the cars. Soon a group of locals came together with the idea of building a bridge and Nutty Narrows was born. Built by Amos Peters, it's a 60 feet catenary bridge with a centre section resembling a suspension bridge. It was installed on March 19, 1963 and had cost around $1,000 to assemble. The bridge became an instant 'hit', with the squirrels, who started using it from the very next day. They were even seen teaching their little ones to use the ropes. The bridge got a lot of media attention and a considerable fan base. Its popularity and success inspired the construction of six other squirrel crossings in the state. A tourist attraction now, the original Nutty Narrows was added to the US National Register of Historic Places in 2014.

*(Nutty Narrows Bridge, Washington, Photo :Tom Banse)*

35. There's a sexual phenomenon named after President Calvin Coolidge. Once he and his wife were touring a farming facility. While inspecting the chicken enclosure Mrs. Coolidge observed a rooster sexually very active. On enquiring how often the rooster mated, she was informed- a dozen times a day. The story goes that she probably told the tour guide to communicate that to the President, when he came to that side. The guide did as was instructed to, Mr. Coolidge asked him if the rooster engaged with the same hen. When the guide said No, Mr. Coolidge slyly told the guide to let Mrs. Coolidge know that. That's how 'Coolidge Effect' came to be named.

36. Bullet proof vests, fire escapes, windshield wipers, and laser printers were all invented by women.

37. The first instance of global electronic communications took place in 1871 when news of the Derby winner was telegraphed from London to Calcutta in under five minutes.

38. The first ever traffic ticket was issued in 1899, to a taxi driver Jacob German for Speeding. He was driving at 19 km/h on Lexington Street, New York City.

39. Since it's rare to find a complete fossil of the dinosaurs, most of them are identified from just a single tooth or a bone. The archaeologists study whatever is available to them, such as teeth, bones, or tracks in order to identify and classify its type.

40. Everyone on Earth is at most fiftieth cousin with everyone else. And people that share the same ethnicity and live in the same country are likely to be related within 10 past generations.

41. When they get too hot, the lithium batteries in the electronic devices such as cell phones, tablets, laptops, E-Bikes, electric toothbrushes and tools etc., release more than a hundred toxic gases, lethal for humans.

42. Nestled in a small grotto at the base of The Eternal Flame Falls in New York burns an eternal flame. This 30 inch tall fire is believed to consume 2 pounds of gas a day, constantly supplied by the high concentration of methane underneath. Legend has it that Native Americans lit it thousands of years ago.

43. Around 90% of the most advanced chips are produced in Taiwan. It is also the unmatched leader of the global semiconductor industry, accounting for 50% of the world market, making the country almost indispensable for global economy and technological development.

44. Nobody knows who gave Earth its name, but the word itself can be traced back to the Indo-European word for "ground". All the planets in our Solar System, other than the Earth, have been named after the Greek and Roman gods.

45. Face feelers are also known as "sensory scientists". Their job is to use their hands to feel the difference in the product testers' skin both before and after they've used lotions and creams.

46. 'Point Nemo' is a spacecraft graveyard in the South Pacific Ocean.

47. People living in the Arctic regions have been protecting their eyes from snow blindness by using 'snow goggles' carved out of whalebone, horn and ivory for the past 4000 years.

48. Carbon dating only works for objects that are younger than about 50,000 years.

49. Water released by corn plants into the air is called corn sweat. A one acre corn crop can release 3,000-4,000 gallons of water per day and can raise the humidity levels of that area by up to 10%.

50. The 'five-second rule', which claims a food item safe for consumption even though it was dropped on the floor or on the ground, provided it was picked up under the stipulated time of 5 seconds, is a food hygiene myth. The origin of this false notion has no base, nor is there any scientific consensus on the factuality of this rule.

51. A tyre is one polymer with a large molecular weight, hence we can say that a rubber tyre is made up of only one molecule.

52. For long linseed oil was used in paint manufacturing. The First World War however, changed the scenario. An acute shortage of supply of linseed oil forced the manufacturers to find newer options. The result was the invention of artificial resins, which were both economical and long lasting.

53. In 2007 while researching the rate of melting permafrost, using Google Earth and NASA technology, a Canadian-based Ecologist Jean Thie noticed a beaver impoundment. Surrounded by heavily forested marshland, the 850 metre stretch of the beaver dam, the largest in the world, lies in the Wood Buffalo National Park. Using the earlier images of the park and aerial photography, he concluded that this supersized architectural project, visible from space, began in the 1970s. Though the beavers create these dams to store food and protect them from the predators in the forests, these sturdy and lasting structures modify the natural environment in such a way that they often reroute rivers and streams, thereby altering entire ecosystems of the regions in favour of wetlands and flourishing diverse populations of plants and animals.

*(An Aerial view of the beaver dam: PARKS CANADA)*

54. Lego mini-figures have little holes in the top of their heads to allow air to pass through should a child ever get one stuck in their throat.

55. Cradled between the islands of Cancun and Isla Mujeres of Mexico, 'The Cancun Underwater Museum' (Museo Subacuático de Arte) is the biggest underwater museum in the world. With about 500 sculptures on display, the tourists can view these art pieces via glass bottom boats, while the snorkelers and scuba divers can move in between the exhibits. The sculptures are created with pH-neutral marine concrete, so as not to harm the sea life.

56. Paper bags aren't any better for the environment than plastic ones are.

57. Prior to the 20th century, squirrels were one of America's most popular pets.

58. In an effort to prevent obesity the Japanese Government introduced 'Metabo Law' in 2008. It requires people between 40 and 74 ages to have their waist circumference measured annually, which limits 85 cms approx for men and 90 cms for women. Companies and local governments are fined for not meeting specific targets. NEC, a Japanese multinational IT and Electronics Corporation, noted that the government collected an amount of US$19 millions from the fines imposed.

59. When Nikola Tesla died in 1943, the US Office of Alien Property confiscated his belongings and unreleased inventions from his hotel room in New York. Tesla had claimed to have created a powerful particle-beam weapon, the "Death Ray", and in the absence of any satisfactory response from the authorities it's still a mystery to this day. Although in 1952, a US court had declared Tesla's nephew Kosanovic the rightful heir to all his properties, it is said that while the FBI had originally recorded 80 trunks among Tesla's possessions, only 60 arrived in Belgrade. Some 20 odd boxes with Tesla's stuff went mysteriously missing. All Tesla belongings are housed at Nikola Tesla Museum in Belgrade, Serbia. Despite the US government's calling the invention of the 'beam weapon' only a speculation, Tesla's biographer Seifer claims that even senior military officials such as Brigadier General L.C. Craigee opines that "there's something to this--the particle beam weapon is real."

60. The original name for the search engine Google was Backrub. According to Larry Page, the idea of creating Google actually came in his dream. He was 22 then, when he dreamed that he managed to download the entire web and kept all those links. Google was finally launched in 1998.

61. Japanese scientists have designed a 'robotic girlfriend's hand' for people who feel lonely and low and just want a hand to hold on to. The hand is able to heat up and even sweat like a real human's.

62. A limestone cliff in Bolivia is home to over 5,000 dinosaur footprints belonging to 10 different species from the Cretaceous Period. Some of these date back to nearly 68 million years. Since new prints are continuously being found, efforts are being made to preserve these. Cal Orcko has been brought under the UNESCO World Heritage list.

63. Once the crew of Gemini 3, astronaut pilot John Young snuck a corned beef sandwich onto his space flight for a six-hour mission. There being zero-gravity conditions inside the cabin, the sandwich began to fall apart the moment he took it out to eat. The sandwich had to be kept away before it could make any considerable damage to the shuttle. NASA was made to assure a strict vigilance on future missions after this episode.

64. In 1975, Jack Hetherington, a professor at Michigan University, had written a physics paper covering aspects of 'atomic behaviour under different temperatures', for an American Physical Society Science Journal. In those days Physical Review Letters published notable works, but only when it had multiple authors. Hetherington, who had reservations about including other researchers, found a solution. He added his family cat's name as his co-author. Stating he had no regrets for this deceit, in an interview he disclosed how the idea struck him. Chester, his cat, a Siamese, was sired by a Willard. All he did was to add genus to his cat's name. He added the initials F D (Felis Domesticus) and thus created F.D.C. Willard"- the joint author. The paper went on to become exceptionally influential. Once the truth was out, Chester, the cat, was invited to join the university's Physics department full time.

65. To counter any kind of future threat to biosecurity of Antarctic region, which might arise due to human presence- whether through on-going research programmes, governmental operations, tourism, or other commercial activities, that involves constant importations, the Protocol on Environmental Protection to the Antarctic Treaty prohibits entry of any non-native species of plants or animals in the region.

# The Ancients

*No Man Ever Steps In The Same River Twice, For It's Not The Same River And He's Not The Same Man.*   - Heraclitus of Ephesus

1.  Recent technologies reveal that the sculptures made by Ancient Greek and Roman were not white, as we see them today. They were painted with different colors, however over the period of time, the paints faded and disappeared due to weather.

2.  The Vikings discovered America nearly five hundred years prior to Columbus. Leif Eriksson of Greenland was the first European to land on the Island of Newfoundland.

3.  Ancient Greeks had a system where citizens could vote to exile a politician for 10 years.

4.  There was a belief in Ancient Greece that the "redheads will become vampires after death".

5.  In Ancient Greece, men usually wore tunics and those who sported trousers would be mocked at. Trousers in those days were considered effeminate.

6.  Ancient Egyptians considered Lotus as a symbol of resurrection, because it can bloom in flooded areas and not only survive for years during droughts but even bloom again when it is watered.

7.  Prostitution was a common aspect of ancient Greece culture and contributed a significant amount to the Greek economy. The prostitutes used to mark the soles of their footwear with "AKONOYOEI MOI", which translates to 'follow me'. This imprint on the floor was to lure the potential customers.

8.  Commodus, a Roman emperor, got so obsessed with the gladiator fights that he himself started participating in them. Since it was against the law to harm the Emperor, no gladiator would dare touch him. He won some 735 gladiator contests.

9. Ancient Greece had public toilets, made of marble slabs. In winters it wasn't unusual for the wealthy to send their slaves to sit on the seat to warm it up before they came to 'do' the thing.

10. Roman Emperor Marcus Aurelius Antoninus, was a philosopher, a humanitarian and the last of the Five Good Emperors. Once his wife Faustina confessed her passion for a combatant. The 'Good' humanitarian king ordered her to strip and have physical relations with the gladiator in question. While in the act, the gladiator was murdered and she was obliged to bathe in his blood. After cleaning up, she was to come back to her husband Marcus.

11. It was common in Ancient Egypt to give radishes, onions and garlic as wages to the workers.

12. The sweat of gladiators was believed to be an aphrodisiac. Women even added them into their makeup products. It was said to improve their beauty and complexion. Romans also used to drink gladiator blood because they believed it would cure them of diseases like epilepsy.

13. In ancient Egypt, whenever the pharaoh moved out, the accompanying servants would be smeared with honey to attract flies away from the pharaoh.

14. It wasn't only the Ancient Egyptians, even Elizabethan England used mice as remedies. The Ancient Egyptians put a dead mouse in their mouth when they had a toothache. The people in Elizabethan England used mice as a warts remedy.

15. Cocoa beans were not only used as currency by the Aztecs, it was even accepted as taxes from the other people.

16. The first mentions of Oxford University date back to the year 1096, which makes it nearly two hundred years older than the Aztecs. The Aztec Empire is said to have originated with the founding of the city of Tenochtitlán at Lake Texcoco by the Mexica in the year 1325.

17. The Great Pyramid at Giza built by Snefru's son, Khufu, is the most famous of all the pyramids in Egypt. The pyramids were basically tombs of pharaohs, who were believed to ultimately become gods in the afterlife, hence these tombs were filled with things a ruler would need to support himself in the next world. The Great Pyramid, constructed some 4,500 years ago, is Egypt's largest pyramid. It has a base that covers over 13 acres and stood 481 feet high, (now 450 ft), and was the tallest building in the world for 3,800 years. It has 8 sides and not 4, which distinguishes it from other pyramids. The concavity of the sides was so subtle that it wasn't until the advent of aviation that it was noticed.

*(The Great Pyramid at Giza, Egypt : Getty Images)*

18. Ancient Athenian boys went to school when they turned 7 and from then on these boys were put under the custody of the Spartan army. These boys were housed in dormitories with other boys, where they were trained as soldiers. Spartan men were not allowed to live with their families until they left their active military service at age 30.

19. Sisamnes was a corrupt royal judge during the reign of Cambyses II in Persia. His notoriety for taking bribes and passing unfair judgments, made the king arrest him as a prevaricator and get him flayed alive. His skin was used to upholster the judge's seat, on which his son, Otanes, would sit. His father's skin on the seat was there to always remind him to be prudent and impartial in his judgement and never indulge in corruption.

20. The Aztecs regarded childbirth as a form of battle—women who died in childbirth were thought to go to the same heaven as male warriors.

21. The Mayans would get their skulls deformed because it was considered beautiful. It was also common to drill holes in the teeth and insert jewels there.

22. The Aztecs imposed penalties like head-shaving, property destruction, and death upon people who were repeatedly found to be drunk.

23. A cave near the Greco-Roman city of Hierapolis in southwestern Turkey was believed to be an entrance to Hades, in the ancient times, probably because the cave emits poisonous gasses. During excavations, the archaeologists discovered a column nearby bearing a dedication to the god of the underworld.

24. Roman Emperor Caracalla, who ruled from 198 CE to 217 CE was a bloodthirsty tyrant who killed anyone who opposed him, which included his own family members such as his brother, his wife and even close friends and relatives. It is estimated that about twenty thousand Egyptians who were involved in either making or watching a play mocking him, were slaughtered by him.

25. In Ancient Rome the head of the family used to be the oldest living male, called the "paterfamilias" and he held full control of his family. Such arbitrary powers were entrusted with him that he had legal rights to decide whether a newborn gets to live or die. He could sell, disown or even kill his family members if he so wished. He headed the family's business affairs and properties and performed all religious rites on their behalf. His sons only received an allowance to manage their own households.

26. Meymand, a very ancient village located in Kerman Province, Iran is believed to be a primary human residence in the Iranian Plateau, dating back to 12,000 years ago and still has residents living in 350 hand-dug houses, amid rocks and boulders, of which some have been inhabited for as long as 3000 years. Before the advent of Islam, it was a Zoroastrian settlement, and before that Sun worshipping Vegan people. According to a theory, Meymand was built by a group of the Aryan tribe about BCE 800 to BCE 700. In 2005, Meymand was awarded the UNESCO-Greece Melina Mercouri International Prize for the Safeguarding and Management of Cultural Landscapes.

*(Meymand, Iran's 12,000-year-old settlement. Photos by (1) Ehsan Kamali, (2) Leman Altuntas and (3) Hamid Sadhegi)*

27. Doctors in Ancient Greece and Rome often used spider webs as bandages for their patients. It was believed that spider webs have natural antiseptic and antifungal properties, which would prevent infection. And the presence of vitamin K in the web would help clot the blood and heal the wounds fast.

28. Stonehenge, the prehistoric monument on Salisbury Plain in England, took nearly 1500 years to build. Radiocarbon dating suggests that the first bluestones were raised between BCE 2400 and 2200. It is said that they are so heavy that each one might weigh around the same as a blue whale.

29. Both the Greeks and the Romans used human urine as a mouthwash. They believed that the ammonia found in urine not only disinfected the mouth but also helped keep teeth pearly white. But it were Romans who went way higher in their madness, so much so that they imported human urine from Portugal and the market became so big that the emperor Nero famously levied a tax on all such imports.

30. It was customary during the Hellenistic times for a Greek man to pursue a younger boy as a lover. Upon seeing a boy, who the man was enamoured of, gift a live rooster, a valuable gift in those days. And thus the relationship would begin and as was the norm, would be over when the boy began to have his facial hair. It was time for him to look for another companion. The Greek men would always be on a lookout for the best-looking gym defined young bodies, who they could show off. Interestingly a relationship with coevals would be frowned upon.

31. Phryne, an incredibly beautiful courtesan, and one of the wealthiest women, who lived in Ancient Greece in BCE 300, had inspired several paintings and statues by famous artists of her time. But she is best known for her trial for impiety, where orator Hypereides, apparently her latest lover, defended her. The legend is that Hypereides called Phryne up in front of the judges, pulled her robes off and said, "Do you really want to kill this!" Bedazzled by her stunning beauty, the jury seemed to melt and she was acquitted immediately.

32. Human urine was treated as a valuable commodity by the Ancient Romans. It was used for tanning and laundering the white togas. Its substantial usage allowed the enterprising types to collect and sell it on profits. The immense possibilities of making big money, made it taxable by the government. The levying of taxes on the acquisition of urine, got us the popular Latin phrase "pecunia non olet", meaning 'money does not stink', its value is in being, not the source it's acquired from.

33. The enigmatic queen Cleopatra VII, was born to Greek Macedonian parents who were first cousins. She was 12 when her mother died and her elder sister became Egypt's new queen, but was murdered by her own father. Five years later he too died and Cleopatra, now 17, became the queen. According to the traditions, she married her 13 year old brother, Ptolemy XIII, who although very young, was a brilliant strategist which Cleopatra despised. Sensing her yearning for power, Ptolemy soon banished her from Alexandria on the charges of conspiracy against him. Not easily giving up Cleopatra approached Julius Caesar. Already blinded by her charms, he agreed to help. Ptolemy XIII was killed by Caesar in a war and Cleopatra's younger sister was captured and detained in Rome. Now with power in her hands, Cleopatra got married again, this time to her youngest brother, Ptolemy XIV, who was only 12 then. Two years later she got rid of him too. After poisoning him she claimed Egypt's crown for herself. Meanwhile Caesar had been killed and she had developed an affair with Marcus, Caesar's ally. This didn't go well with Octavius, Caesar's grand nephew, who imprisoned them, where Marcus and Cleopatra committed suicide. She was only 39.

34. Aristotle's philosophy on women would be not just misogynistic but blatantly degrading women by today's standards. Interestingly his philosophy had dominated the Western civilization well into the early modern period and never appalled anyone. Aristotle believed that Nature always aimed at perfection, and anything less than perfect was deformity, which is to say "women are imperfect men" and are born due to some kind of defect that had occurred during the time of conception, else a male would have been born. He found women to be inferior because their bodies were "too cold to produce seed (semen)". The ancient Greeks who glorified a male body, tended to view women as being passive and weak and not worthy of being treated as a man's equal.

# The World Of The Royals

*It is an old prerogative of kings to govern everything but their passions.*
-Charles Dickens (The Pickwick Papers)

1.  The first ever engagement diamond embedded ring was commissioned by the Archduke Maximilian of Austria for his betrothed, Mary of Burgundy in 1477. This spurred a trend for diamond rings among European aristocracy and nobility.

2.  Back in the 18th century, King George I, declared all pigeon poop to be the property of the crown. It was used as a vital ingredient in the manufacture of gunpowder. It was mixed with saltpetre, sulphur and charcoal to give it a bang. So important was this pigeon poop that George even appointed guards in the places where pigeons regularly perched in order to claim the 'property'.

3.  The conquest of the Ming Dynasty by the Manchus in the 17th century, brought a considerable change in the way the Chinese began to dress. Once annexed, the Manchus established the Qing dynasty. The new emperors forced the masses to wear not just their ethnic Manchu styled long robes and magua but even wear their hair in a style called the "queue." The queue was a shaved forehead and long braid down the back. It was deemed a criminal offence if a man tried to remove the queue or wear their hair in a different style. Chopping off the queue was a sign of rebellion against the government.

*(Hair styles of Qing & Ming dynasties: Image Credit: Quora)*

4.  In 1451, Philip, Duke of Burgundy, gave a four-day banquet. The high point was a Pie- which, when its lid was lifted, revealed twenty eight musicians playing inside it.

5.  Akbar had 300 wives and an additional 5000 women in his harem, which included dancing girls, concubines and sex slaves. The size of Akbar's harem grew in direct proportion to his empire, with each new conquest new additions were made. According to historians Akbar was "a typical mughal in his attitude towards women whom he collected in much the same way as an obsessive philatelist amasses stamps'. The harem would be guarded by a legion of eunuchs, where no man other than Akbar had an access. Most of these eunuchs were young men and boys, who had been forcibly castrated, either as punishment following defeat in a battle, or after having been donated by the rulers. Once emasculated, they were easier to exploit for their servitude. Eunuchs were heavily employed in harem for labour works, security and spy on the women and pass any relevant information to the emperor. Thus eunuchs with no families of their own were at mercy of the emperor, with no one to turn to, they became trusted and dependable slaves.

6.  Louis XIX was the king of France for just 20 minutes, which was after his father had renounced the throne. Ironically enough, Louis XIX also abdicated about 20 minutes after his father appointed him to the throne. Louis XIX shares the 'twenty minute ruler' record with Prince Luís Filipe of Portugal, whose father King Carlos I was murdered in an attack in which Luís Filipe too got so badly injured that he outlived his father by just about 20 minutes, and during these minutes, he was king of Portugal.

7.  Elizabeth Bathory, the Hungarian countess is said to be the most prolific female serial killer in European history. She is accused of allegedly killing and torturing hundreds of girls between 1590 and 1610, with the help of her loyal servants.

8.  Raja Jai Singh of Alwar, India, had a fleet of Rolls Royce which were employed to transport the city's waste. The story goes that the Raja, visiting London, was insulted by a Rolls Royce salesman, who took the ordinarily clothed Raja to be a commoner. Outraged, immediately after his return to India, the Raja ordered a fleet of Rolls Royce & put these luxury cars in the garbage collection duty. This dent in the reputation of the Rolls Royce made them tender an official apology to the Raja, after which the cars were withdrawn from trash transportation.

9. Louis VI, who stank badly, had his shirts rinsed with a perfumed concoction called 'Aqua Angeli', made with flowers, herbs and spices such as aloes-wood, nutmeg, storax, cloves and benzoin boiled in rosewater. After simmering for twenty four hours, a pinch of musk grains with water of jasmine and orange flowers were added to this mixture before soaking his shirts in it. This kept both his clothes and himself, pleasantly scented. He had commissioned his perfumer to create a new scent for each day of the week. With fountains & bowls filled with flower petals, furniture and draperies sprayed with perfumes, Versailles palace was seriously fragrant. Little wonder then that the French court became to be known as 'the Perfumed Court'.

10. Marie Antoinette, the queen of France, who was married at 14 had her first child after 8 years of marriage, which made it such an eagerly awaited event, that reportedly 200 people witnessed the birth of Princess Marie-Thérèse in 1778. According to the historians, to avoid any scandals, such as substituting the living baby for dead child or switching a royal baby girl for a desired boy, the practice of Royal mothers giving birth in front of a large crowd had been in trend for a long time in Europe. This practice was finally discontinued in England by George VI, when his daughter Elizabeth II, gave birth to the present British monarch Charles III.

11. Russian Empress Catherine had multiple lovers, several of them younger than half her age. She knew how to use sex as a tool to garner political power. After her successful coup in 1762 against Peter Ill, her husband, Catherine realised that marriage would mean conceding her power. Instead, she aligned herself with the high military officials and relied heavily upon her noble favourites. She was rather generous with her lovers, in return for their favours she showered them with expensive gifts, titles and wealth. Catherine ruled for 34 long years before dying in 1796.

12. Mary Tudor, Queen of England and Ireland, later the Queen of Spain was nicknamed "Bloody Mary" for her aggressive attempts to reverse the English Reformation. Following in the footsteps of her father Henry VIII, who had executed about 72,000 of his Protestant subjects, she, in her three years of rule, had about 300 of religious dissenters burned at stake. Some prominent religious figures like Thomas Cranmer, the archbishop of Canterbury, and bishops Hugh Latimer and Nicholas Ridley fell to the Marian persecutions.

13. Krishna Raja Wodeyar IV, the Maharaja of Mysore, used a customised Rolls Royce to shield his servants from the sun. The car, crafted in 1911, was auctioned a hundred years later, in 2011 fetching a whopping £400,000. With his personal assets worth £35 billion at the time of his death, the Maharaja was one of the world's wealthiest royals in the 1940s.

14. Swans, which were a delicacy once, were killed indiscriminately throughout Britain. In the 12th century the British royal family laid a claim to the ownership of every single bird in the UK. Since then injuring or killing one, is considered an act of treason. Even if a dead swan is found by someone, it must be turned over to the Crown, to someone known as the official Swan Marker. The present King Charles III has some 32,000 swans under his protection.

15. The law of the land entrusted unlimited powers with the French king. He wasn't just the master but the owner of the bodies and properties of all his subjects and therefore, was saluted as "a visible divinity". For instance when 4 year old Louis IV was proclaimed the king, he became the owner of the bodies and property of 19 million French people. Which meant he could do whatever he wished with them or their properties and they had no legal say in it.

16. So devoted was Queen Victoria to her deceased husband, Prince Albert, that from the day of his passing away in 1861, until she herself died in 1901, she wore only black. She was nicknamed "Widow of Windsor", by the English people.

17. In 1662 Catherine of Braganza had to travel to England to marry King Charles II. After alighting the ship, she stunned the welcoming party by demanding for a 'dish of tea'. Other than using it as medicine, tea hadn't yet caught up with the English. Portugal, however, had its nobility completely into traditional tea drinking due to its trade relations with China and Japan. The credit of introducing tea as a fashionable beverage to the British Royals goes to Princess Catherine.

18. The modern mind would be appalled at the concept of hygiene that existed in Europe. Let's check out a few of them- Spanish king Phillip II had prohibited regular bathing and banned public bath houses in 1576. Queen Isabella boasted that she had bathed only twice in her life, the day she was born, and the day she married. While Queen Elizabeth I bathed once a month, her successor, James VI reportedly never bathed. Louis XIV bathed "only three or two times throughout his life", that too on the recommendations of his doctor. Scottish royalty, including King James VI, wore the same outfits for months on end. Marie Antoinette, the French queen seldom bathed. Russian Czar Peter, took bath only occasionally and its reported that he would often urinate on the palace walls. British King James I was said to never bathe, causing the rooms he frequented to be filled with lice. Anne of Cleves did not believe in bathing or washing her hands even before eating. It is said that before she was presented to Henry VIII to be his wife, her advisors worked hard on the 'stinky' princess, and made her take bath. Since Catholics believed bathing to be sinful and "unreligious" behaviour, Spanish king Ferdinand disallowed that in their colonies too. Even the lice infected wigs did not deter them from their continual usage. Changing of clothes or washing them regularly was unimaginable for the common people. Before the 19th century, hair washing was not practised. Royal households later started changing their inner wear and linens, unpleasant body odours were removed using perfumes generously. Peter Ward in his book "The Clean Body: A Modern History" says, "The idea of being clean wasn't closely associated with water in the 17th century anywhere in the western world", and we can't agree more.

19. In 16th century England, any kind of blemishes on the face were seen as a mark of God's discountenance. These were believed to be the consequence of sins committed or the disoriented thoughts such as lewd or lascivious fantasies, which 'bubble up' from one's private parts and show up on the face. Since the marks were associated with sins, women used 'Venetian Ceruse', a skin whitener made of lead, to manifest flawless complexion. Elizabeth I, whose skin was left pitted after she was infected by smallpox at the age of 29, used to wear layers and layers of Ceruse, without removing the previous ones, lest her face should show the pockmarks.

20. French ruler, King Charles VI held a strange conviction that he was made of glass. He dressed himself in special clothing which had iron rods to 'support and protect his fragile' body. No one was allowed to come near or touch him, lest it should shatter him to pieces. In 1392, in a spurt of anger and paranoia he even slaughtered four of his own knights. He would roam his palaces howling like a wolf, sometimes wouldn't recognize his wife and children and with the help of alchemists even attempted to discover the philosopher's stone that would turn lead into gold. In 1396 Charles married his 7 year old daughter Isabella to the 29-year-old Richard II of England, and then 19 year old Catherine to 34 year old Henry V, after declaring his own son illegitimate. According to scholars Charles, who suffered 56 mental health episodes, was bipolar. In November 1405, Charles, who hadn't had a wash for 5 months, was covered in infected sores and lice, and had to be forcibly bathed. Nicknamed 'Charles the Mad', ruled France for 44 long years.

21. Mir Osman Ali Khan, the Nizam of Hyderabad, a Princely State during the British Raj in India, owned the world's largest diamond, a Jacob Diamond worth $200 million which he found in the toe of his father's shoe and decided to use it as a paperweight. Featured on the cover of Time magazine as the richest individual on the planet in 1937, he is said to have the wealth equivalent to 2% of the US GDP in those days.

22. In a Christmas feast, hosted by King Richard II of England in 1377, some three hundred sheep and twenty-eight oxen were served to the guests.

23. Mary Stuart was just six days old, when she was crowned the Queen of Scotland. In 1567 when she was 24, she was forced to abdicate the throne in favour of her one-year old son. A three times widow, she was perceived as a threat by her cousin, the English queen Elizabeth I, who kept her captive for 18.5 years and then got her executed at Fotheringhay Castle on 8 February 1587. Mary Stuart was just 44.

24. It wasn't just the food, which required testing for poisoning, Henry VIII even had his bed kissed every morning by the servants who made it. Every part of the linen- the sheets, pillows and blankets they had touched was to be kissed, to prove they had not smeared any of it with poison.

25. Vajiralongkorn, the present king of Thailand, is the wealthiest monarch in the world. He is protected by one of the most strictly enforced laws, which gives the royals and their pets an immunity of sorts. Any criticism can land one in prison,(up to 35 years) along with heavy fines. A number of international journalists, publications, television channels have either been punished or banned by Malaysia. He has his private residence in Bavaria, Germany where he resides. According to the German foreign ministry, they have objected to "having guests in our country who run their state affairs from here", Vajiralongkorn stays there claiming that his PM runs the kingdom. With 7 children from 4 wives and a number of mistresses, the controversial monarch enjoys polygamy despite a law against it in his own land. His 3rd wife, came in the limelight in November 2009, when a leaked WikiLeaks video showing the king in casuals, and his wife Princess Srirasmi Suwadee, wearing only a G-string, in attendance of several formally dressed servants, celebrating the birthday of the their dog, Air Chief Marshal Fufu. In 2011, Germany seized his aircraft in lieu of non-payment of €30 million, a 20-year-old debt. During the pandemic, in 2020, the monarch reportedly went into a self isolation, along with his entire harem of 20 mistresses to a Bavarian high end hotel.

26. King Vlad III Dracul, who ruled Wallachia (Southern Romania), was so cruel that he surpassed history and almost became a myth. He is believed to be the inspiration for Bram Stoker's 1897 novel 'Dracula'. Disemboweling, beheading, skinning, boiling alive were some of the methods that were used to kill, but his favourite and probably most impactful was impaling, which involved the insertion of a metal or wooden spike through the genitals to the victim's neck or mouth, giving him the most prolonged and excruciating pain. It is estimated that Vlad killed about 80,000 people, which includes 20,000 who were impaled and exhibited outside the city, rotting, slowly dying, and being pecked by birds of prey. Whatever the world viewed him as, to the Romanians, he's a national hero, who consolidated power and brought stability and kept the equally cruel Ottomans at bay until his death in 1476. He won praises even from Pope Pius II.

27. Unlike the Islamic rulers, the Chinese emperors were bound by rules to maintain a harem. It is estimated that besides the four official wives of the Emperor, there were some 40,000 women and girls- singers, dancers, concubines and maids in the Forbidden City, who all received a living allowance. There were strict rules for meeting or communicating with the Emperor. For instance, the emperor could sleep with his wife only once a month and with the highest ranking concubines five times a month. The belief was that a queen, unlike the concubines, had the highest and the most pronounced feminine nature, hence would conceive in one attempt. The overall management of the Harem was carried out by eunuchs. It was not the emperor but they, who picked up the concubine for the emperor. Before entering his bed chamber the girl was stripped naked (this was done to ensure that the girl wasn't carrying any hidden weapons in her dress). Once she stepped in, a eunuch would record every minute detail of what went in, in red ink. The emperor was not allowed to keep his concubine until morning, the Chief order of the House would knock on the doors to ask the emperor to send her away in case she overstayed. He would ask several questions about the performance of the concubine, whether she needed to be kept or let go. If the emperor showed an interest, a corresponding entry was made in a special book. The emperor could visit his wives on his own will, but that needed to be recorded too. It is believed that all such 'records' became the basis for Chinese erotic writings later during the Qing Dynasty.

28. Empress Anna Ivanovna is called "the worst-ever ruler of Russia- with terrible manners, unpleasing looks and barely literate", became a widow just 2 months after her wedding. Desperate to marry again, she wrote her family more than 300 letters, but in vain. This turned her so bitter that she began penalising those who were 'happily married'. One such nobleman was Prince Mikhail, who she turned into a court jester - his job was to sit on a nest of eggs and pretend to lay them, and welcome guests sitting in the same position. Not satisfied with inflicting this humiliation, it is said that she got a massive ice palace constructed in 1739 and forced Mikhail to marry one of her ugly old maids in clown's clothes. She then made them spend a night inside this ice palace- naked on the ice bed hoping to see them freeze to death. Though not immediately, the maid did die in a few days time. Russia got rid of this psychotic empress the following year, to a kidney failure.

29. Peter, the Great, is credited with modernising Russia, revamping Russian calendar and alphabet, building its first navy and updating the army. But there is a dark side to him which overshadows all these initiations. Peter was a cruel, erratic and dangerously intolerant ruler. His sheer disregard for human sensibilities was appalling. During one of his trips to Britain, while staying at John Evelyn's mansion, Peter and his friends trashed the place, damaging invaluable furniture, practising pistol shooting on the precious paintings, destroying the beautiful gardens, vomiting and urinating on the carpets and floors. Back home, he imposed a 'beard tax' on his officials. Being unhappy with his wife, he sent her away to live in a convent. He was dangerously homicidal and any defiance or revolt was met with mass executions. He crushed the Streltsy uprising of 1698, inflicting gruesome tortures, killing 1,200 captives. His own son was condemned to death. His project St.Petersburg, which was built under adverse weather and geographical conditions, took more than 100,000 lives. Peter ordered a yearly conscription of 40,000 serfs for the construction of the city, and who "died like flies from exhaustion, exposure, starvation and disease", making St. Petersburg literally a "city built on skeletons".

30. Excessive brutalities by Ashoka earned him the epithet "Chandashoka" (Ashoka, the Cruel) during his lifetime. From usurping the throne, initially with the help of Greek mercenaries, to killing all the male adversaries in his family, including his 99 half brothers and hundreds of loyalist officials, Ashoka went on to eliminate all possible rivals and enemies in his kingdom. 'Ashokavadana' eulogizes his acts of putting to death about 18,000 Ajivikas in Bengal alone and beheading about 500 officials with his own hands. A few years after converting to Buddhism, a political decision rather than remorse for violence and bloodshed as popularly believed, Ashoka went on to attack Kalinga. His own inscriptions on this invasion in BCE 262, speak of 100,000 killings, and an even larger number of wounded and hungry civilians, who later succumbed to death. This was in addition to 150,000 who were taken away as captives. His depiction as a 'Great' king, is a 19th century creation, based on almost no substantial historical evidence of him being great.

31. George IV's coronation, held on July 18, 1821, is so talked about not only because of being the most expensive and extravagant coronation in British history, but also because the king did not allow his wife, Queen Caroline to attend it. In fact the doors of the Westminster Abbey, the coronation venue, were slammed on her face. The Royal couple, who were also first cousins, had a short and disastrous married life. George had found her repulsive- "her looks, body odour, and lack of refinement"- it was 'despise' at first sight, but he agreed to marry her only because he was crippled under heavy debts and this marriage meant an increased allowance from the Parliament and strengthening Britain. Shortly after their marriage, he banished her from the kingdom and kept their only daughter Charlotte under his own custody. He pressured his wife for a divorce, which she refused. He then set up a secret commission "Delicate Investigation" to prove her guilty of infidelity, which too, fell flat. He didn't stop here. He neither let her attend Charlotte's marriage, nor informed her when she died a year later. Caroline was later stripped of her title and proven guilty. Despite the King's best attempts to decry her, Caroline retained a strong popularity among the masses, and subsequently it led proponents of women's rights and political reforms.

32. Some of the Royal court records reveal that several monarchs including the French King Francis I, the English kings Charles II and William II and Christian IV of Denmark and many more followed cannibalism. In his book, "Mummies, Cannibals and Vampires", Richard Sugg says, "Over in continental Europe, where the axe fell routinely on the necks of criminals, blood was the medicine of choice for many epileptics." Charles II, often distilled the human skull himself in his private laboratory. He had bought the recipe for $6,000. The royals, the monarchs, the nobles and the rich, who could afford, "applied, drank, or wore powdered Egyptian mummy, human fat, flesh, bone, blood, brains and skin", which were easily available at the apothecaries and physicians, sold to them by town executioners. The general belief was that even though a person passed away, some essence of the life force still remained in the body, particularly of those who did not have a natural death. Such a premature demise, deprived a person of his natural life span, and by consuming their body parts, the remainder of the life of the dead, would be ingested by the one consuming the dead.

33. The title "Groom of the Close Stool" refers to the man in charge of the furniture piece (stool), used as a toilet- to monitor and assist the king in his toileting needs. It is debated as to whether the job involved cleaning of the royal bottoms after the business was done, or not. Seemingly ignoble, it was a most coveted job. Owing to close proximity to the king during his private moments, an unobstructed access to him, travelling with him everywhere, in time became a powerful position. He, in a way, was privy to the king's trust and would often learn many court secrets. Not surprising then that the sons of noblemen or members of the gentry were usually awarded this job. King George III, is believed to have employed nine, the most number of Grooms during a single reign, including John Stuart who later went on to become the Prime Minister of Great Britain! The office was exclusively, one for serving male monarchs, but with the accession of Elizabeth I in 1558, it was "neutralized", and replaced by the First Lady/ Gentleman of the Bedchamber. By the 1660s, it became the office of Groom of the Stole (robe), and remained so until 1901 when King Edward VII decided to abolish it.

34. Ming dynasty's Zhu Houzhao was notorious for his idiosyncrasies and cruelty. His reign was marred by rampant corruption, ineffective administration and appointment of eunuchs to key positions, particularly Liu Jin, who later was executed in a most merciless manner for squandering millions. While the rise of corrupt eunuchs continued throughout the Emperor's reign, he remained entirely in pleasure-seeking, spending recklessly on his amusement. His harem was so overcrowded with concubines, that many of them starved to death due to lack of supplies. He even built palaces for exotic animals outside the Forbidden City and instead of the court, he spent majority of his time there. He even gave himself an alter ego, General Zhu Shou and indulged in capricious military expeditions. Once when a revolt was quelled before he reached, he ordered the captured prince to be released so that it would be he, who would catch and kill him. Houzhao once burned down the entire palace by storing gunpowder during the lantern festival. He had set up a commercial district in his palace where all his ministers, soldiers and servants were expected to act as commoners, merchants and street vendors while he walked through the scene pretending to be an ordinary person. Anyone who did not kowtow would be punished severely. Hundreds of officials who criticised his ridiculous ways, were tortured, suspended, demoted or even killed.

# The Victorian Era

*The Victorian world is extremely dark and extremely bright.*
*- Harry Treadaway*

1   One of the first homeless shelters were built in Victorian England. Although eerie looking, this coffin-shaped bed greatly helped hundreds of thousands vagrants, in finding a warm place during the cold nights. It could be rented by the homeless Londoners for four pennies each, from the Salvation Army.

2.  Body modification was a fad with the Victorians. In order to achieve the 'wasp waist', which was an impossibly narrow midriff, they would tighten up lace with super-snug corsets, which barely allowed them to breathe. A long- term pressure on growing ribs and vertebrae would compress the internal organs, leaving permanent indentations in the women's bodies. According to the doctors of the time, this madness to achieve an hourglass figure, was fatal for most women, but it didn't 'discourage' them from following the fashions of the day.

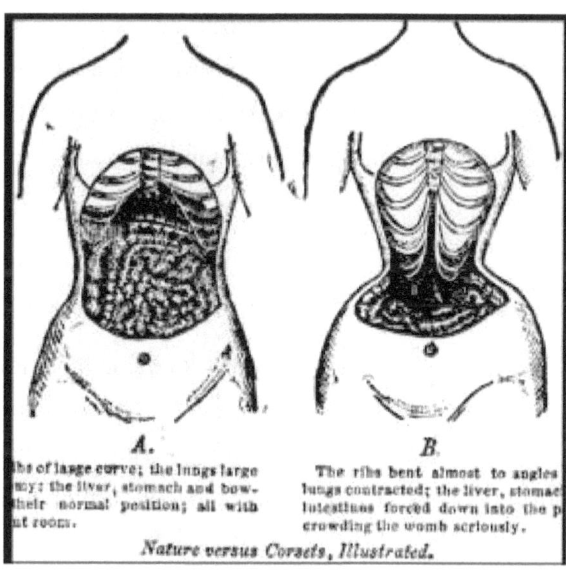

(A: Normal body B: Wasp waist :Image: www.alamy.com)

3.  The fear of being buried alive, which had peaked during the cholera epidemic, led to the invention of "life preserving" or "safety coffins". These coffin boxes were equipped with a mechanism. A device such as a cord was attached to a bell, so that the interred person, who was prematurely buried, could pull and communicate to the outside world that he was alive. However, a major problem arose, as the bodies decayed and naturally swelled, they would activate the bell system, thus giving false alarm.

4.  Victorian vacationers and visitors to Egypt would often bring a mummy as a souvenir. They would even hold the 'Mummy Unwrapping' parties, where the guests would gather to see what lay beneath the mummy's wrappings. One such printed invite sent by a host reads : "Lord Londesborough at Home: A Mummy from Thebes to be unrolled at half-past Two." Seeing such a rising demand for mummies, Egyptians even began transporting them from less-visited ruins to areas that got more tourists.

5.  The Victorians seem to have had a fascination for the gnomes and hermits. The wealthy ones who could afford, hired real-life humans to serve as ornamental garden hermits on their property. An advertisement put up by a certain Charles Hamilton shows this : "..he shall be provided with a Bible, optical glasses, a mat for his feet, a hassock for his pillow, an hourglass for timepiece, water for his beverage, and food from the house. He must wear a camlet robe, and never, under any circumstances, must he cut his hair, beard, or nails, stray beyond the limits of Mr. Hamilton's grounds, or exchange one word".

6.  Mummy brown", a colour made from the ground-up mummies, though expensive, was quite popular among the Victorian painters.

7.  Valentine's cards weren't meant only for the lovers, in the Victorian times. A lampoon of valentine's cards called Vinegar Valentines, enjoyed as much popularity. Some millions of vinegar valentines, with verses that humiliated a person, were sold between the 19th and the 20th centuries. Some of these cards were so mean that they reportedly led to the recipients committing suicide.

8.  Crinoline, French crin (horsehair) and Latin linum (thread or flax) was a stiff fabric used as underskirt and as a lining too. These underskirts or petticoats became so popular among the fashionable European women that in 1856, R.C. Millet, a Parisian designer patented the steel-hooped cage crinoline. This new steel frame crinoline soon caught the fancy of the British women too. Between 1850 and 1870 the mass-production in the factories across the Western world went up to tens of thousands a year. A crinoline could reach 18 feet wide at the base. It is estimated that the crinoline dresses took the lives of thousands of women- apart from catching fire due to their incredibly flammable nature, the hoops would get caught in the carriage wheels, machinery, gusts of winds or other obstructions which turned out to be fatal for them, but that was no deterrent, they kept wearing these.

*(A lady customer trying a crinoline : Image: Pinterest)*

9.  Unlike modern mental asylums, the Victorian ones would have criminals locked away along with the people with learning disabilities and mental illnesses. If Harriet Martineau, a social reformer, is to be believed, the public asylums contained "chains and strait-waistcoats, three or four half-naked creatures thrust into a chamber filled with straw, to exasperate each other with their clamour and attempts at violence; or else gibbering in idleness or moping in solitude." In short, people with mental disorders and those who were criminals, were treated alike by the Victorian law agencies.

10. Makeup was considered tacky but achieving a translucent white skin was a craze. Their favourite cosmetics were riddled with arsenic. One Dr. James P Campbell' Safe Arsenic Complexion Wafers even claimed to get rid of freckles, pimples, wrinkles, blotches and other "facial disfigurements." This might sound weird but they nibbled on the arsenic - advertised as "perfectly harmless". While women used the carcinogenic poison, to fight wrinkles the men presumably swallowed arsenic tablets as an aphrodisiac.

11. After his visit to Jerusalem in 1862, Edward VII started the trend of tattoos. Soon it became a craze. According to one estimate, more than 100,000 Londoners sported tattoos in the Victorian era.

12. High heel shoes and umbrellas were in great demand. In case someone was planning to empty their chamber pots into the streets, an umbrella would come in handy and the high heels saved the clothes from being soiled from the filth that the streets were covered with. Such was the condition of stenchy city roads of Victorian London.

13. One of the boorish practices that was popular among the Victorians was 'Corpse medicine'. Interestingly similar practices of cannibalism in the New World would be denounced, but claiming the use was for medicinal purposes, the Europeans unabashedly used it for themselves. It involved ingesting certain parts of the human body as a way of curing certain ailments. There were cookbooks and medical texts which explained how to optimally prepare these body parts, which could be easily procured from an executioner, though pharmacists too sold these in their pharmacies.

14. Victorians had this weird belief that digestion could best be achieved by eating in the dark, so most of them built their dining rooms in the basement.

15. For the Victorians "electrotherapy" was the solution for most kinds of health issues. From gout to muscular ailments, they believed everything could be fixed. However, a visit to the therapist, who shocked the problem area, did little to ease the ailments, all it did was leave ugly scars on their bodies.

16. When photography was invented, Victorians didn't flock to the photo studios just with the family members, in fact they even went for postmortem photographs. The dead family member or relative would be propped up with the help of wires or cords and photographed with the rest of the family.

17. The Victorians dressed both boys and girls in white frilly dresses until they were about big enough to go to school. The wealthier the more bows, buttons, ribbons, and lace these dresses would have. Even wearing bonnets wasn't restricted to girls alone, little boys too wore them.

18. Victorians' demands of modesty didn't allow women to openly plunge in water, but when recreational swimming became popular in the 18th century, it kickstarted a service industry that provided equipment for decent beach life etiquette. A 'beach bath' meant renting bathing machines, which were essentially covered wagons that were human or horse pulled. These consisted of a bench, a flannel gown, and towels and offered privacy - to change clothes and take a dip or just spend some time there. Soon this trend caught up with countries such as the US, France, Germany and even Mexico. However, with the dawn of the 20th century, when gender segregation was no longer mandatory on beaches in Britain, these bathing machines became redundant. Though at some beaches they were permanently stationed to be used as changing rooms, they gradually disappeared completely.

*(Women enjoying a beach day on their Bathing Machines, each marked with a number :*
*Photo: www.whizzpast.com)*

19. The Victorians had elaborate funeral services and families saved for years to pay for a good funeral service. Such was their obsession with death that women frequently made their own shrouds and carried it along in their wedding trousseau.

20. Exhibitions featuring exotic animals, deformed and physically challenged people and populations from unknown lands, were a fad with the Victorians. Historian Michael Diamond, quotes Queen Victoria's coronation as an example, which included entertainment in the form of "a display of giants, dwarfs, a two-headed woman, living skeletons, and the pig-faced lady." During her reign the 'human zoos' prospered. The 1895 African Exhibition at the Crystal Palace, was such a kind of human zoo in London, which presented some 80 Somalians along with two hundred African animals.

21. One of the insane fashions that was a rage with the Victorian women was to don live beetles as jewellery, and adorn gowns with dead butterflies and moths. That this lunacy pushed some species to the brink of extinction, won't be an exaggeration. An article that appeared in 1890 reads: "Not content with her slaughter of the innocents in the matter of birds, Dame Fashion has extended her murderous designs to moths and butterflies."

22. One of the most fatal diseases in the Victorian period, Cholera, killed thousands in London alone. Despicable hygienic conditions, raw sewage draining into the Thames, dumping of garbage in the open streets, contaminated water, were some of the most terrifying reasons for London becoming a cesspool and a disease hub.

23. Grave robbing was one of the most lucrative criminal ventures during the Victorian era. A shortage of cadavers for medical schools led to the black marketing of the corpses. Soon the 'business' began to thrive. Riots would occur when the families found bodies missing from the cemetery, but that did little to stop the freshly buried bodies from being stolen.

24. The Victorians took the mourning rather seriously. They had a specified mourning period depending upon the type of loss. If it was a husband, the widow would be expected to wear mourning clothes for two years- one year in full mourning and then next would be half mourning. During this period she was to wear only black and stay home. She was, however, allowed to attend church. The mourning women would wear elaborate jewellery and collect their tears in bottles to show how they shed tears over the dear departed. Men weren't bound by such rigid practices, however, in case of someone who died leaving behind no widow, there were women available on hire to cry over the grave.

25. When Italian astronomer Giovanni Schiaparelli claimed that through his telescope he spotted some artificial waterways which meant aliens were planning travel or commerce. Many affluent Victorians, who believed some sort of life existed on Mars, went on to leave behind money in their wills, to be used for making contact with the aliens.

26. It had been a long existing belief that the unborn baby had no gender until it exited the womb, therefore divine intervention was sought through ritual prayers to influence God. The expectant mother was made to lie in a dark chamber, which was believed to bring in a male child. The agony of labour and delivery were seen as an innate part of a woman's existence, which was closely associated with biblical doctrine - the fall of Eve in the Garden of Eden. (Genesis 3:16 -"I will make your pains in childbearing very severe; with painful labour you will give birth to children".). The Christian belief that women were destined to suffer, was one of the major reasons painkillers were never induced despite excruciating pain. In one case, in 1591 a woman in labour was burnt at stake after she asked for pain relief during the birth of her twins. Queen Victoria was probably the first Royal to ask her physician to do something about relieving her pain. Dr John Snow administered chloroform, which calmed her immensely. The queen went on to have 9 children. Women across Britain should be grateful to her for ushering a new era of pain relieving drugs during labour.

27. In the times when legal separation was a complicated process and far too expensive, wife-selling was viewed as an easy way out of the marriage. All a guy had to do was to take the wife to something like a livestock market, an inn, a marketplace or any such public place where he could find both the public and the bidders. The wife was often taken like a cattle - a halter around her neck and hands tied with a rope. Once sold, the existing marriage would be annulled. Even though it would be 'the highest' bidder, most of these wives were sold rather cheaply- "as low as a bullpup and a quarter of rum", reports the North-Eastern Daily Gazette in 1887. Though the custom of wife selling was practised throughout Britain since the 16th century, the Victorian period saw it at its peak. Although more prevalent among the common folks, the purveyors of their wives came from higher classes too. Henry Brydges, the 2nd Duke of Chandos, who was an MP too, bought his second wife for half a crown in 1740.

*(Wives on Sale in Britain  Image: Wikipedia//Atlas Obscura)*

28. There was a large-scale employment of children in the hazardous areas during the Victorian century. Little children laboured for hours in terrible conditions for a small sum of money. Despite the 1833 Factory Act, which tried to regulate the excessive exploitation, little changed the scenario on the ground. The law banned children under 9 from being employed, but allowed 9-13 years to work for 9 hours and 13 and above, 12 hours a day. Reportedly in the 1870s, some 30,000 children worked in Britain's brickyards alone.

29. By and large the Victorians remained unimpressed by the Railway boom. The feeling in general was that the sounds and motions of train travel, which they referred to as "railway madness," would turn people into lunatics. Many cases would get reported of inexplicably strange behaviour of people on the trains. For instance in 1864, a newspaper reported the story of a sailor who swore, shouted, and attacked people in his carriage. That same year, the Victorian Railways posted a new rule isolating "insane persons ... in a compartment by themselves." The appreciation for this revolutionary means of transport came much later.

30. Industrialization led to mushrooming of factories in the cities, which led to massive amounts of black smoke being pumped into the air, making it extremely toxic. With pollution at its peak, London would remain under a thick layer of smog for long periods. The factory pollutants stained both the Londoners and their buildings which made the environment stenchy and dirty, creating enormous laundry problems. This was one of the primary reasons Victorian men preferred wearing black to hide the unsightly stains formed by the sooty London air.

# Customs & Traditions

*Sometimes tradition and habit are just that, comfortable excuses to leave things be, even when they are unjust and unworthy.* - Matthew Scully

1. 'Bomena', translated as 'Prowling for girls', is a traditional 'courtship' custom practised in some parts of Bhutan even to this day. Bachelors sneak into the rooms of the marriageable girls in the village to spend a night there. If caught, they must either marry the girl, or as a punishment work in fields of the girls' father. A similar night hunting custom called Yobai or 'night crawling' was widely prevalent in Japan until the beginning of the 20th century.

2. Slovakia has a strange Easter tradition, where men throw water and whip their women in the belief that it'll keep them fresh and beautiful for the next year. Grateful women reciprocate by serving drinks to their menfolk.

3. Indonesia's Tidong community has a bizarre custom, which forbids the newly wed couple from using the toilet for the first three days of their marriage. During this period they're under the supervision of their relatives. Breaking the rule is believed to be a bad omen for the family. The couple goes about their routine life after the stipulated time is over.

4. The Yanomami tribes living in the Amazon rainforests, after cremating the dead body, collect the ashes and the bone powder. The family and the relatives then mix this powder in a plantain soup which is then consumed by all the members. By doing this, they believe the soul of their lost loved one will come to reside within them.

5. 'El Colacho' is a tradition followed by a small Northern Community in Spain. Men dressed as the Devil run between and jump over infants laid on mattresses along the streets, in the hope of keeping the real devil away.

6.  An interesting custom in Turkey is that of the bride offering the groom a salt spiked coffee just before the wedding. The belief is if the groom drinks it without a word of complaint, the marriage is for the keeps.

7.  In medieval times "Cat-burning" was an accepted practice thought to bring good luck. It was custom to burn a barrel full of live cats over a bonfire and as they got roasted inside, the people shrieked with laughter. French Kings often witnessed it and even ceremoniously started the fire.

8.  In Ancient Rome men gave their brides rings made of ivory, flint, bone, copper, or iron. Post marriage the wives wore rings attached to small keys, indicating their husbands' ownership. Anthropologists believe that the tradition of giving an engagement ring in the Christian marriage originated from this Roman custom.

9.  The tradition of the bridesmaids dressed alike dates back to ancient Rome and China, where a bride might have to travel far off to her groom's place, making her susceptible to attacks by bandits or rival suitors. With all the bridesmaids identically dressed, identifying the bride wasn't easy. Over the period of time it became a legal requisite for ten witnesses uniformed in matching colours to attend a wedding ceremony. Also, brides wore veils in order to mask their faces from the wedding crashers.

10. The term "best man" comes from Germanic Goths in 200 CE. The best man at the wedding was the best swordsman, whose job was to protect the couple during the ceremony and stand guard as a sentry outside of the newlywed couple's home after the wedding.

11. According to an estimate around 15,000 blood fiestas are celebrated annually in Spain alone. Similar practices exist in Brazil, Mexico, and Portugal too. Blood Fiestas celebrate the killing and torturing of bulls. The practice includes chasing Bulls, pouring hot wax on the injured animal, and stabbing them to death with sharp objects.

12. Between July and September months, the Hauts Plateaux of Madagascar celebrate the custom of Famadihana, which is 'turning of the dead'. The deceased relative's body is exhumed and the remains are re-wrapped in fresh cloth. It's party time with drinks, music & dance and food. They seek blessings from the dead and ask them the things they might need in the world of their living, before reburying it.

13. Although its origins are not known, there's a long standing Danish custom, where a person who is still single after turning 25, gets splashed with water and then have their body covered in cinnamon- a fun occasion for family & friends.

14. Phra Prang Sam Yot temple in Lopburi, Thailand, has a unique tradition. On the last Sunday of November, a lavish banquet is laid out in honour of thousands of macaques there. The belief is that this brings good luck for Lopburi town. Dances are performed in monkey costumes and heaps of fruits and vegetables are put for the monkeys to enjoy the feast.

15. In the Satare Mawe tribe in Brazil, the young boys have to prove their bravery and courage by placing their hands in a basket filled with angry bullet ants.

16. Dani tribe in Indonesia have a rather inhuman way to express their grief over the dead. A woman who has lost her loved one, has to get the top joint of her finger amputated, this too in a most shocking way. A string is tied very tightly around the finger until it goes numb and then a family member chops it off. The severed part is then burnt to stop the bleeding and prevent infection. This is a symbolic expression of the pain being suffered after the departure of the dear ones and to keep their spirit away from the family. No such expectations are from the men in the tribe!

17. Archaeologists have unearthed more than a 1,000 years old stone carvings and urns filled with human ashes and rubber, buried deep under the city of Toniná in southeastern Mexico. They are of the opinion that possibly the Mayans turned the remains of their rulers into balls for the popular sport of pelota during the 8th century C.E. According to researchers this process represents a "transformation of the body" that allowed their rulers to live on in the culture's sacred game.

18. Some of the wedding traditions that are followed even in modern weddings actually stem from a time when brides were routinely kidnapped. Such a one is that of the bride standing on the left side of the groom. This would leave the groom's right hand free to draw his sword and fight off hijackers or attackers.

19. The Yanomami, a group of approximately 35,000 indigenous people living in the villages in the Amazon rainforest on the border between Venezuela and Brazil, refrain from killing the exotic birds there. They believe that the birds have the soul of a family member and they cannot be hurt. Thus help in conserving the exotic creatures.

20. Although the Bachelor/ Bachelorette parties are a 'big affair' for the French, it's nothing like what you have in the west. The French have a tradition of what they call "enterrement de vie de garçon" (EVG)/ jeune fille", which literally translates to "funeral of the life of the young man/ woman". The French groom and his bride-to-be wear comic tombstones or costumes to signify the end of their youth and freedom, which needs to be buried. It involves "kidnapping" of the bride and the groom on Saturday morning and whisk them away for a rocking weekend full of fun, games, drinking, and eating. It's usually planned by the friends of the bride and the groom.

21. When they harvest honey from high in the trees, the Soliga people have a tradition of leaving some of it near the ground for tigers who they consider their family. They do so because tigers cannot climb trees to get it for themselves, it's the harvester's responsibility. (Soliga tribe is from the southern Indian states of Karnataka and Tamilnadu).

22. During the Ming Dynasty rule, it was customary for the emperor's mother or a senior female maid of honour or someone of a similar hierarchy, to be present by the bed chamber of the Chinese emperor, when he was in bed with a concubine. They would stay until the end of the 'act', and in case required, would advise her the best way to please the emperor.

23. Balinese undergo an extremely gruelling and excruciating experience of tooth filing in preparation for marriage. Smoothly filed teeth mark the passage into adulthood and are symbolic of control on sinful emotions such as lust, greed, anger and jealousy.

24. The tradition of celebrating birthdays with a cake lit with candles is believed to have started in Germany in the 1400s. The superstition that demons and evil spirits lurked around and harm the child on his birthday made the worried parents put candles for the child's age and add an extra one symbolizing the coming year. The lighted candles were believed to drive away the evil spirits. The tradition of candles today may not mark what they did then, but the tradition still continues.

25. The ancient Egyptians had a tradition where, in the event of the death of a pharaoh or some influential official, their personal servants were killed and buried close by, in the belief that these servants would be required by the master to attend to him in his afterlife.

26. Scotland has a pre-wedding ritual for the bride, which involves people throwing all sorts of disgusting things like eggs, spoilt milk, fruits etc at her. This "blackened bride" is then taken around the town. It's believed that this would prepare her for the tough life after her wedding.

27. The tradition of organising weddings in the May-June months, in the west, is said to have emerged out of the availability of water to bathe, which they seldom did. Winters were tough months, but summers provided the opportunity to bathe and clean oneself. The spring provided flowers, which the brides could carry to cover up any residual unwelcoming smells they still had. The popular tradition where the bride throws her bouquet to the bride's maids, is believed to be in the hope that pleasant fragrances will get them someone from among the guests to marry.

28. Brides and flowers have a long history. In ancient Rome, brides wore flower garlands in the hope of new beginnings, fidelity and fertility. In the Middle Ages, strong-smelling herbs and spices made their way. They were believed to ward off evil spirits, bad luck, ill health and help mask the body odour. Dill, the herb of lust was especially popular. Its consumption by the bride and groom during the reception was thought to increase intimacy in the couple. In the Victorian era flowers became part of the wedding bouquet which even modern weddings follow.

# Christmas Trivia

*Christmas is the season for kindling the fire of hospitality.* – Washington Irving

1.  The exact date of the birth of Jesus is not known. However, historians believe that he was born between the 6th and 4th century BCE. Though Jesus was born in the Spring Season, it was sometime in the mid 4th century, that December 25 was chosen to celebrate Christmas. Some historians posit the Winter date was decided intentionally to coincide with the pagan festival of Saturnalia, which is celebrated from 17 to 23rd December in honour of the agricultural god Saturn with gift-giving and merrymaking. This way the pagans, converted now to Christianity, too had something to celebrate during the Saturnalia festival period.

2.  The Christkindlesmarkt in Nuremberg, Germany is one of the oldest and the largest Christmas markets of Europe. It was first held in 1570. It sells all kinds of Christmas goodies including gluhwein (spiced, mulled wine), sweets, sausages, and Christmas decorations and ornaments. Germanisches Nationalmuseum among other treasures has a small inscription that reads: "Sent to Regina Susanna Harßdörfferin by Miss Susanna Eleonora Erbsin on the occasion of the Christmas Market of 1628."

3.  In the olden days, Santa Claus would gather up mischievous children, shove them in his basket and whisk them away to the North Pole where he would keep them to serve as his slaves. That's where the legend of Santa's elves comes from. However, Santa's elves can be traced back to the "nature folk" of pagan religions.

4.  Standing over 150 feet tall and weighing 225 tons, the copper made "Statue of Liberty Enlightening the World" is considered to be the largest Christmas gift ever. The statue was given to the U.S. by France in 1886 to commemorate their commitment to democracy and honour the late president Abraham Lincoln.

5.   The English speaking countries know him as Santa Claus, but he is known by as many as thirty different names around the world. For Brazilians he is Papai Noel, for Hungarians he goes by Mikulás, Père Noël to the French, Julenisse to the Norwegians, La Befana to the Italians. While Russians call him Dueshka Moroz ("Father Frost"), he is Kriss Kringle to the Germans and those in Japan refer to him as Hoteiosho. These are but just a few examples.

6.   The song "We Wish You a Merry Christmas" originally was sung by servants during the festive period, to demand alcoholic drinks from their masters. "We won't go until we get some, so bring some out here", was the original lyric.

7.   Rio de Janeiro, Brazil has the largest floating Christmas tree in the world; it is 278 feet tall.

8.   When James Lord Pierpont first wrote 'Jingle Bells', in 1857, he had meant it to be sung at Thanksgiving and not at Christmas. The original title of the song was "One Horse Open Sleigh," but that was changed to "Jingle Bells", when it was reprinted in 1859. Today Christmas is unthinkable without this classic- Jingle Bell song.

9.   Two towns claim to be Santa Claus' home- the town of the North Pole in Alaska, and the town of Rovaniemi in Finland. The US Postal Service website, however gives an altogether different address- Santa Claus, 123 Elf Road, North Pole, 88888.

10. A law passed by Oliver Cromwell in the Seventeenth century, banning the eating of mince pies on Christmas Day has not yet been repealed.

11. One of the four known handwritten copies of Clement Clarke Moore's 1860 poem, "A Visit From Saint Nicholas" ('Twas the Night Before Christmas), was purchased by a business executive for an insane amount of $280,000 in an auction in 2006. Reportedly the buyer read it out at a private holiday party, but he preferred to remain anonymous.

12. Santa Claus, white bearded, reddened cheeks, large stomach, little glasses, a beaming smile and clad in a red outfit is a twentieth century creation. Though American cartoonist Thomas Nast in the 1870s did put Santa in red, it wasn't until 1931, when Coca-Cola hired Haddon Sundblom, an illustrator to portray a 'jolly old elf' for magazine ads, that Santa got the modern day makeover. The pre-Cola pictures of St. Claus were anything but charming. Thanks to the beverage company, now kids see a friend in Santa, who they can communicate with, write letters to, send their wish lists and even 'receive gifts from him'!

*(Santa Through Time by Erin Sweeney Design. Transformation of Santa Claus from the original St.Nicholas- the last two images are, Thomas Nast's Santa Claus and Coca Cola's Santa Claus respectively)*

13. The festive tradition of the Christmas tree dates back thousands of years to the Romans and Ancient Greeks.

14. "Happy Christmas", which is still traditional in England, was replaced by "Merry Christmas" because clergymen felt that the traditional greeting was associated with insobriety!

15. Rudolph the Red-Nosed Reindeer was created in 1939 by a US department store, Montgomery Ward as a marketing campaign to get children to buy Christmas colouring books. Robert L. May, the artist was asked to compose a poem for the colouring fun books. It was how Rudolph the reindeer came into being. Rudolph's story about embracing even those who are not like you, instead of bullying them, made him an instant hit.

16. The much loved Christmas treat, the 'hooked' candy cane, which dates back to 1670, is believed by some to be symbolic of the shepherd's crook. However, those who refuse to see any symbolism, argue that the candy was shaped into a 'hook' to enable it to hang on the Christmas tree. According to The National Confectioners Association of the US, neither of the beliefs have a ground. The origins lay elsewhere. During the marathon church services, which often became tiresome for children, the choirmaster would give the red-and-white-striped sugar sticks to choirboys to keep them quiet during the sessions. The candy cane was introduced to the Americans by a German-Swedish immigrant, who decorated his Christmas tree with candy canes in 1847. In the years to come, they became popular as a Christmas confectionery.

17. When the world was first introduced to Santa's reindeers, through a 1823 poem 'A Visit from Saint Nicholas', the two of the flying creatures, who we know as Donner and Blitzen, were originally called Dunder and Blixem, which is a Dutch way to refer to "thunder and lightning."

18. The Christmas tree tradition was initially introduced to the Americans in the 1840s by the German Lutheran immigrants to Pennsylvania. Seen as pagan symbols and not Christian, they were frowned upon by the puritans. It was only in 1851 that Christmas trees began to appear in the US stores.

19. The first artificial Christmas trees put on display in the year 1856, were made either of goose feathers dyed in green or the material that the hula skirts were made from - green raffia.

20. When initially letters were sent for Santa, some generous hearted Canadian post office workers started replying to these letters. But with time when things really began to grow big, the need arose for an altogether independent postal code. Under the "Santa Letter-Writing Program" initiative, now there are numerous volunteers who keep up with his correspondence. Santa's address reads : Santa Claus, North Pole, HOH OHO, Canada.

21. The world's first commercially produced Christmas card came in 1843. It was designed by John Callcott Horsley for Henry Cole and hand-coloured by a professional colourer Mason. A thousand cards were lithographed and sold at a shilling each, at the time when an average man's weekly wage was one shilling, only wealthier classes could afford them. Also, a controversy surrounding the depiction of a small child drinking wine arose and the card got highly criticized. It wasn't until 1848 that the second Christmas card, designed by William Maw Egley, arrived on the scene. In the US, Louis Prang, a Polish immigrant, who is known as "the Father of the American Christmas card", introduced Christmas cards to the Americans in 1875. Rest is history!

*(Image credit: Vintage News. The card, a triptych showing a family celebrating the holiday, with the side panels depicting the images of charity work.)*

22. How intricately woven Christmas is into the social and administrative fabric of the country can be seen from the sincerity and seriousness with which efforts have been put in to make the festival celebration an industry in the US. The campaigns such as 'Operation Santa' which has been running for decades has hundreds of volunteers, whose responsibility is to reply to letters from children that are addressed to Santa Claus. The festival season sees a boom in the economy, for instance the holiday retail sales in 2022 have gone up to $942 billion.

23. The Christmas wreath symbolises Christ. While the holly represents the crown of thorns Jesus wore at his crucifixion, the red berries stand for the blood he shed.

24. The idea of Santa Claus draws from a 4th century Dutchman, Sinter Klaas, who, when alive, is believed to have done a lot of charity work. The English called him St. Nicholas. In the Netherlands 6th December, the date when Sinter Klaas died, is observed as a day for giving out presents. The Dutch settlers in America brought this tradition of Sinter Klaas celebrations, that of giving away gifts, to Christmas celebrations in the US, and with time, exchanging gifts became common to Christmas celebrations across the globe.

25. In order to facilitate his annual travel round the globe on Christmas Eve, the government of the United States issued an official pilot's licence to Santa Claus. It was presented to 'him' in 1927 by the Assistant Secretary of Commerce for Aeronautics, William P McCracken.

26. Until 1849 Santa Claus had been talked about as a bachelor. But James Rees created Mrs. Claus' character in his short story "A Christmas Legend" and made him a married man.

27. The US Christmas market is worth $380 million. About 30 to 35 million Christmas trees- Pine, Fir & Spruce grown on 295 acres of land are cut annually for the festival sale. Oregon is the highest Christmas tree growing state in the US. During the Christmas festival around 120 million trees are cut across the world resulting in a carbon footprint of between 2-3 billion kilogrammes. Additionally about 33 million trees are cut down across the globe for Christmas cards alone. Such massive scale cutting of trees to celebrate a festival negatively impacts Global Ecological Health- both the Present and the Future world .

28. According to the Smithsonian, the origin of the tradition of hanging stockings on Christmas Eve, is based on a popular legend which goes thus- St. Nicholas was wandering through a town and learnt about the plight of a poor widower with three marriageable daughters. At night, he slid down the chimney of their house and filled the girls' recently laundered stockings, drying by the fire, with gold coins. In the morning, the family found the gifts, and the daughters became eligible to wed. 'Twas a Christmas miracle'.

29. There is an interesting story about how the 'Santa Tracker' started in the US. In 1955, Sears Retail Store put an ad in the newspaper with a phone number of one of their stores where children could call Santa Claus to tell him what they wanted for Christmas. However, the number got misprinted. The one that got printed turned out to be the hotline number of the NORAD (North American Aerospace Defense Command). Since then NORAD has taken upon the responsibility of acting as, "Santa Tracker". Each Christmas they provide flight information on the internet, TV news, and on a special iPhone App.

30. On 16th December 1965, Wally Schirra and Tom Stafford, two astronauts on board the Gemini 6A alarmed their Mission Control when they announced that they saw an "unidentified flying object" which was about to enter Earth's atmosphere, travelling in the polar orbit from north to south. Before things could go out of hand, they interrupted the broadcast with "Jingle Bells," played on harmonica accompanied by tinkling of small sleigh bells. Thus 'Jingle Bells' made history by becoming the first song to be played in space aboard NASA space flight.

31. James Edgar, a Scottish immigrant, and the owner of Edgar Boston Store, was the first person to come up with the concept of putting on the costume of Santa Claus. During Christmas he used to dress up as a clown and entertain children visiting his store. But in 1890, he dressed up in a custom-made red Santa suit, and thus brought Santa Claus to life- the first ever Santa in a store, for Christmas.

32. The first ever mention of Santa having reindeers and the sleigh occurs in the 1812 writings of the American author Washington Irving, where he talks of St. Nicholas as "riding over the tops of the trees, in that self-same wagon wherein he brings his yearly presents to children".

33. Between 1644 and 1660, Lord Protector Oliver Cromwell, banned the celebration of Christmas. As a Puritan, he abhorred drinking, dancing, or having fun, which according to him was against the spirit of Christmas. In Scotland there were no Christmas holidays or celebrations for over 300 years, from 1640 to 1958. Meanwhile, between 1659 and 1681, in the United States colonies, anyone caught making merry on Christmas would face heavy fines. In fact, Christmas, like any other day, was a regular working day. The Congress even held their first session on 25th December in 1789.

# Olios From The Past

*If you don't know history, then you don't know anything. You are a leaf that doesn't know it is part of a tree.* - Michael Crichton

1. Silk production, which was China's monopoly until the fifth century, ended in 552 CE, when two monks smuggled out the eggs of silkworms in their walking sticks from China to the Byzantine Empire, thus bringing silk manufacturing to Europe.

2. In the 1860s the Russian Empire was vast and powerful but to maintain it, funds were required. Russia, therefore, felt that selling Alaska, which had a very small population of Russian settlers there, to the United States wouldn't just get them the money needed but will help offset Europe's power also. On March 30, 1867, the Alaska Purchase Treaty was signed between the two for a price of $7.2 million. Even though it was dirt cheap, roughly two cents an acre, the Alaskan purchase was ridiculed in the US, calling it "Seward's Icebox". History, however, made it one of the most valuable land grabs by the Americans.

3. Sudan has 225 pyramids, which is more than any other country in the world. With 138 pyramids, Egypt is the closest second.

4. 'Chinese Head Tax' was imposed by Dominion of Canada on the Chinese immigrants between 1885 and 1923, majorly to discourage new settlers from the Far East. Interestingly, no other ethnic group was charged any such tariff. Initially it was $50 which rose to $500 by 1903 and this was the time when these migrants wouldn't even be earning a dollar a day.

5. Just to confuse the German bombers, the French built a fake Paris during the First World War. In order to make it look real, the replicas of all important landmarks, including the Eiffel Tower were set up.

6. It was common for the doctors to use the teeth of the dead soldiers as prosthetics, when the dentures hadn't been invented.

7. On 1st May 1840, the world's first adhesive postage stamp was issued in a public postal system in the United Kingdom. It was called the Penny Black and featured the then queen of England, Queen Victoria. At the same time a second, a blue one (for philatelists' interest- this is ten times rarer than penny black), too was issued but it didn't go into circulation. This was the first time a pre-paid postage was being used, until then it was normal for the recipient to pay postage on delivery, charged by the sheet and on distance travelled. Sir Rowland Hill, a teacher, is credited with coming up with the idea of a prepaid adhesive stamp. However, frauds couldn't be controlled. Since the original red postmark on penny black was removable, people could easily reuse these stamps. When the postmark was made black, it couldn't be seen on the black stamp. It was then the Penny Red was developed, which remained in circulation for next four decades. Within three years of the institution of the stamp in the UK, Switzerland and Brazil, a little later the United States too introduced postage stamps in their countries and by 1860, 90 countries around the world had started it. In India the British penny Postage Stamp was first initiated on 1st February 1901, for sales at the Post Offices.

*(Penny Black was a flat rate, domestic stamp, hence it doesn't mention the country name in its design.*
*Image: Reuters)*

8.  The 16th century Philippines used yo-yo as a weapon. In 1929 however, it was introduced as a toy, in the United States. Unlike today, the yo-yo at that time used to be 4 pounds and had a 20-foot-long cord.

9.  Until the 19th century 'Pillory' was a common punishment in England. The last person to be pilloried in England was Peter James Bossy in London on 22 June 1830. A pillory was a wooden frame with holes for neck and hands. When bound to a pillory, victims could neither run away nor use hands to protect their faces from whatever things were thrown at them, and could be blinded, severely injured or even killed. This inhuman punishment was abolished in 1837.

10. William Henry Harrison, the 9th President of the United States had the shortest tenure in Presidential history. He died in just 31 days after his Inauguration on March 4, 1841. Historians had maintained that he died of pneumonia. However, recent research suggests that septic shock, not pneumonia per se, was the reason for his death. The notes and records by Dr. Miller, his personal physician, hold enough evidence to prove that the insanitary conditions at the White House proved fatal for the President.

11. The "Pinky Promise" originally indicated that the person who breaks the promise must cut off their pinky finger.

12. The middle finger has been used as a derogatory gesture for at least 2800 years.

13. Indian territory of Himachal Pradesh was created in 1948 by merging some 30 small ruling states.

14. Greeting by shaking hands has an interesting origin. Initially handshakes meant that you were unarmed. The hand clasp proved that your hand was empty and shaking was meant to dislodge any weapon concealed up the sleeve.

15. Prince Albert, Queen Victoria's husband believed that any food that was rectangular in shape resembled a coffin and hence unlucky. It is said that since then the British royal family has never been served sandwiches with right angles- the corners are rounded off.

16. During WWII, the US and the British intelligence agencies got the United States Playing Card Company (USPCC) to manufacture spotter cards which were distributed as Christmas presents to the POWs of allied forces. These innocent looking decks of cards couldn't raise any suspicion. But these seemingly ordinary cards- on moistening and peeling apart, would reveal a hidden map with escape routes, directions and other valuable tips. Thus the information enabled the POWs to flee from German prison camp Castle Colditz, notorious for its "incorrigible" security, and reach friendly lines or cross the border into a neutral country. Reportedly there were some 300 escape attempts made, however only 32 POWs, mainly high-value detainees like pilots and officers, could succeed in fleeing.

*(Castle Colditz/A soldier with a spotter card revealing the hidden map of escape route: http://warhistoryonline.com)*

17. Installed in 1410, the Prague Astronomical clock, is the world's oldest astronomical clock still in operation. It was created by clockmaker Mikulá and Prof. Jan Sindel, a mathematician and an astronomer.

18. A lottery ticket in 16th century England came with the added bonus of getting a 'get out of jail free card.' Every participant was granted immunity from one arrest, as long as the crime wasn't real serious, like murder or treason.

19. After the death of Chaim Weizmann, the first President of Israel in 1952, Albert Einstein was proposed to become the President but he turned down the offer stating that he didn't think he was a 'great peoples person'.

20. During World War II, the Obo Monuvo tribe of the Philippines 'fought' the Japanese invaders by serving them "Kollut", a poisonous variety of yam. Kollut can be safely eaten only after subjecting it to several tedious processes. Since the Japanese had no idea about this, they consumed it, only to be affected by it and then being hacked to death by the tribes.

21. The 'holed' coins were still in use in Chinese until the beginning of the twentieth century. Like a beaded string, these coins too could be slid on a cord through their holes and be worn like a necklace or a girdle or even hung from their belts. Large payments could be made in strings of 100 or 1000 holed coins.

22. A cemetery containing 300,000 mummified cats was found in Egypt in 1888. About 20 tonnes of the mummies were shipped to the UK. Later sold at an auction for £4 per ton, probably used as fertiliser.

23. It is believed that Hernán Cortés, the Spanish conquistador initially brought the tomato seeds for the ornamental purpose in the gardens. In the 1700s, the aristocrats started eating tomatoes. Death of many people after consuming tomatoes convinced them that the fruit was poisonous. The fact was the lead content in their pewter plates got enhanced by the acidic tomato and it was the lead poisoning that people died of not the tomato.

24. George Shillibeer was an English coach builder, who was inspired by the public bus service in Paris and he wanted to start one of his own. However before he did that, Newington Academy for Girls, a Quaker school in Stoke Newington, near London, commissioned him to build one for the girl students. In 1927, Shillibeer built a 25-seater omnibus for girls. This three horse drawn omnibus became the first school bus in history.

*(Shillibeer's first omnibus (1927) Photo: Wikipedia)*

25. The Dutch-Scilly War or Three Hundred and Thirty Five Years' War was the longest war fought without a single shot fired. It is said to have been extended by the lack of a peace treaty for 335 years from 30 March 1651 to 17 April 1986.

26. After a statute of 1324 that declared whales and dolphins as "fishes royal", these fishes officially came under the British Crown. In the later times the law was expanded to include sturgeon and porpoises too. Also under the same law, the monarch can claim any of these sea creatures captured or washed ashore within three miles of the boundaries of the United Kingdom.

27. Roman Catholics in Bavaria founded a secret society in 1740 called the Order of the Pug. It was imperative for the new members to wear dog collars and scratch at the door to get in.

28. The city of London had a gigantic cesspit constructed under its 200,000 houses but it often overflowed into them, resulting in most terrible situations for the residents. In the 1840s cesspits were abolished and it became mandatory for every household to have their individual lavatories. However, the planners did not realise that diverting the sewage into the river Thames would prove hazardous. In 1858 summers, the city of London suffered 'the worst smell in the city's history', often referred to as the 'Great Stink' which was the consequence of the city's entire sewage being dumped into the river Thames.

29. Windsor Castle, built in 1070 by William I, is the oldest inhabited castle in the world. It's home to the British Royal family.

30. Between 1840-1900, a new trend caught up with the Londoners - the craze for ice cream. This was long before the refrigeration units came by and the city could not get enough of it. It was then Carlo Gatti, an Italian Swiss entrepreneur came up with an idea. He built two vast wells in the basement of his premises in Kings Cross in central London. He then imported tons and tons of ice from the frozen lakes and rivers of Scandinavia and filled these wells. He would sell these on high profits to the ice cream makers in the United Kingdom. Gatti died in 1878, but his ice wells can be visited even today via the London Canal Museum.

31. Cleopatra was able to speak eight different languages, including Hebrew and Arabic.

32. Playing cards came to Europe sometime in the 15th century. In next hundred years, the French card-makers standardized the suits of Spades, Hearts, Diamonds & Clubs and designated to the four kings- SPADES - David, (king of Israel, Old Testament) CLUBS - Alexander (king of Macedonia), HEARTS - Charlemagne (king of France) and DIAMONDS - Julius Caesar (Roman commander). By the 18th century however, they stopped being emblematic, and became something like the modern day ones, which represent no specific king.

33. Maison de Jeanne, in Sévérac-le- Château, Aveyron is the oldest house in France. Built some 600 years ago, this 15th century house has a unique construction style- reverse construction- smaller ground floor and significantly larger upper floors. This construction style was adopted probably to save taxes, which were imposed on the ground-floor square footage. Since the upper stories weren't built directly on the ground, they remained tax exempt, hence the architectural design.

*(The 15th century top-heavy house in Aveyron, France. Image Credit: MailOnline)*

34. The British Empire has been the biggest coloniser in world history. In the 1920s, it controlled almost one fourth of the world's population. There are only 22 countries in the world that the British couldn't invade or attack.

35. During the 16th and 17th century, it wasn't uncommon among Europeans to commit murders just to get executed. They believed suicide to be a crime and their soul would remain eternally condemned to hell. Unlike murdering somebody, where a sincere repentance would open the doors to heaven. So a criminal committed only that exact crime, that would bring them death.

36. During the middle ages, it was believed that sperm produced from the left testicle begets girls. To ensure a son, men would often get it removed.

37. In 1518, a "dancing plague" took over the town of Strasbourg in France. People seemed to have contracted a strange disease where they kept dancing nonstop for weeks. Reportedly, as many as 400 people danced until falling unconscious from exhaustion.

38. Clinking of wine glasses when saying cheers dates back to the times when people feared that their drink might be poisoned by their enemies. Subsequently, this 'ritual' became a practice. In order to prove that the drink was safe, the host would pour some of his guest's wine into his own glass or goblet and take a sip first which later evolved into crashing tankards or chalice together in such a way that a little of both would spill into each other. In due course of time clinking the wine glasses became a practice.

39. Almost as many people were killed by guillotine in Nazi Germany as in the French Revolution.

40. Early colonists in the US had a single tool to clean all- their ears, nails, and teeth. The twentieth century excavations revealed tools which were used by the early settlers. The ones related to personal hygiene are of special interests, it included a sharp silver ear picker and a little scooping tool found at Jamestown's original fort. These ear-picks were used as toothpicks, fingernail cleaners, and other hygiene activities.

41. The horrific massacre at Nanking is one of the worst atrocities committed during World War II. During the occupation of Nanking city in 1937, the Imperial Japanese Army soldiers inflicted unimaginable sufferings upon the Chinese civilians there. More than 200,000 innocent people were murdered and at least 20,000 women including children were brutally raped.

42. Stalin had his pictures edited to suit his political agenda. He got his photographs modified by completely removing all the traces of his political rivals, it was rumoured that probably those people were 'removed' in their real life too.

43. Due to the scarcity of rubber during WWI, German manufacturer Victoria created a spring wheel as a substitute for rubber tyre.

*(A 1905 Herrenrad Victoria Model 12 German bicycle with Mauser GEW 88 rifle: Credit: Colin Kirsche's online museum)*

44. 'Trenches' were the stale slices of bread, used as plates during the Middle Ages in Europe.

45. Eyam, an English village, became infected with the bubonic plague in 1666. Instead of fleeing the villagers quarantined themselves to stop the disease from spreading. The epidemic took the lives of about 260 villagers.

46. The German state-owned brewery Weihenstephan in the city of Freising, Bavaria, is believed to be the oldest and still functional brewery in the world. It can trace its history back to 104 CE.

47. When Mary Queen of Scots returned to her native Scotland from France, she was quite displeased to see male guests at the banquet, eating with their hats on. It was later explained to her that this was in no way to show any disrespect to the queen, but a necessity to keep the long hair from getting into the food and also to prevent head lice from falling into the plates.

48. Benito Mussolini, the leader of the Fascist party, was the Prime Minister of Italy between 1922 and 1943. He was anti-church and referred to the priests as "black germs", but after rising to power in 1922 he began finding ways to please the Roman Catholic Church, so much so that he baptised his children, closed down wine shops, local nightlife, and the use of contraception and abortion. He even barred women from going out to work, all this just to stay in power with the support of the Catholic church.

49. During the colonial era, between 1765 and 1938 Britain drained almost $45 trillion from India. Which calculated in today's time would be over 14 times more than the UK's annual GDP.

50. 'Scheveningen', a city in the Netherlands, is a shibboleth (a peculiarity of pronunciation that distinguishes a particular class, a group or set of persons). During World War I, the Dutch identified Germans by asking them to pronounce the city's name.

51. A popular form of punishment in Europe was a 'Scold's bridle', which finds its earliest reference in Geoffrey Chaucer's 1380s' work, wherein a female character is made to wear it. A Scold's bridle served the same purpose as does a barnacle, which is put on a horse's muzzle to curb and control it. The bridle was often used on women who were deemed 'troublesome' or 'spoke too much'. Such a punishment accomplished two goals- humiliate the "offender" before their community and titillate the spectators, who had gathered around. The device would be fastened around the woman's head and the attached metal plate would go inside her mouth and press down on the tongue to keep her from speaking. It was believed that such women have come under the influence of a devil and hence needed to be chastised.

52. Madame Tussauds wax museum has a dark past. Marie Grosholtz (maiden name), was a Wax artist, who taught sculpting to King Louis XVI's sister. It was at the onset of the French Revolution that Marie would sculpt plaster casts and death masks of beheaded victims of public executions, many of whom she knew personally which included her patrons the King, his wife queen Marie Antoinette, Maximilien Robespierre and several others. Later she was thrown into the prison along with her mother. According to her in a forced show of her allegiance to the revolutionaries, she was compelled to create Death Masks of the executed ones. Eventually she left France, taking her waxworks on a travelling show through Britain. The next three decades saw her marry, separate, travel and add more and more to her collection - from English royalty and famous politicians to dioramas of notorious criminals and their grisly crime scenes. Eventually she settled down in London where she founded the Wax museum in 1835. Despite being immensely popular, the museum was criticized for selling "human tragedy". Punch magazine even called it "Chamber of Horrors". With over 300 wax statues today, Madame Tussauds at Baker Street London, is one of the most iconic tourist places.

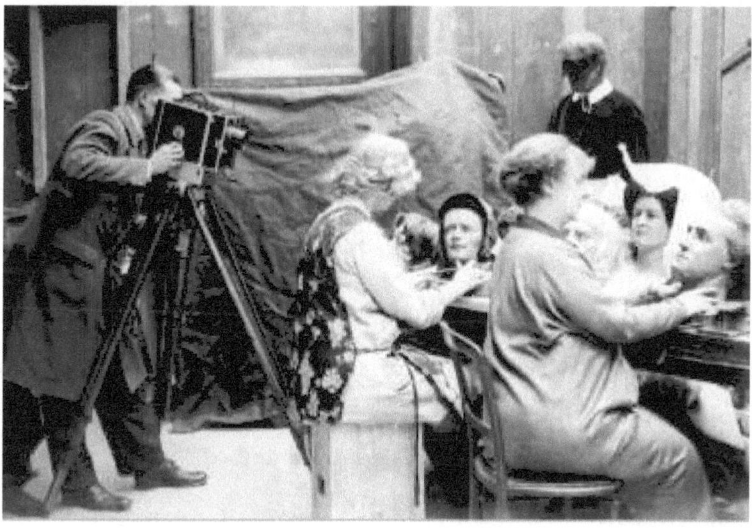

*(Women artists sculpting wax heads for an exhibition at Madame Tussauds, London in 1928, while a cameraman films them. .Image: National Geographic)*

53. Laying of sewer in the major cities in the US and Europe began only in the nineteenth century. The waste disposal practised prior to this, was to empty chamber pots into the streets. The castles had garderobes, which were small cupboard like structures, with a hole that allowed waste directly into the moats built around. This open disposal was one of the biggest reasons for frequent epidemics. Such a one which killed about a quarter of the people in Europe, was 'Black Death' in the 14th century.

54. Forks were first introduced in Italy in the 11th century. But using them was seen as blasphemy. It was so because these 'artificial hands' were an insult to God!

55. Polish writer Stanislaw Jerzy Lec, tried to escape the German concentration camp in Ternopil, where he was imprisoned. His second attempt at escaping wrought him a death sentence in 1943. He was given a shovel to dig his own grave under the supervision of a guard. Lec killed the guard with the shovel, and escaped in the guard's uniform. He went on to become one of the greatest writers of post war Poland and one of the most influential aphorists of the 20th century.

56. In the 1950s, CIA and MI6 conducted a joint exercise "Operation Gold", to install wiretaps to listen to the communication of the Soviet Army headquarters in Berlin using a tunnel they dug into the Soviet-occupied zone. Although, even before its construction began in September 1954, the Soviets had already been informed about it by their mole in the British Intelligence. However, in order to protect his identity, they allowed the construction to continue. In the meantime the US is said to have recorded about 90,000 communications. When it was felt George Blake, their man, was safe, USSR "accidentally" discovered the 1,476 feet long tunnel on 21 April 1956. Both sides claimed victory. Later Blake's espionage came to light and in 1961, he was arrested, tried and convicted.

57. People switched from night gowns to wearing pyjamas sometime during World War I. It was to remain prepared in case they needed to run outside at night amid air raids in England.

58. Ravindra Kaushik was a deep-cover agent planted in Pakistan by RAW with a new identity. He studied Law from Karachi University and subsequently joined the Pakistan Army. His passing on the confidential information between 1979 and 1983 helped India immensely. This earned him the title of 'Black Tiger', by none other than the then PM Indira Gandhi. He got caught, when he was given away by Inyat Masiha, another undercover RAW agent, during an interrogation by Pak army. Ravindra was just 29 then. He was arrested on the charges of espionage and tortured for next 2 years but he didn't give into the pressure. In 1985, the Supreme Court of Pakistan awarded him a death sentence. "Had I been an American, I would have been out of this jail in three days," he wrote before his death in November, 2001. His father died of a heart attack when his family in Jaipur was informed through a letter about Ravindra's death. Despite spending 26 years away from his homeland, Ravindra never received any recognition. Initially the family would receive Rs 500 a month then later Rs 2,000 until 2006 when his mother too passed away. According to his brother, Ravindra "saved the lives of about 20,000 soldiers", but he himself died of lack of medicines and "the Indian government did nothing"!

59. Hanns-Joachim Gottlob Scharff, often called the "Master Interrogator" of the Luftwaffe, was a German interrogator during WWII. He never used physical means of torture to interrogate. His tactic was more psychological- which he did by being extremely nice to the subject. His methodology included- disarming the subject with informal chitchat, gossip about things, nature walks without any security guards close on heels, baking them homemade food, drinking beer, cracking jokes, and gradually extract required information. So effective were Scharff's interrogation techniques that he was often called upon to assist in other interrogations too. After the War, the US military not only incorporated his techniques in their interrogation schools' curriculum, he was even granted immigration status by the US government. There in the US, he focused his energies in mosaic creation and became a world renowned mosaic artist, which he remained until his death in 1992.

60. Since there were no divorce courts in the Middle Ages, Germanic law allowed couples seeking separation, to resolve it through a combat. Hans Talhoffer, a German fencing maestro was the first to document this outlandish practice of spousal bloodshed in his 1467 manuscript Fechtbuch, a book on fencing. The combatants were expected to follow a codified set of rules. While the woman had free movement around the arena, the man had to stand in a waist-deep pit with one arm tied behind his back. The woman fought with 1-5 pound stones wrapped in a cloth, the man was allowed to use only three clubs, but they forfeited one every time they touched the sides of the pit with their hand or arm. If the man lost the fight, he would be publicly executed and if it was the woman who lost, she would be buried alive.

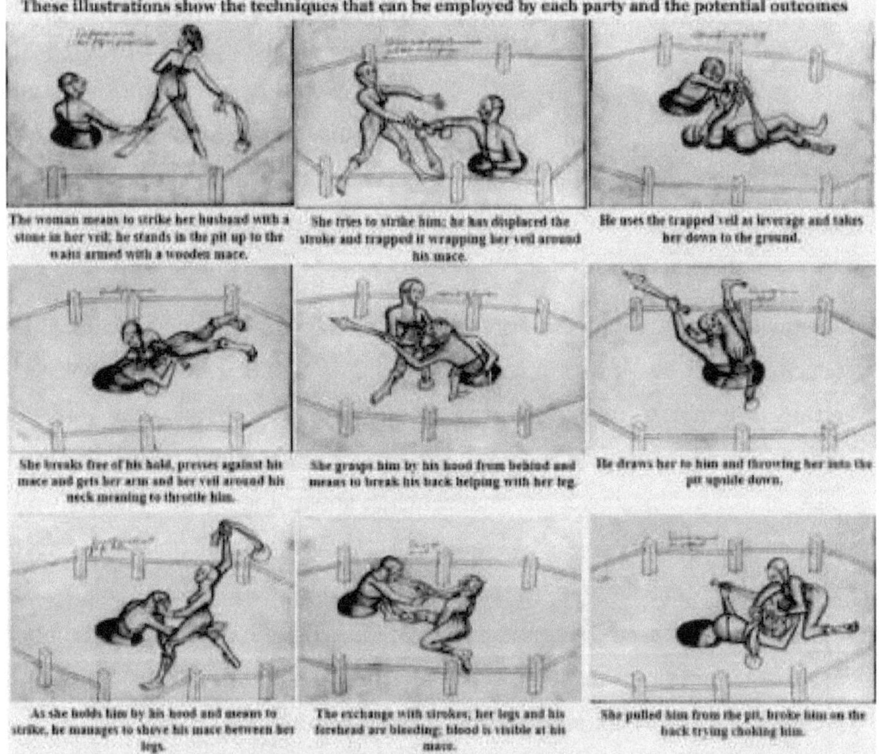


*(Image Courtesy: The Cellar - Illustrations depict the process of martial duel and techniques used by each opponent)*

61. It was a common practice for the soldiers during WWII, to keep family pictures, under clear grips of their 1911 pistols. These were called "Sweetheart Grips".

62. In 16th and 17th centuries Europe, when the sewage used to be thrown into the streets, it was considered good etiquette for a gentleman to walk on the insides of the streets while escorting a lady, which meant that he was in the way of sewage falling, while the lady remained safe.

63. Wiping clean, after 'doing' their job, definitely had its own challenges in the past. Until the 19th century Europe used dried corn cob, which was needed to turn on its axis to clean the region, a handful of leaves or straw, torn rugs, even a sea sponge, which would be attached to a handle and washed in a bucket of vinegar or salt water. Later even the newspapers, magazines, catalogues, in short whatever they could lay hands on, became their 'wipers'. It's widely believed that China invented toilet paper in the 6th century. In the West patents related to toilet paper started appearing in the second half of the 19th century, but it was only in the beginning of the 20th century that toilet paper began to be mass produced. Interestingly the most hygienic and comfortable method of cleaning bums by using water directly, never occurred to the lot. But then perhaps 'hygiene and comfort' together was unthinkable at that time.

64. Canada and Denmark had been fighting a war to take control of Hans Island near Greenland, in a most unusual way. In 1984, Canadian soldiers hoisted the Canadian flag and left a bottle of Canadian whiskey there. Offended, the Danish Minister of Greenland Affairs himself visited the island the same year, and brought along a Danish flag, a bottle of Schnapps, and a letter stating "Welcome to the Danish Island". After this the two countries had continued their 'Whisky War', - putting their flag, and leaving alcoholic beverages. Although the two had agreed to resolve the issue in 2005, it wasn't until 2022, during the Russia-Ukraine conflict that the three decades old "Whiskey War" finally got sorted out.

65. Spread over 38 square miles of area, at Mount Li, is the incredibly lavish mausoleum of China's first emperor Qin Shi Huang. It was in BCE 246, when he was 13, and had just ascended the throne that the construction of the grand tomb complex was started, involving some 700,000 conscripted workers. Following the unexpected death of the Emperor in BCE 210, it is believed that all 3,000 of his concubines and hundreds of artisans working there were made to follow the emperor into his tomb. The funerary art with some 8,000 life-size soldiers in terra-cotta, one of the biggest of its kind, was discovered in 1974. The other terracotta figures found at the four partially excavated pits are that of officials, acrobats, strongmen, musicians, rare animals, horses and bronze cranes and ducks but no concubines. A museum complex has since been constructed there. Buried in the massive tomb for over 2,200 years, the exhibits of the Terracotta Army have been one of the biggest crowd pullers ever, across the world. The necropolis has anomalously high levels of mercury around the area, which slowed down the process of excavations.

*(The Terracotta Army excavated from the pits next to the Qin Shi Huang's tomb, Xi'an China: Photo by Zhang Tianzhu/For China Daily.)*

66. On 12th August 1952, popularly called "The Night of The Murdered Poets", Stalin ordered the execution of 13 Soviet Jews, including 5 Yiddish poets, by falsely accusing them of treason. He had plans to purge the Soviet Union of Jews, but before his wish could be materialised, he himself died.

67. There were about 200,000 pigeons enlisted in the US Military during WWI and WWII. Cher Ami, was one such enlisted homing pigeon who, during WWI carried a crucial message from the 'Lost Battalion' of 545 American soldiers left stranded without food or ammunition, surrounded by Germans on one side and the Allied forces on the other. The exchange of fire from both sides led to heavy casualties. As a last resort Major Charles Whittlesey, who was wedged behind enemy lines in France with the 194 surviving soldiers, sent a message to the headquarters through Cher Ami, explaining their position. Although being badly wounded from the shots by the Germans, the brave bird managed to fly 25 miles in 25 minutes to the pigeon loft at the American base and thus saved the soldiers' lives. In recognition of his heroic services the French government decorated him with the Croix de guerre Medal. Cher Ami had suffered serious injuries and died within a year's time, in 1919. He became one of the first recipients of the "Animals in War & Peace Medal of Bravery", which was bestowed on him posthumously in November 2019 in Washington.

68. Bank notes were issued in the US in 1862 during the time of Civil War. The first face to appear on the $1 bill was that of Salmon P. Chase, who was the Secretary of Treasury at that time and had designed the country's first currency. George Washington had appeared on Washington cent in 1783, which was in commemoration of the end of the Revolutionary War. However, it wasn't until 1869, that the President got featured on a dollar note.

69. George Washington, at the time of his inauguration on April 30, 1789, had just one of his own natural teeth, a premolar, the rest were implants. He began wearing full dentures after his last tooth was gone. Dentures in those days had an interesting assembly- human teeth extracted from the slaves or dead soldiers, cow's teeth, hippopotamus ivory, and metals like brass and gold. The dentures were kept in place with metal fasteners, with attached springs. Interestingly the poor selling their teeth to make some money existed in the Western world even during the Middle Ages. These teeth were sold as dentures or as implants to the rich clients. Records show that Washington bought a total of 9 teeth from unknown slaves.

70. The Constitution of India was originally written in both Hindi and English. While the Hindi version was handwritten by Vasant Krishan Vaidya, the English one was calligraphed by Prem Behari Narain Raizada. The illumination, beautification and decoration on the original scripts were done by Nand Lal Bose and Beohar Rammanohar Sinha. On being asked about his charges by Nehru, the calligrapher said all he wanted was his name on each page and his grandfather's on the last page of the seminal document, which was honoured. It took 432 pen nibs and 6 gruelling months to finish the 251 pages manuscript weighing 3.75 kilograms. These original copies of the Constitution of India are still kept in helium-filled cases in the Library of the Parliament of India.

*(The original manuscripts in Hindi and English. The paper and Black ink used for writing were specially imported from Birmingham(UK). Image available on public domain)*

71. In 1853, William Ewart Gladstone, the then Prime Minister of England, introduced "Death duties", a tax that the widow/widower had to pay after the spouse's demise. This tax later began to be called Inheritance tax.

72. In September 1666 Central London was swept by a major conflagration, popularly known as The Great Fire of London, that gutted the entire area inside the old Roman city wall, destroying over 13,200 houses. The casualties reported were surprisingly too small, just 6, and it's this figure that is being challenged by the historians today.

73. New York was initially a Dutch colony, which they called New Amsterdam. It was in the late 17th century that New Amsterdam got renamed to New York, after the Duke of York, who had helped the English in capturing it. New York, the most populous US city today, had served as the country's first capital between 1785 and 1790. George Washington was sworn in as the first President from here on April 30, 1789. The following year on July 16, 1790, Congress declared the city of Washington in the District of Columbia, the permanent capital of the United States. It is said that although the best, New York is the rudest of all cities in the US.

74. The first newspapers are credited to Julius Caesar. His handwritten reports on new pieces of information were posted in public places in Rome in BCE 59 onwards. China had newspapers from about 713 CE, however the first newspaper printing appeared in Germany in 1609, while America's first successful newspaper - the Boston News Letter, came up in 1704.

75. A popular 16th century book on health, "This is the Myrour or Glasse of Helth", says : "Use not baths or stews, nor sweat too much, for all openeth the pores of a man's body and maketh the venomous air to enter and for to infect the blood." This sort of advice that bathing or sweating opens the body pores which let the poisonous air enter the human body, infecting the blood, made not just the people in general, but even the physicians to believe that washing was dangerous. Such was the apprehension that astrologers were consulted to predict the auspicious time for bath.

76. In 1233, Pope Gregory IX, the bishop of Rome, ordered extermination of all the cats, which he linked to devil worship. This "war on cats" resulted in an unprecedented rise in the population of rats, which subsequently spread the bubonic plague in the 1300s.

77. Swedish warship "Vasa'. which was touted as one of the most powerfully armed vessels in the world, sank on its maiden voyage on 10 August, 1628. It could not even sail a mile, leading to the death of 150 sailors and soldiers in it. Vasa was salvaged in 1961 with a largely intact hull. Now 400 years later, it's housed at the Vasa Museum in Stockholm. One of the most popular tourist attractions, Vasa is the world's best preserved 17th century ship.

*(Photo Courtesy: Vasa Museum, Stockholm)*

78. Agnès Sorel was the first recognized mistress in the history of France. Her mesmerizing beauty made her the subject of several paintings and works of art in France, including Jean Fouquet's "Virgin and Child Surrounded by Angels". Charles VII was so enamoured with her that he gave her the title of maîtresse-en-titre. He even left his pregnant queen for her. Agnès was famous for her extremely revealing dresses and popularizing low cut gowns. Her complete hold over the king and her extravagant tastes, earned her strong enemies. She had four daughters with the king but died very young- just 28. Her death at that time was attributed to dysentery. However circumstances surrounding this enigmatic woman's death always raised suspicions, so much so that more than six centuries later, in 2005 her body was exhumed and the forensic reports determined that Agnès died of mercury poisoning.

79. Kerala is home to the first mosque and the first church built in India. Constructed in 629 CE, Cheraman Juma Masjid was built on the orders of the successor of Cheraman Perumal, the Chera King. This Sunni mosque, which resembles a traditional Hindu temple, is the second in the world where Juma (Friday) prayers were started. Similarly St. Thomas Church in Palayur in Kerala is the oldest church in India and one among the oldest Catholic Churches in the world. It is believed to have been built in 52 CE by Thomas Didaemus, one of the 12 apostles of Jesus Christ, who converted both Jews and Hindus at Palayur.

80. World War II saw the genocide of about 6 million Jews. Feeling a deep sense of injustice, some 50 Jewish young men and women, who had been a part of resistance, came together to form a group codenamed Nakam, (Hebrew for vengeance), which sought a more comprehensive form of punishment for the Nazi war criminals. A strong belief in "Zionism", which is the Jews deciding their own fate instead of letting others dictate theirs, on April 13 1946 carried out mass poisoning of former SS men in an American prisoner-of-war camp, by coating some 3,000 loaves of bread with arsenic. Despite what the investigations revealed, that the amount of arson was enough to kill about 60,000 persons, none died. To this day, it remains a mystery as to why the poison failed to kill Nazis.

81. During his studies at Trinity College, Cambridge, Lord Byron, regarded as the greatest among the English poets, had to send away his beloved pet, a Newfoundland dog, Boatswain, because rules forbade dogs on the premises. Upset, he got a tame bear, the authorities were helpless as no law prohibited that. Upon graduating he took it with him to his home. His estate didn't have what an ordinary animal lover would usually keep, he had ten horses, three monkeys, eight dogs, five cats, five peacocks, a tame wolf, a bear, two Guinea hens, one Egyptian crane, one falcon, one eagle, and one crow. It's among them he found solace.

82. It was in 1942, during WWII, Polish soldiers bought a Syrian bear cub in Iran. The cub became so popular that he was soon made an unofficial mascot and nicknamed Wojtek. Being a part, he travelled along with the unit. It was when the Polish soldiers were to travel to Italy on an assignment, that the British Transport ship which forbade pets and mascots, barred Wojtek from travelling. To deal with that Wojtek was officially drafted into the Polish Army as a Private. As an enlisted soldier with his own paybook, rank, and serial number, he lived with the other men in tents or in a special wooden crate. During the Battle of Monte Cassino, Wojtek helped his unit by carrying heavy ammunition. This service earned him promotion to the rank of Corporal. After the War, he moved along with his unit to Scotland, where his popularity won him an honorary membership of the Polish-Scottish Association. After the demobilization of his unit, Wojtek was sent to Edinburgh Zoo, where he lived until his death in 1963. There are many memorials and monuments dedicated to him in different countries.

*(Wojtek with the fellow soldiers. Image: Edinburgh News)*

83. Using soap was regarded as an exclusivity for the privileged class in Europe. Since it was considered a luxury product, in 1712, heavy taxes were imposed on soap along with other 'luxury' items such as playing cards, windows and wall paper. This resulted in black marketing and smuggling of soap. Soap tax being a significant source of revenue for the government, the entire manufacturing process began to be closely supervised by revenue officials, who took to locking the soap-making equipment overnight. Additionally the soap makers were forced to manufacture a minimum quantity of one imperial ton at each boiling. With such tough legislation, a considerable number of soap makers were forced to immigrate to other countries, leading to big losses for the government. However, it was only a century and a half later in 1853, that the soap tax got repealed.

84. India's first passenger train was pioneered by Hon. Jagannath Shankarsheth Murkute, an Indian Philanthropist and Educationalist along with Sir Jamshedjee Jeejeebhoy, a merchant, a philanthropist, and later a British knight and baronet. Nana Shankarsheth approached the British government with the proposals of constructing railroads in India, which led to the formation of the Indian Railway Association in 1845. Soon East India Company entered the contract of railroad construction and in course of time the association evolved into the Great Indian Peninsula Railway. Although the Railways were to be constructed in India, the company had 23 British board members and just 2 Indians. India's first passenger train ran on 16th April 1853 between Boree Bunder and Tanna (Thane) covering a distance of 33.8 km in 45 minutes. Fourteen carriages carrying 400 passengers including Director Nana Shankarsheth, were hauled by 3 locomotives named Sultan, Sindh and Sahib. Since private investors were encouraged, soon independent kingdoms in India began to lay their own rail systems. By 1901 a Railway Board was established, however the WWI impacted the leased out railroad badly and this was a good excuse for the British Government in India, to take over the management. The Great Crash of 1929 saw a withdrawal of 11 million rupees from the Railway funds by the British government. Although WWII had further worsened the situation, for India, it was the partition in 1947, that gave Indian Railways a severe blow. With almost 40% of the railway network lost to newly created Pakistan, it took some time for independent India to systematise the entire network. It was on 5th November 1951, that all the private players were removed and the Central Railway was formed. Today India has one of the largest rail networks in the world.

85. When tea was first introduced into Europe in the late 17th century, it became a valuable commodity, so much that people stored it in special boxes. These 'tea chests', as they were called, had metal compartments within to keep different types of tea leaves and were secured with locks. Soon tea consumption became a status symbol and as its demand shot up, smuggling and adulteration became a practice. Twigs, sawdust, ash leaves boiled with sheep dung, iron filings and artificial flavors began to be commonly added. There's a reference of a village near London, which in the 1770s, is said to have been producing more than 20 tons of adulterated material annually for the tea merchants. An exclusivity then, Tea has now become the second most consumed beverage after water. Today as many as 3,000 different types of teas are available in the market catering to both- the elite and commoner alike and it no longer requires to be kept under lock and key.

*(A tea chest/ caddy which held containers with different types of teas & sugar.*
*Image: http://collections.vam.ac.uk)*

86. The Romani or Roma people are perhaps the most persecuted and least talked about ethnic group in the world. From being forced into slavery in the Balkans, to being killed in England, Switzerland and Denmark, throughout the mediaeval era they "were sold, bartered, flogged and dehumanised" for their artisanship and labour, Roma face oppression and discrimination, and are denied basic human rights even to this day. An estimated 2 million Roma were killed in concentration camps under the Nazi Germany and its allies including Italy, Czech Republic, and Russia. About 90,000 Romani women were forcibly sterilised in the Czech Republic and Slovakia (1970-1990). In 2013 France expelled some 10,000 Roma and destroyed their camps. Italy has denied housing to Roma families. There are countless reports of their torture - from abduction of children, to hot iron branding of men, defacing their women, banning their language and marriages in their own community, to social exclusion, and depriving them education or employment. A 2016 survey across 9 European countries indicates that about 80% of the Roma live in conditions of poverty. Genomic studies reveal that the first migration began during Alexander's invasion and then due to constant raids and barbarity by Mahmud of Ghazni, which forced some 2 million Hindus, living in the Punjab and Rajasthan regions, to leave their lands. This westward migration occurred in waves in 500 CE. The Roma are known for their rich musical heritage, which has over the years influenced jazz, bolero and flamenco music. Ernő Rubik, Charlie Chaplin, Elvis Presley, Rita Hayworth, Bob Hoskins, Alfie Best, President Washington Luís, Michael Caine, Tracey Ullman, David Morley, Charlie Smith, Mary Teresa Bojaxhiu (Mother Teresa), Michael Costello are some of the famous Romani people. In 2016, the International Roma Conference was held in India, where Roma were assured that they would be treated as Indian diaspora abroad.

# The Arts

*The one thing that you have that nobody else has is you. Your voice, your mind, your story, your vision. So write and draw and build and play and dance and live only as you can."   - Neil Gaiman*

1. Indian classical music has its roots in the Vedic period. Sāmaveda (c. 1200-600 BCE), talks about melodies and chants. Music, in the Vedic times combined three arts- syllabic recital (vaadyā), melos (geet) and dance (nratyā). As these fields developed, sangeet became a distinct genre of art. Between the 12th and 18th century a slow and progressive divergence of Hindustani (North Indian) and Carnatic (South Indian) classical music or Sangeet evolved. Today the two traditions are considered sufficiently distinct at an aesthetic and stylistic level, though still retaining commonality in terms of principles of consonance and technical aspects.

2. A violin is a complex instrument. Some seventy different pieces of wood are put together to craft this string instrument (for that matter even viola, cello and bass too, are similarly created). Giuseppe Guarneri, an Italian luthier made the world's most expensive violin in 1741, which was appraised with a value of $18 million.

3. Listening to loud music interferes with your vision. This is why even though you were listening to loud music while driving, you reduce the volume when looking for parking.

4. The Mona Lisa which has been in the Salle des États of Louvre museum since 1797, suddenly went missing in 1911. Stolen by an employee at the museum, it was brought back after a brief period of time. Interestingly the empty space it had left during its absence, attracted more visitors than the actual painting had.

5.  Havergal Brian's Gothic symphony requires a thousand performers. Among them, there are 800 singers, and the remaining 200 make up the orchestra.

6.  Capoeira, an art form that combines the elements of martial arts, acrobatics, dance, music and spirituality was born out of the melting pot of enslaved Africans in Brazil, indigenous Brazilians and Portuguese influence. Since African slaves were prohibited from practising martial arts, they developed this dance form which combined dance steps with self defence moves, thus camouflaging it as a dance while ensuring the preservation of their cultural heritage.

7.  Beethoven, the renowned pianist, went to Tirocinium, a Latin school, where he was taught some maths, but he couldn't learn multiplication or division. The story goes that once he needed to multiply 62 by 50, he wrote 62 down in a line 50 times and added it all up to get the product.

8.  Louis-Antoine Jullien, a nineteenth century French conductor and composer of light music had a 40 words long name. The story goes that at the time of the baby's baptism, his violinist father was performing in a concert by Sisteron Philharmonic Society. He politely asked one of the members to be the baby's godfather. The other members of the society too, wished to be considered for the privilege. Thus, persuaded, Louis was christened with the names of all 36 members of the local Philharmonic Society.

9.  The Earliest Known Oil Paintings go back to the 14th Century, when the artists would mix the dried pigments into a paste using egg yolk!

10. Linda Manzer created a guitar with four necks, forty-two strings, and two sound holes in 1984. Interestingly this bizarre looking guitar sounds quite normal when played.

11. There's a town in Poland where everything is decorated with paintings of flowers.

12. Finland has the most metal bands per capita. In 2019 the country had some 70 bands per 100,000 people, outnumbering all the other European nations.

13. There is a music piece that has neither lyrics nor music, only the sounds of the environment that the listeners hear while it is performed on stage. American composer John Cage released it in 1952 with the title "4'33". The song lets the audience listen to the silence for four minutes and 33 seconds. The idea was to show Silence is not the absence of Sounds!

14. Varamoortheeswarar temple at Ariyathurai, Tamil Nadu, India, is believed to be more than a thousand years old, although legend has it that it could be over 6,000 years old, because of its connection to sages Romar and Mukunthan. The temple has images of fertilisation carved on stone walls showing the stages of foetus development. The carvings, it is believed, are inspired by The Garbha (womb) Puran, one of the Hindu literary ancient encyclopaedic books.

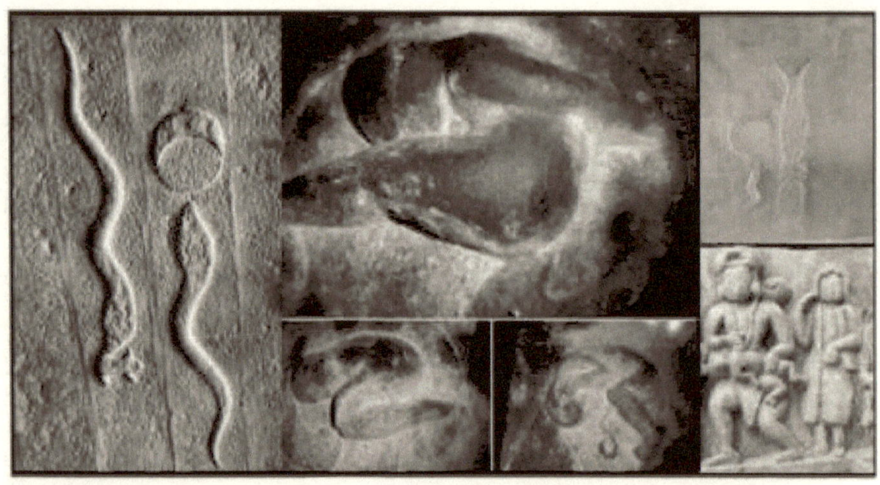

*(Temple wall carved with the process of fertilization and the different stages of fetus development.*
*Image Credit: Reddit)*

15. The famous charcoal painting of Kate Winslet you see in Titanic was drawn by the movie's director James Cameron.

16. It is estimated that in his lifetime, Picasso created some 147,800 pieces of artwork which include: 13.5K paintings, 0.1 million prints and engravings, 300 sculptures and ceramic works, 34K Book illustrations and 300 poems. As per the Art Loss Register, as many as a thousand of his works are listed as lost, stolen or disputed.

17. Karaoke is a clipped compound of the Japanese word 'Kara' which means empty or missing and 'ookesutora' (orchestra). The word "karaoke" existed in Japan's entertainment industry even before the first machine was invented. Karaoke, then meant the use of instrumental recordings as facilitator for the singer in case the live band couldn't be made available. Though crude, Daisuke Inoue, who is called the father of Karaoke actually created the original karaoke machine using car stereo with pre-recorded music and a coin box in the 1970s, but he never got it patented. Roberto del Rosario, a Filipino national got the patents in 1983 and 1986 for more sophisticated versions of karaoke machines.

18. Even after about five decades of his death, Elvis Presley is still the best selling solo artist in the world, with an estimated one billion sales worldwide.

19. Andy Warhol was an American visual artist, film director, and producer who was a leading figure in the visual art movement - the Pop Art. Over the course of the last 13 years of his life, starting in 1974, he consigned 300,000 of his everyday possessions to 612 sealed cardboard boxes. These 'Time Capsules' were boxed up with random objects that include a 17th-century German book on wrestling, postage stamps, drawings of 1950s icons, a mummified foot, Christmas decorations, autographed underwear, fan letters, unopened Campbell's soup tins and so on! Housed in Andy Warhol Museum in Pittsburgh, this unlike art, 'artefacts' collection is a popular tourist attraction today.

20. In 2017, as a part of Canada's 150th anniversary, the world's longest concert consisting of multiple artists was organised. The concert lasted for 453 hours, 54 minutes, and 40 seconds.

21. On 18th October 1961, New York's Museum of Modern Art put on an exhibition of Henri Matisse's works: "The Last Works of Matisse: Large Cut Gouaches," unaware that one of his works, Le Bateau, was hung upside down. The error wasn't discovered for 47 days of the exhibition by curators, museum staff or even 116,000 odd visitors, which included Matisse's own son Pierre, an art dealer. The only one who did, was a Wall Street stockbroker Genevieve Habert. She tried convincing the officials about the flipping of the painting but by the time the fact dawned upon them, it was time to deinstall the exhibition.

22. Now widely regarded as one of art history's greatest painters, Vincent van Gogh officially sold only one painting - 'The Red Vineyard' in his lifetime. He committed suicide in 1890.

23. John James Audubon was an American self-trained artist and ornithologist whose work, a colour-plate book titled 'The Birds of America' (1827-1839), is regarded as one of the finest ornithological works ever completed. This archetype of wildlife illustrations contains 435 life-size watercolours of North American birds. Although there are some inaccuracies in his understanding of bird anatomy and behaviour through his field notes, Audubon's contribution to both the world of Art and the birds of America is unique. He is credited with discovering 25 new species and 12 new subspecies. The book, which has 119 copies left, majorly held by libraries and museums, serves as an important record of those birds which are now extinct. In 2010, one of the copies of Birds of America received a whopping $11.5 million, at an auction, making it the 8th most expensive book ever sold.

24. Mozart sold the highest number of CDs in 2016 despite Adele, Drake, and Beyoncé having Grammy-winning hits that year. It became possible because Universal Music Group released a box set commemorating the 225th anniversary of Mozart's death. Each set contained 200 discs and each disc included in the box set was counted as one CD sold. Hence the number!

25. London based artist Tim Knowles known for his 'Tree Drawings', attaches artists' sketching pens to the branches of different kinds of trees, and then places sheets of paper under them, he then lets the winds do the rest of the work. These natural motions or stillness create art, which are recorded. They have produced some interesting results too!

26. The founder of the iconic electric guitar and bass brand and Rock and Roll Hall of Fame inductee Leo Fender never learned to play either instrument.

27. Orchestras don't always need a conductor. There are orchestral pieces that are for performances without a conductor. They usually go back to the 17th or the early 18th centuries.

28. One of the most remarkable paintings by Michelangelo is the fresco ceiling of the Sistine Chapel- including the most intricate one depicting the God giving life to the first man: "The Creation of Adam". It took the artist four years' time between 1508 and 1512 to paint the ceiling, all this had to be done standing up on scaffolds, especially designed to attach to the chapel walls with brackets.

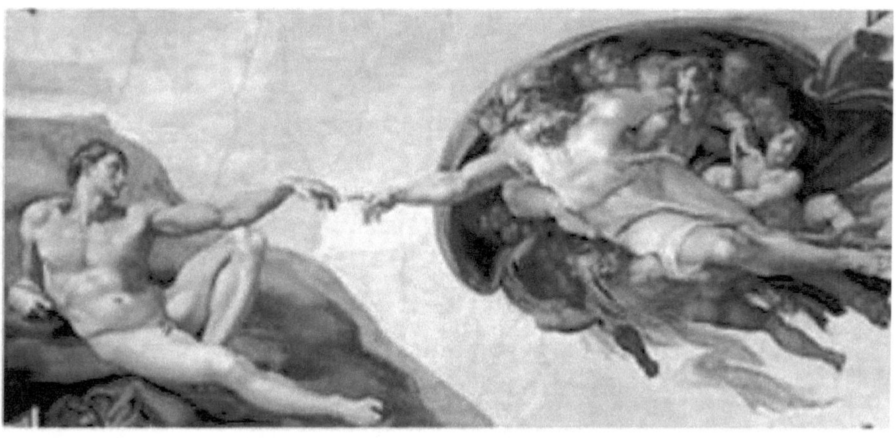

('The Creation of Adam' Fresco painting by Michelangelo. Photo : Encyclopedia Britannica)

29. The Mona Lisa has her own mailbox in the Louvre. She receives hundreds of love letters, gifts, poetries and flowers from her admirers from all over the world which are stored here.

30. British naval officers play Britney Spears songs- "Oops I Did It Again" and "Baby One More Time" to scare away Somali pirates off Africa's eastern coast. The rationale is, apparently, Somali pirates have a strong dislike for western culture and music, which would make the bandits move on as quickly as possible.

31. A study on 12,665 pop artists who passed away between 1950 and 2014 found that they have shorter lifespan than your average man.

32. A song that gets stuck in your head for whatever reason, is called an earworm. Earworms could be triggered by experiences that bring up a memory of a song, such as feeling an emotion which you associate with the song.

33. A prey to Mona Lisa's bewitching smile : Luc Maspero, a French artist, threw himself from the fourth floor of a Parisian hotel in 1852. His suicide note read: "For years I have grappled desperately with her smile. I prefer to die."

34. Sthanumalayan Perumal Temple in Suchindram, Tamil Nadu, India, is dedicated to the Trinity of Hindu Gods: Brahma-Vishnu-Shiva. It dates back to the 9th Century. The granite statue is a masterpiece of engineering in art. It has a hole of 0.5 mm width and 400 mm length.

*(A devotee measuring the size of the hole in the statue's ear. The sculptor/s of the statues are unknown : by Veludharan)*

35. Sculpting 525 busts and 225 large bronze statues has earned Jasuben Shilpi the sobriquet "the Bronze woman of India". Some of the renowned personalities she sculpted are Rani Laxmibai, Rani Chenamma, Vivekananda, Gandhi, Sardar Patel and Martin Luther King Jr. and many more. She got her name into the 'Limca Book of Record' in 2005 for her statue of Rani Laxmibai riding on a horse. Her largest creation is a 28.8 feet tall Hanuman idol which clinched the world record of being the tallest bronze statue created by a woman. Winner of Abraham Lincoln Artist Award- USA and the Miracles World Record Certificate, Jasuben at the age of 64, left for heavenly abode on 14 January 2013.

36. Over 2,000 items belonging to Elvis Presley including his clothes, letters, his school report cards and 29 dry-cleaning bills were sold at an auction in Las Vegas in 1999.

37. Jackson Pollock, an American painter often used cigarettes to paint.

38. The Romans often sculpted statues, the ones meant for public places, with detachable heads. This was quite convenient and practical as well- the body would be a generic one which could be fitted with the sculpted head of a new king or a hero, as the situation demanded.

39. According to the experts, the petroglyph rock art at Daraki-Chattan in Mandsaur district of MP, India, is estimated to be 2-5 lakh years old, making it the world's oldest rock art.

40. Fine Art Logistics, an art storage company in London, had to pay £350,000 in damages for mistakenly throwing away a valuable piece of art into a skip where it got destroyed. The said abstract work was created by Turner Prize winning Sculptor Anish Kapoor and was bought by a Swiss art collector Ofir Scheps, who had left it with the storage company.

41. Rock band Metallica became the first musical act to play a concert on all seven continents in one calendar year. They set this record after performing for 120 scientists and competition winners in a transparent dome at Carlini Station in Antarctica in 2013.

42. Ferdinand Cheval, a French postman spent 33 years creating an incredible building, Le Palais Idéal, in Hauterives with the pebbles he collected on his beat. Cheval started building this palace in 1879, using only sandstone pebbles. He carved into it mythological figures, animals, the religious places such as a Hindu temple and a mosque, structures like an Egyptian tomb, a mediaeval castle, a Swiss chalet, the tower of Barbary and other monuments. Famous quotes and poems adorn walls. One of the most impactful inscriptions reads: "1879-1912 10,000 days, 93,000 hours, 33 years of struggle. Let those who think they can do better try." Le Palais Idéal, designated as a cultural landmark of France in 1969, stands as a unique example of naive art/ architecture.

*(Palais Ideal - a palace from pebbles! Image: Wikipedia)*

43. One of the most prominent street artists working today is Banksy, who has to his name as many as 4218 artworks. Even though he displays his works on publicly visible surfaces, no one seems to have ever seen him in action. He is said to have printed his own money, modified street signs, clandestinely hung his own work on the museum walls and other conspicuous places. The England based artist is not just a graffiti artist but a political activist and film director too. His urban interventions that display disparaging wit and a biting political edge has made him quite popular. Even though his real name and identity remain unconfirmed to this day, he has quite a strong fan base in the world of art.

44. Leonardo da Vinci took 16 years to complete painting Mona Lisa, of which twelve years were spent just to create that bewitching smile on her face.

45. Established in 1958, the early Grammy Award trophy used to be made of lead with a fully hand-made gold-plated exterior. In 1990, the Recording Academy changed the design. John Billings created the new Grammy with a special proprietary zinc alloy called "Grammium". Since it is handcrafted, each piece takes fifteen hours to make. This 24K gold personalized trophy is handed over a few weeks after the actual show. What we see being presented to the artists on the stage, is just a dummy..

46. The Louvre Museum in Paris, is the largest art museum in the world. About 66% of all artwork in the museum is created by French artists. Before the Louvre became a museum, it was a 12th century fortress, which was renovated into a royal palace in the 16th century. People have claimed it to be haunted, which isn't strange, most old monuments world over have such stories attached to them.

47. A study on the impact of music on plants, conducted by South Korean scientists from the National Institute of Agricultural Biotechnology Jeollabuk-do, found that plants grew faster when music was played around them.

48. "Happy Birthday to You" dates from the late 19th century, when the Hill sisters Patty and Mildred introduced the song "Good Morning to All", to their kindergarten class in Kentucky. According to the Guinness World Records, "Happy Birthday to You", is the most recognized song in the English language, followed by "For He's a Jolly Good Fellow". Warner Chappell bought its ownership rights for $15 million in 1990. Today the "Happy Birthday" song brings in $2 million a year in royalties alone, which comes to $5,000 per day. The song costs $25,000 to use in a movie or TV show.

49. John Cage's musical piece, "As Slow as Possible", based on avant-garde composer, started in 2001 and is still running at St. Buchard Church in Germany. It's not just the slowest but the longest as well. The show is so slow that the visitors have to wait months for a chord change and the organ it's played on was not even completed before the concert began. Pipes were added to keep the music steady in 2008. The performance is scheduled to conclude in 2640, which is 639 years in all.

50. Claude Monet, a renowned 19th century French painter and founder of the Impressionist Movement in art, is seen as a key precursor to Modernism. His father disapproved of his artistic bent of mind and insisted that he focused on being a grocer. Imagine the Loss to the world of Art, had Monet succumbed to his father's will !

# Language & Literature

*A Person Who Won't Read, Has Literally No Advantage Over The One Who Can't Read.   - Mark Twain*

1.  The phrase "win hands down" comes from horse racing. When a jockey would win a race even without pulling the reins of the horse or whipping the horse, it would be referred to as a 'hands down' victory.

2.  'Mellifluous' is a sound that is pleasingly smooth and musical to hear.

3.  The word "bankrupt" comes from the Italian phrase 'banca rotta', meaning "broken bench". It refers to an old custom that involved literally breaking the bench of money dealers who ran out of funds. According to the Online Etymology Dictionary, the word "bankrupt" grew out of this phrase that literally refers to breaking something-not just the bank.

4.  French was the official language of England for about 300 years from 1066 till 1362. The Norman invasion in 1066, established French as the official language of the court, parliament and aristocracy. It impacted the mannerisms, fashions, food, lifestyles, art and literature of the elite English. As for the common people, they still spoke the old English. It is not surprising therefore that English vocabulary which was highly influenced by French, has about thirty percent of French words in it.

5.  The phrase "spending a penny" originated sometime around the 1890s when the British authorities set up the first public lavatories, fitted with penny-coin-operated locks.

6.  The nursery rhyme "Mary Had A Little Lamb," is based on an actual person. Mary Sawyer, an 11- year-old Boston girl had a pet lamb who followed her to school one day. It is believed that in the late 1860s, she contributed money to an old church by selling wool from the lamb, which made her a darling of the townsfolk and hence the poem.

7. During the evolution of the English language, there was a time when "girl" meant child, or a young person, and not a specific gender. In modern times it's specifically used for females.

8. The symbol '#' isn't officially called hashtag or pound. Its technical name is octothorpe. The "octo" means "eight" and refers to its points, though reports disagree on where "thorpe" came from. Some claim it was named after Olympian Jim Thorpe, while others argue it was just a nonsense suffix.

9. 'Lemniscate' is the technical name for the infinity sign.

10. While 'aristarchy' is a system where the government is run by the most able rulers, 'kakistocracy' is a government of the worst, least qualified, or most unscrupulous citizens. The modern governments which have been labeled as kakistocracies are Malaysia under Pakatan Harapan, Philippines under Rodrigo Duterte, UK under Boris Johnson, Egypt under Abdel Fattah Al-Sisi are a few notable ones.

11. Cherophobia is a phobia where a person has an irrational aversion to being happy. The term comes from the Greek word "chero," which means "to rejoice." When a person experiences cherophobia, they're often afraid to participate in activities that many would characterize as fun, or of being happy.

12. The word for someone giving an opinion on something they have no knowledge about, but speak as an expert, is called an 'ultracrepidarian'.

13. The word 'barbecue' originated from an indigenous American word 'barabicu' used by Arawak people of the Caribbean and the Timucua people of Florida, meaning a 'frame of sticks'. The word was first used in the English language in 1648 as 'barbacado' but the first recorded use in its modern form was by Edmund Hickeringill in his book Jamaica Viewed in 1661. According to linguists before the word came to be used in English, it had already found its way into the culinary lexicon of Spanish, Portuguese and French languages. Barbecue might have been used as a verb in its earliest usage, in the present times, it is used as a noun, a verb as well as an adjective.

14. The word "school" comes from the ancient Greek word for "free time."

15. "Horizontal refreshment" was 19th century slang for sex.

16. "What in tarnation?" is literally just another way of saying, "What the hell?"

17. Paraskavedekatriaphobia is the fear of Friday the 13th.

18. The word for the day after tomorrow is "overmorrow'.

19. In German idiom, "Leben wie die maden im speck" translates to "to live like a maggot in bacon" is a jargon for having a luxurious lifestyle.

20. The expression "dog days" of summer has its origin in ancient Roman history. The ancient Romans saw the Dog Star, Sirius, rise with the sun in July and early August.

21. A noodle strand is spaghetto and a plate of it is spaghetti. In Italian, an 'i' at the end of a word implies a plural form, while an 'o' or an 'a' is indicative of its singular status. For instance raviolo and ravioli, gnocco and gnocchi, l'uovo and le uova, fettucino and fettuccine, are singular and plural respectively.

22. The 'D' in the D-Day, which is often mistakenly understood as 'Doomsday', is actually 'day' - Its Day-day. The D-Day was the start of Operation 'Overlord'. On D-Day, 6 June 1944, Allied forces launched a combined naval, air and land assault on Nazi-occupied France and the term began to be used to describe the first day of any large military operation.

23. Coming from the Greek words "arachi" (ground nut) and "butyr" (butter), Arachibutyrophobia', refers to the irrational fear of peanut butter getting stuck to the roof of the mouth. Actually arachibutyrophobia has nothing to do with the peanut butter as an object, but the 'sensation', that one feels, of having it stuck inside the mouth. Although it may occur alone, it's often rooted in a more generalised phobia of choking (pseudodysphagia) or of sticky textures such as peanut butter.

24. There was no word as 'woman' to refer to a female in the English dictionary earlier. Word 'Woman' was a distorted etymology of 'whyfman' or 'wife'-man'.

25. Sanskrit, Hebrew, Basque and Sumerian are the oldest documented languages of the world.

26. The illegible handwriting is usually scribbled by doctors, lawyers, or even the journalists— this "careless handwriting" is referred to as "griffonage".

27. Not Italian but Florentine, an Italian dialect that is the official language of Italy.

28. The phrase : "Pardón my French", was meant to be used when apologizing for swearing.

29. The word "gorilla" is derived from a Greek word meaning, "A tribe of hairy women."

30. Rollin Kirby's cartoon, "On the Road to Moscow", which portrays the suffering of the Soviets under the 1921 famine, where Grim Reaper is leading them to Moscow, was awarded the inaugural Pulitzer Prize for Editorial Cartooning in 1922.

31. There is a misconception that Korean spoken by the two Koreas is the same. The fact is North Korean and South Korean are two different languages, with different sets of grammar rules, vocabulary and accent.

32. In the times when the china cups weren't as strong as they are today, the practice was to pour milk first to neutralize the temperature and then the boiling tea, so as not to crack the cup. However over the period of time when the quality of Chinaware improved it was no more necessary to follow that order. But how you serve your tea became an indicator of your social status- pouring milk last meant you had a superior quality of China. That's how the expression "rather milk in first" began to be used for those who were from lower class.

33. The word "camel" comes from Arabic and means "beauty" if translated directly.

34. A jiffy is an actual unit of time. It's 1/100th of a second.

35. The last letter added to the English alphabet was 'J'. The letter dates back to 1524, and before that the letter 'i' was used for both the 'i' and 'j' sounds.

36. The word "nerd" was actually coined by Dr. Seuss in his 1950 book "If I Ran the Zoo."

37. An eccedentesiast is an individual who prefers to hide emotional pain with a smile and/or laughter.

38. Located in Oceania, Papua New Guinea may not seem a very big name on the world map, but this small country with 17 million population has the world's most number of languages spoken in a country- its 840!

39. What we call a division ( ÷ ) sign is technically an "obelus". Centuries ago, the obelus was used as an editing tool to mark factually questionable passages in the manuscripts.

40. The random symbols used as a group eg. "$¥%#!$", in text as a replacement for profanity, it's called "grawlix ". The term was coined by American cartoonist Mort Walker.

41. NASA scientist Rick Briggs maintains that Sanskrit is the only unambiguous language in existence. It has about 103 billion words, which is the largest for any language in the world. Studies claim that owing to its structured science, Sanskrit not only makes it one of the most computer friendly language but even develops one's logical and analytical skills. A US university dedicated to Sanskrit has a NASA department in it for research work on Sanskrit manuscripts. As per the reports, the proposed 6th (in 2025) and 7th generation Super Computers (in 2034), which the US is creating are based on Sanskrit language.

42. The word 'microscope' was proposed as a term in a letter to Federico Cesi, Duke of Aquasparata and founder of Italy's Accademia dei Lincei, by Johannes Faber of Bamberg, Germany in 1625.

43. Left-handedness is also known as "sinistrality". It comes from the Latin word for left. There were huge prejudices against left-handed people, who were once thought to be unlucky and evil.

44. More than 1,000 different languages are spoken on the continent of Africa.

45. The word clue comes from the Greek word 'clew'. When Minatour - a monster with a bull's head and a man's body, trapped Theseus in a labyrinth. Theseus was able to escape using a ball of yarn, a 'clew'. The yarn helped him to keep track of the path he took. So, in its English usage a "clue" came to mean something that guides you, gives you a hint or suggestion. Over the period it began to be used in the sense of offering guidance to discover a truth, or giving a piece of information that helps you solve a problem.

46. In the 1870s, Irish farmers faced a crisis that could result in a terrible famine. In order to prevent this, they formed a group that campaigned against rent increases and evictions landlords were proposing. Charles Boycott, a British army captain, who tried to evict farmers, was ostracised by the community. Gradually his name 'boycott', began to be used as a protest strategy.

47. It's popularly believed that the word "wannabe" was coined by the Spice Girls. The fact is that the surfer slang for the phrase "want to be" was first used in 1981 and popularised a few years later when Madonna fans began to call themselves "Madonnabes."

48. The English word "alphabet" comes from the first two letters of the Greek alphabet – alpha and beta.

49. The slang term for dollars, "bucks", originates from the early 1700s. It refers to deer skins from male deer, or bucks as they're commonly known. This is because during these early times, deer skins were used as an informal currency.

50. The unclassified Busuu language spoken in the Southern Bantoid of Cameroon has on record only three speakers when last checked in 2005. In 1986 there were just eight people who spoke Busuu. And that makes it an endangered language.

51. Spanish is a Romance language that was derived from a vulgar take on the Latin language.

52. Cryptophasia is a language phenomenon that only twins, identical or fraternal, can understand.

53. Basque is a mystery language that has baffled even the linguists. Spoken by around 700,000 people in the Basque Country in Spain, this language is so unique and unrelated to any other language around that experts aren't still sure of its origin. It even has its own numbering system.

54. The ancient name of Sri Lanka in Sanskrit was Siṃhaladvīpa (Dwelling-Place-of-Lions'- Island), which during the trade with the Arab world gradually got corrupted to Serendib. Horace Walpole was inspired by a Persian fairy tale, "The Three Princes of Serendip", in which the princes "were always making discoveries, by accidents and sagacity, of things they were not in quest of", coined the word 'serendipity' in 1754 to mean "the faculty or phenomenon of finding valuable or agreeable things not sought for".

55. Most know Michelangelo as a famous Italian sculptor, painter, and an architect, but he was also an established poet. He produced hundreds of madrigals and sonnets during his career.

56. A "buttload" is a real measurement of weight.

57. Greek poet Dionysios Soloms' 158 stanzas long poem, "Ode to Freedom", written in 1823 was adopted as the national anthem of Greece in 1864, making it the longest national anthem for a country.

58. The term 'Arab' is often used to describe the race of those who hail from the Middle East part of the world. Actually 'Arab' is a cultural term that refers to the people who speak Arabic as their mother tongue and they need not necessarily be from that particular part nor be following a particular religion- Islam.

59. Ciao, a common Italian salutation for hello or goodbye, comes from the Venetian phrase "sciao-vostro', meaning 'at your service. It's now a part of the English vocabulary, used as a greeting at meetings or parting.

60. After winning independence from Britain, a need was felt in the US to break away from the shackles of their language too. Noah Webster, an American lexicographer, political writer, editor, and author, led this crusade. He urged Americans to be free from "the clamor of pedantry" that had plagued British English. He rejected the notion that knowledge of Greek and Latin was elementary to the study of English grammar. He even started a private school and wrote a series of educational books, including the "Blue-Backed Speller". He removed or substituted what he thought was unnecessary in word construction. In 1806, Webster published his first dictionary. For the compilation of his next- An American Dictionary of the English Language, which took 26 years to complete, Webster learnt some 28 languages including Sanskrit, Greek, Latin, Hebrew, Russian, and Arabian to evaluate the etymology of words. His Merriam-Webster dictionary is one of the most popular English dictionaries in the world today.

61. This one will definitely blow your mind away. Forbidden from formal education, women in Jiangyong Prefecture, Hunan Province, in the 19th century developed their own script called Nüshu or "women's script". The invention helped the women to communicate with each other, write songs, poems, or any other piece of information they felt important. Until the 1980s, outsiders did not know about the existence of this secret script.

62. It is estimated that Franz Kafka burned 90% of his total work due to his persistent struggles with self-doubt. In his will, Kafka instructed his literary executor and friend Max Brod to destroy his unfinished works, including his novels The Trial, The Castle, and Amerika, but Brod ignored these instructions, and had much of his work published. Even with only ten percent of his work published, Czech writer Franz Kafka is the most influential writer of the twentieth century.

63. The lint that collects in your pockets is known as "gnurr".

64. While Caliology is the study of bird nests, Oology is that of bird eggs.

65. William Shakespeare was the first person to use mother insults.

66. It is estimated that by 2050, the US will become the largest Spanish speaking country in the world.

67. The Tale of Genji, (Genji monogatari), written by Murasaki Shikibu in the 11th century, a classic work of Japanese literature, is considered to be the world's first novel- first psychological novel. The novel ends abruptly mid sentence. Opinions vary on whether this was intended by the author or there are missing chapters.

68. E. E. Cummings, regarded as one of the most important American poets of the 20th century, had to face rejection from as many as 14 publishing houses for his collection of poems. Undeterred, he self-published the collection under the title -"No Thanks," which his mother financed. Bound like a notepad, with a top spine, the book has an unorthodox appearance. It is dedicated to those 14 publishing houses who had turned the collection down. The book would become a classic in the times to come. Cummings wrote approximately 2,900 poems, two novels, four plays, and several essays in his lifetime. He was the second most read American poet after Robert Frost.

69. American author Morgan Robertson's novel 'Futility' (later published as "The Wreck of the Titan"), which was written long before the conceptualization of RMS Titanic, has an uncanny parallelism with the real Titanic tragedy. In his book, the fictional ship meets a similar fate as does the actual Titanic 14 years later. Be it the size of the ship, touted as the largest one in line or being regarded as unsinkable. It's carrying about the same number of passengers, who lose their life because there weren't enough lifeboats for all its occupants, or the ship hitting against an iceberg in the North Atlantic Ocean - all these striking incidents repeating in factuality made some people credit Robertson with premonition and clairvoyance, which he denied.

70. The term "happily ever after" was originally used as "happily until they died."

71. Originally published in Russian as "Voyna i mir", War and Peace is regarded as the masterwork of Russian literature. Leo Tolstoy took six years to finish this classic. Initially some parts of its draft were published in a periodical under the title 'The Year 1805', but not really satisfied with that version, he changed both- the title as well as the ending of the story.

72. It was John Dryden, a 17th century English poet, who is said to have made the syntax rule, which considered a sentence ending with a preposition grammatically incorrect. For a long time strict grammarians have cringed over such sentences, students had been losing marks, however, the modern writers do not treat a sentence wrong just because it has ended in a preposition- it might be a poor sentence but definitely not incorrect.

73. Although Harper Lee's 'To Kill a Mockingbird' won a Pulitzer Prize and stayed about 88 weeks on the bestseller list, Lee did not write again. The one book wonder, gave two reasons for not writing again: "One, I wouldn't go through the pressure and publicity I went through with To Kill a Mockingbird for any amount of money. Second, I have said what I wanted to say, and I will not say it again." ( I like that attitude!)

74. While sleeping through the winter is Hibernation, it is 'Estivation' for sleeping through the summer.

75. Mary Shelley famously wrote the horror sci-fi novel 'Frankenstein' at the age of 18. Conceived in 1816, it was first published in 1818. It is said that Mary was holidaying in Switzerland with writers Percy Shelley (her lover), Lord Byron, John Willam Poridori, and her step sister, when one stormy and creepy night she had a nightmare. While stuck indoors in Geneva, Byron is believed to have suggested that the four writers have a ghost story writing competition. Mary used this dream vision in her creation of Frankenstein and she even won the contest. Thus the first true horror science fiction came into being.

76. Dental Fricative is when sounds are pronounced differently although the letters are the same. For instance the 'TH' sounds in 'this' and 'thin' - are pronounced differently. Such Voiced Dental Fricative is typical of the English language.

77. The word 'robot' has its origin in the Czech word 'robota' meaning forced labour. Karel Capek, writer, playwright and critic introduced it in his SciFi play R.U.R. ('Rossom's Universal Robots' , which explores the idea of manufacturing artificial people) in 1920 and popularized the term. Capek had used the expression 'roboti', (robot in English) on his brother Joseph Capek's suggestion, who was also a writer and a painter.

78. In 17th century England, Parishioners were required to pay a tax to supply the church with wax candles, which was called " wax-scot " or wax-shot. The shot meant "discharge of a weapon", which comes from the Old English gesceot meaning "payment". The expression 'scot-free', without having to pay, comes from there.

# Games & Sports



*You win some, you lose some, and some get rained out, but you gotta suit up for them all.   - J. Askenberg*

1. Manchester United was formed as Newton Heath LYR in 1878 by workers from the Lancashire and Yorkshire Railway. It was renamed Manchester United in 1902. It is because they represent all of the Greater Manchester area, rather than just the City, they are Manchester United. The first known captain of this club was E. Thomas in 1882.

2. The temperature of a tennis ball affects how it bounces. While at higher temperatures, the ball bounces higher because the gas molecules inside the ball expand. Lower temperatures on the other hand lead to the shrinkage of the ball which doesn't allow the ball to bounce much. Wimbledon goes through more than 50,000 tennis balls each year to ensure the best tennis balls are used.

3. Jerry Reinsdorf, owner of Bulls and White Sox kept paying Michael Jordan his reported $4 million basketball salary even while he was experimenting with baseball.

4. American President Teddy Roosevelt had threatened to ban football unless the association introduced player safety rules. In response, the rules were revised and the forward pass was introduced. According to the new change, an incomplete forward pass would cost teams a 15-yard penalty.

5. During the Wimbledon Championships in England, on an average about forty two thousand tennis balls are used each year.

6. The longest recorded boxing match in history was one fought between Andy Bowen and Jack Burke in 1893. It lasted 110 rounds and went on for over seven hours. This historical contest of 6 April 1893 was eventually ruled as a "no contest," and it still stands unbroken!

7. Robert Fischer, popularly known as Bobby Fischer, was an American chess grandmaster and the 11th World Chess Champion, who learnt chess at age six and by 14, he had won his first of a record eight US championships. At 21, in 1964, he won with an 11-0 score, the only perfect score in the history of the tournament. Post WWII, Soviet Russia had been dominating Chess, but in 1972, by defeating the Soviet Union's Spassky, Fischer became the first native-born American to win the world champion title (and $156,000 prize money). In 1975 when Fischer was deprived of his championship title for his refusal to meet his Soviet challenger, Anatoly Karpov, he withdrew from serious play for 20 years and returned only to defeat Spassky in a privately organized rematch in 1992. Fischer took Icelandic citizenship in 2005, where he stayed until his death in 2008. The 1993 Academy Award-nominated movie, "Searching for Bobby Fischer" was inspired by him.

*(1964-Bobby Fischer playing 50 opponents simultaneously, winning 47, drawing 2, and losing 1.*
*Image: Rare Historical photos)*

8.  Sheep Counting is an official sport in Australia. About 400 sheep are made to make a dash past ten competitors, who must count them. The closest to estimate the numbers accurately is declared the winner.

9.  Soccer is World's most popular sport, but in the United States it is in fifth place. The first four being Basketball, Baseball, American Football & Ice Hockey, in that order.

10. According to the World's Sports Encyclopedia, although there are over 8000 sports played across the globe, only 200 have recognition from the international governing bodies of some sort.

11. Golf ball divers retrieve golf balls from bodies of water in or around golf courses. The golf balls are then cleaned up, repackaged, and resold.

12. Few people would know that Lumberjack is also a sport with international competitions. The most popular one is the Lumberjack World Championship that features 4 different competitions for women, 9 for men, and 3 team events.

13. Formed in 1857 in England, the oldest soccer team in the world is Sheffield Football Club.

14. Golf is the only sport to be ever played outside the Earth. In 1971, Apollo 14 Commander and original Mercury astronaut Alan Shepard, the first American to fly in space, also became the first to tee off on the lunar surface. The two balls he hit with a six-iron (one that went into a crater another that "sailed for miles and miles") are still there.

15. When he was 26, "Pistol Pete" Maravich, in an interview reportedly said, "I don't want to play 10 years in the NBA and die of a heart attack at age 40". He went on to play 10 years in the NBA, and died during a pick-up game in 1988 due to a heart defect, which hadn't been detected earlier. He was 40. Maravich is regarded as one of the greatest creative offensive talents ever and one of the best ball handlers of all time.

16. Nissan uses number 23 on their vehicles during the Car races, allegedly because in Japanese number two is pronounced as "ni" and three as "san". Together this gives "ni-san".

17. In 1962, former Major League Baseball (MLB) catcher Harry Chiti was traded from the Cleveland Indians to the New York Mets. The player was to be named later. A poor performance by Chiti made him that "player to be named later". Thus making him the first ever player to be traded for himself.

18. To officiate a baseball game was exhausting, gruelling and rather taxing. Therefore the Umpires were allowed to sit. They would sit 20 feet behind home plate in a padded rocking chair. This practice, however, was discontinued after 1859.

19. Players are not allowed to swear at Wimbledon. Therefore, judges have to learn swear words in different languages in order to enforce the rules.

20. Pakistan's Sialkot city produces over 50% of all soccer balls in the world. It all started during British colonial rule. The long unbearable delays in the arrival of the shipments of footballs made them depend heavily on the local artisans for the repairs of the damaged or punctured footballs they had. Impressed with the results, initially as a trial, they placed a small order. The hand sewn footballs were an instant hit. Today, it's the largest football producer in the world.

21. Soccer player Ronaldinho came to media attention when he was just 13. His team won 23-0. All the 23 goals were scored by him.

22. Kite flying is a professional sport in Thailand.

23. When boxer Manny Pacquiao has a fight, it is said that the crime rate in his native Philippines drops to 0%.

24. James Fixx, the creator of the word "jogging" died from a heart attack while jogging.

25. While stitches on a cricket ball may vary - from anything between 65 and 70, a baseball has an exact 108 number of stitches. The first and last ones remain concealed completely. Each ball is hand sewn with 88 inches of waxed red thread. Such precision!

26. The longest tennis match, which took 3 days to complete was played in 2010 at Wimbledon. John Isner of the United States beat Nicolas Mahut of France in a match that lasted 11 hours and five minutes.

27. Michael Jordan makes more money from Nike annually than all of the Nike factory workers in Malaysia put together.

28. The English had banned Golf in 1457 because they considered it to be a distraction from the serious pursuit of archery.

29. Pelé is the only player who was a part of three different World Cup winning teams.

30. Ossip Bernstein a Russian-French chess player and the recipient of the title International Grandmaster was captured by the Bolshevik secret police in 1918, on the suspicion of being a part of 'counterrevolutionary' crime and was sentenced to death. On the day of his execution, as he stood facing the firing squad, a commanding officer who recognized his name from the list of the prisoners, offered him a deal- the two would play a game of chess and if Bernstein won, he would be released but if he couldn't, he would be shot along with the other prisoners. Bernstein won his freedom. Later he quietly left Russia to settle in Paris.

31. The first mass-produced, travel-sized board games were made during the American Civil War. When Milton Bradley, a board game manufacturer saw bored soldiers stationed in Springfield, he began producing these low cost and long lasting small games which the soldiers could play during their down time.

32. Such is the obsession for football, that when the University of Nebraska plays football at home, it's said that the stadium becomes the state's third largest city.

33. In order that no catastrophic situation occurs, a 'black underwear' policy is enforced on the umpires of Major League Baseball during the games, lest they should split their trousers.

34. Until 1949 the grass at Wimbledon used to be two inches long. But after an incident where an English player got bitten by a snake in the deep grass, the grass size got reduced. The grass courts have about 8mm high grass.

35. In 1923, jockey Frank Hayes won a race at Belmont Park in New York despite being dead. It so happened that mid-race he suffered a heart attack, but since he was still seated on the horseback, his body stayed in the saddle until his horse crossed the finishing line for a 20-1 outsider victory.

36. New York's early Dutch settlers wore loose-fitting short pants gathered at the knee called knickerbockers or ( popularly called knickers), which gave the New Yorkers the name "Knickerbockers." The NBA team calls itself "The Knicks" in short.

37. Bowling was invented around 3200 BCE in Egypt.

38. The game "Quidditch" from the Harry Potter novels is now a recognized sport in the real world, with its own leagues and world championships.

39. Since 1992, Finland has hosted the official "Wife Carrying World Championship". The participants have to carry their wives and race through a long obstacle course. The 'prize' that the winner receives is Beer equivalent to his wife's weight.

40. It was in 1960, when the Baseball uniforms began displaying players' names on their backs.

41. The first college football game was played on November 6, 1869, between Rutgers and Princeton, then known as the College of New Jersey, in New Brunswick, New Jersey. Rutgers won.

42. Sir Arthur Conan Doyle, known for creating the famous detective Sherlock Holmes, was a sportsman too. He played goalie for the amateur Portsmouth Association Football Club, which became the Portsmouth professional team and eventually won the FA Cup in 2008.

43. The Sun City Poms is a cheerleading squad in Arizona that only people 55 or older can join.

44. Three-time world champion, Sebastian Vettel once revealed that when driving for Red Bull, he usually wore lucky coins tucked into the laces of his boots and the lucky charm worked for him.

45. The Philadelphia Eagles' old stadium, the Veterans Stadium, had a courtroom and jail to handle their fans who were notorious for indulging in hooliganism. It was later reported by the stadium court that about 95 percent of 'inmates' did not belong to the city itself.

46. The Supreme Court of the United States has its own private basketball court called "The Highest Court in the Land." It was before the 1940s that the top floor of the court building, which used to be a storage area, was turned into an exercise room for the courthouse employees. Later the basketball nets were installed for the employees there. I liked the play on the words - highest and court, the pun intended here- the highest court in the land !

47. Almost half the population of the world watched FIFA World Cup games both in 2010 and 2014. The 2010 World Cup in South Africa was watched by 3.2 billion people from every country and territory on the globe, including Antarctica and the Arctic Circle. The next FIFA World Cup held in Brazil in 2014, drew record breaking numbers again.

48. Initially the baseball caps were made from straw and were first worn by the New York Knickerbockers in 1849. The first merino wool baseball caps came into circulation only after a few years. This cap came with an attached visor which would later be called a bill.

49. In 1930s England, greyhound racing was big business and national news. Arthur Leggett, owner of Romford Greyhound Stadium London, decided that after greyhounds, he was going to bring cheetah racing to the UK. He imported twelve Cheetahs from Kenya, quarantined, acclimatised and trained them. The expectations were great when the race was held on 11 December 1937 however, due to a lot of technical issues, the experiment failed. Leggett decided to introduce a new event for greyhound races called 'Essex Vase', in 1939, which is still popular among the race lovers.

50. The world's first eSport event, the 'Space Invaders', was released for the Atari 2600 in 1980. A massive tournament was organized to determine the champion of Space Invaders. Some 10,000 participants from different regions competed, of which only four were shortlisted to play the finals in New York.

*(Gamers in the 1980 Space Invaders Championship http://earth-azrael.tumblr.com)*

51. In the 1950 World Cup, the English, 'the kings of football', were heavy favourites against the hastily assembled U.S. team, which was composed of semi- professional part- time players. But when the Americans defeated them, apparently many newspapers around the world believed the 1-0 score was a typo and instead printed that England won 10-1 or 0-1. (It's still a disputed fact). Well, the unexpected result of the match was one of the biggest upsets in the competition's history. So inspired by this match, that Professor Geoffrey Douglas later profiled this match in his book The Game of Their Lives, which was made into a movie with the same title in 2005 and later the DVD version came as 'The Miracle Match'.

52. This sounds crazy but the NFL claims that over 100 children are conceived annually at tailgate parties in the Super Bowl parking lot.

53. While running at 120 miles per hour, a Formula One car generates so much downforce that it can drive upside down on the roof of a tunnel.

54. Around 700,000 footballs are manufactured annually for America's National Football League. And to make regulation footballs some 35,000 cows are slaughtered in a batch of 3,000 at a time.

55. America's professional football association- National Football League mandates that during the entire competition period, the Home team must provide 36 footballs for outdoor and 24 for indoor games. Additionally they must be ready to be inspected by the referee two hours before the game.

56. America's National Hockey League (NHL), is considered to be the top ranked professional ice hockey league in the world. Its players are not permitted to tuck their jersey into their pants in the way where the top padding of the pants is exposed outside the jersey.

57. Bill Bowerman, a track and field coach is credited with the design of waffle sole shoes for Nike. Bowerman didn't like the running shoes that the athletes were using in the 1950s. So he created the Cortez shoe, but that too did not satisfy him. He was looking for a much lighter version which could be worn on any surface type. It was in 1970, during a waffle breakfast that the idea came to him of using the waffle texture on the sole of the running shoes. The waffle sole shoe made its appearance in the 1972 U.S. Olympic track and field trials in Eugene, Oregon, USA.

58. Even though it's a square, the boxing area is called boxing "ring". In the early days of boxing, the spectators who came to watch would circle around the combatants in the shape of a 'ring'. That's how the expression 'ring' came. In 1743, Jack Broughton, a bare-knuckle fighter, came up with the first set of modern boxing rules, including the shape. However, it wasn't until the following century the boxing ring became a "squared circle." When the Pugilistic Society revised the rules in 1838, they built the first square boxing ring and it has been used ever since.

59. A golf ball has over 300 dimples. While the American golf balls have 336 dimples, there are some special ones which may have as many as 500, with an average depth of about 0.010 inch each. A smooth ball hit by a professional golfer with the same precision, would travel much lesser distance as against the dimpled ball. These dimples affect both the drag and lift and help increase the ball's flight range almost by double.

60. Four of the American Presidents had been cheerleaders in their student days. President Franklin Roosevelt, was a cheerleader for Harvard College, Dwight Eisenhower, the 34th President was for West Point Academy. The 40th President Ronald Reagan had cheer led Eureka College, Illinois and the fourth one to do so was the 43rd President George W. Bush, who cheer led at Yale University.

61. Major League Baseball, a professional Baseball organization, spends about $5.5 million on the sport. According to an estimate about 850,000 balls are used per season.

62. Cheerleading originally began as an expression of dissent against the harsh and abusive treatment that the students faced at the hands of teachers and faculties after the American Revolutionary War in the 18th century. The male students initially reacted violently, but later used more subtle ways to register their independence. They began by organizing their own extracurricular activities outside their professors' control and soon college sports teams were formed. In the 1860s, the trend of cheering and chanting in unison for their favourite player had begun in the UK, and before long it travelled to the US too. On November 6, 1869, the first Intercollegiate Football took place, which saw "Sis Boom Rah!" cheer shouted by students in unison. Twenty nine years later, on 2nd November, 1898, organized cheerleading got official recognition as an all-male activity. Though in 1923 the women were permitted to participate, it was only around WWII when collegiate men were being recruited for war that the opportunity for more women to make their way onto sporting event sidelines was created. As of today 97% of all modern cheerleading participants are female.

63. It's interesting to know how the word "Soccer" that got coined in Britain, is used by Americans and not by the British. In 1863 England's Football Association drew some rules. The game played under the Football Association's rules became known as association football. Students at Oxford University, began to use words like "rugger" for Rugby football and for the association football "assoccer", which was further shortened to "Soccer". Meanwhile, in the 19th century a sport emerged in the US, which borrowed elements from both rugby and association football which came to be known as "gridiron football". Later gridiron got dropped and just football stayed. Before long, it became more popular than either of them. The United States Football Association, formed in the 1910s, as the official organizing body changed its name to the United States Soccer in 1945. This is how the "Soccer" has stuck!

# Olympics



*The world never puts a price on you higher than the one you put on yourself.*
- Sonja Henie

1.  The first Olympic Games took place in BCE 8 in Olympia, Greece. They continued to be organised every four years until being banned in the 4th century by Emperor Theodosius I, a Roman ruler, for being a 'non-Christian' or a 'pagan festival'. They were revived in the 19th century, with the first modern Olympics taking place in Athens, Greece, in 1896.

2.  The first recorded Ancient Olympic race, held in BCE 776, was won by Corubus of Elis, who was a chef, a baker and an athlete. He won the stadion race which was a 200-yard sprint.

3.  Stadion, a sprint event of 600 feet run, is the oldest Olympic sport. The length of the stadion varied because the foot differed from place to place. For instance the Delphi stadion was 177,55 m while at Olympia it was 192,28 m long. Similarly the distance that the women ran in the Heraia was 5/6 of the length of the stadion for men. The Olympic stadion race for men was run in honour of Zeus while the women ran in honour of Goddess Hera which was measured in shorter feet.

4.  Athens 1896, officially known as the Games of the I Olympiad were the first international Olympics, organised by the International Olympic Committee (IOC), founded by Charles Pierre de Coubertin, a French educator and historian and the father of modern Olympic Games. Athens 1896 was an all male event ( women began to compete from 1900 Paris games onwards), with about two third athletes from Athens. In all 14 nations and one Mixed Team participated. Winners were rewarded with a silver medal and the runner up, a bronze. The Gold medal got introduced to the Olympics in the 1904 St. Louis games, which was a solid gold medal.

5. China, which hadn't won even a single Olympic medal until 1984 went on to win a hundred medals in the 2008 Beijing Olympics.

6. Modern Olympics founder Baron Coubertin proposed an Olympic event combining a 14km race and a written essay on it, to show prowess in mind and body. It never took place. Thankfully so! What would be judged athletic skills or creative abilities?

7. The 1900 Paris Olympics had the freakiest of competitions - Live pigeon shooting. Some 300 live birds were killed mercilessly, leaving a gory sight of blood shattered bodies of pigeons scattered everywhere- and all in the name of sports. Each participant was to shoot the birds released in front of him, much in the way clay targets are fired out of traps these days. Belgium's Leon de Lunden topped with 21 kills, closely followed by French shooter Maurice Faure with 20. Donald MacIntosh, a Scot finished in third. The prize money of 20,000 French franc was shared among the top 4 winners. Probably the event didn't go down well with people, the IOC distanced itself declaring it not an official sport. And thus pigeon shooting was never repeated as an Olympic discipline.

8. The 1900 Paris Olympics, was the first international competition that allowed women to compete, even though it was just a couple of events. Croquette was one of the sports that saw women participants, but the competition didn't see the audience- just 1 person bought a ticket to watch the women's event. Croquet has not appeared again on the Olympic roster.

9. Originally Chicago was to host the 1904 Olympics. St. Louis, which was organizing the Louisiana Purchase Exposition, wanted the Olympics to be held in their city. The idea was to club together -the Olympics and the Expo. Such was the determination that they even threatened to stage rival events if Chicago did not yield the Games. Eventually Chicago had to bow down and the Olympics were held in St. Louis, Missouri.

10. In the times when Olympics Games included a competition for music, entries were submitted on paper, but not performed, making it rather tough for the judges to give them a score.

11. The Olympics were initially a summer event. The winter games were introduced in 1924. Until 1992, the Winter and the Summer Olympics took place in the same calendar year. In the present times they're organized on separate cycles and alternate every two years.

12. In the 1904 St. Louis Olympics, American marathon runner Frederick Lorz reached the finish line first and was even declared the winner, however it was found that due to exhaustion Lorz had stopped running after 9 miles. His manager gave him a lift covering a distance of 11 miles. After which Lorz continued on foot back to the stadium. Lorz accepted the allegations and Thomas Hicks, another American athlete went on to become the real winner.

13. Tug-of-War was contested as part of the track and field programme in every Olympics between 1900 and 1920. Since it used to be the Clubs participating, a country could be represented by more than one team for the same event. As a result the US clubs won all three medals in 1904. Tug of War had become too controversial for the Olympics. For instance during the 1908 Olympics the U.S. team accused the Liverpool Police team of wearing extra-heavy boots, but they declined when the Liverpudlians offered a shoe- less rematch. Britain won all the three medals in 1908.

14. In the history of Olympics only two sportspersons have won Olympic medals in such contrasting disciplines as Sports and Art. The first being the multi talented Walter W. Winans, an American marksman, horse breeder, sculptor, painter and a writer, who won a gold medal in Shooting at the 1908 London Olympics and then went on to win two more medals in 1912 Stockholm Olympics- silver in Shooting (in the running deer team competition) and a gold for his sculpture 'An American Trotter'. The other achiever was from Hungary, Alfréd Hajós, who won two gold medals in Swimming at the 1896 Athens Olympics. Twenty-eight years later in the 1924 Paris Olympics he secured a silver medal in Architecture for 'Plan for a Stadium', which he had co-designed with Dezsó Lauber.

15. The Olympic gold medals that the players are awarded today aren't solid gold. Actually they are made from sterling silver and feature a very small quantity of gold, just enough to plate it. For instance the 2016 Rio games versions were only 1.34 percent gold. The last of real gold medals were awarded in 1912.

16. Visual and Fine arts, such as Literature, Music, Sculpting, Architecture and Art based on sports-themed paintings, prints, watercolours, engravings and oils, were Olympic disciplines between 1912 and 1948.

17. During the 1928 Olympic Games Australian rower Bobby Pearce had to stop rowing midway during the race to let ducks in front of him cross. Despite a loss of time, he won against eight other competitors in the match.

18. In the 1936 Berlin Olympics, twenty one year old Jesse Owens created history which remains unbeaten to this day. He set five world records and equalled a sixth in 45 minutes.

19. Probably the first time or perhaps the only time in the history of Olympics, a tie in a competition led to cutting of the medal. It was in the 1936 Berlin Games, where two Japanese pole-vaulters tied for second place. So the problem was solved by cutting the silver and bronze medals in half and fusing the two different halves together. Now both the athletes had a medal each which was half-silver and half-bronze.

20. Nadia Comaneci, Romanian gymnast, 5 times Olympic Gold medalist all in individual events, was the first gymnast to be awarded a perfect score of 10.0 at the age of 14 in 1976 Montreal games. During her career, Comăneci won nine Olympic medals and four World Artistic Championship medals.

21. It was due to "royal courtesy." that Princess Anne, daughter of Queen Elizabeth Il, did not have to undergo gender verification at the 1976 Montreal Olympics. She participated in the three-day equestrian competition.

22. During the Beijing Olympics in 2008 Usain Bolt ate only chicken nuggets, apparently it was the only meal he recognized from home. Food in China may have put him in a fix, his performance on the field was anything but confusion. He won three gold medals with this diet.

23. Kabbadi, a native game to India, may be a lesser known sport to the world today, but it did receive international exposure during a demonstration in the 1936 Berlin Olympics. Although the Kabaddi moves had immensely impressed Adolf Hitler and the Olympic Committee members, it couldn't be included in the Olympics competitions and we have no idea why.

24. Chintamoni Kar, a renowned sculptor from Kharagpur, born in British-India won a Silver medal in Sculpting in the 1948 London Olympics. Although Indian, he won the medal for Great Britain because technically he had British citizenship at the time of the competition. In 1956 he returned to West Bengal, where he lived till his death in 2005.

25. The word gymnasium has its roots in Greek, 'gymnásion', which literally translates to 'nudity' or 'place to be naked'. The gymnasiums in Ancient Greece did not just function as the training facility for competitors in public games, but were also a place for socialising and engaging in intellectual pursuits. Since the athletes practised nude, only adult male citizens were allowed to use the gymnasium. The early gymnasiums were made near a spring or on a riverside. A small stretch of area with packed earth and shaded trees served as a place for practice. The earliest recorded examples of gymnasia date back to the 6th century BCE. Some of them can be seen at the sites like Delphi, Olympia, and Nemea.

26. Oksana Aleksandrovna Chusovitina, the only female gymnast ever to compete in 8 Olympic Games and one of the only two female gymnasts to compete at the Olympics under 3 different national teams: the Unified Team (1992); Uzbekistan (1996, 2000, 2004, 2016 & 2020); and Germany (2008 & 2012). She has also competed in 16 World Championships, 4 Asian Games and 3 Goodwill Games. She holds the record for the most individual world championships medals in a single event.

# The Show Business



1. For the character of Harry Potter more than 16,000 children from the UK and US contested. Ultimately we know Daniel Radcliffe grabbed this hotly contested role and did absolute justice to it.

2. Netflix founders had to struggle initially to conceptualize a catchy name for the streaming platform. Marc Rudolph then came up with "Kibble'! Of course, it wasn't meant to stay on forever. Marc eventually came up with the word 'Netflix' and it's been entertaining us since 1997.

3. In 1997 some six hundred eighty five children were rushed to hospitals in Japan after an intense Pokémon episode that caused dizziness, vomiting, and seizures.

4. Amzad Khan, who has immortalised the iconic character of Gabbar was almost dropped from Sholay, because Javed Akhtar deemed his voice too weak to do justice to the role of Gabbar Singh.

5. Originally to promote the upcoming movies, the trailers of the new films would play in the cinema halls after the movie got over. Running these trailers proved completely ineffective as the audience wouldn't stay to watch them. These days, even though we see them either in the beginning of a movie show or during the intermission or even on social media platforms, the term 'trailer' is still stuck to it.

6. In the movie 'Babe', which is a story about an orphaned pig, the characters are played by a combination of real and animatronic pigs and Border Collies. The breed used for the main character was 'Large White', which grows rather fast. As many as 46 different piglets of the required size were used during the course of the filming.

7.  In order to get a big break, James Cameron sold the script of 'The Terminator' for $1 and the assurance that he'd get to direct it.

8.  The 'Joker's' scars were inspired by a torture method used by Scottish gangs in the Twentieth century. These gangsters in Glasgow would punish their rivals by cutting the victim's mouth open in the shape of a demented grin - which we know as "Glasgow smile." The cut was made from one or both ends of the victim's mouth, sometimes all the way to the ears, resulting in a terrifying scar that marked the wearer for life.

*(The Joker with 'Glasgow Smile' :Image: Pinterest)*

9.  With almost a billion dollars worth of worldwide ticket sales, the 'Saw' franchise is the highest earning horror franchise ever.

10. In 1933, the first drive-in theatre opened in Camden, New Jersey, which screened the British comedy "Wives Beware". People paid 25 cents per car.

11. Shekhar Kapoor, an eminent film director and actor, had to undergo the horrors of the partition of India in 1947. His father, who was a doctor and had a flourishing medical practice in Pakistan, was forced to leave everything and go to India. While on train a massacre took place, killing almost all the passengers. Kapoor and his sister were able to survive only because his mother, pretending to be dead, threw herself over them.

12. The Pokémon franchise is worth over $24 billion.

13. New Zealand pop star Ella Marija Lani Yelich-O'Connor or better known as Lorde has an unusual Instagram account "onionringsworldwide" where she rates Onion Rings from around the world.

14. James Cameron once confessed that more than the movie, it was his yearning to dive down "to the shipwreck" of the ill fated ocean liner, that he sought funds to make Titanic.

15. H.J. Whitley, popularly known as the "Father of Hollywood", states an interesting episode in his diary regarding the christening of Hollywood. When he initially came to Hollywood, it was a rural settlement of 18 families. It was during his honeymoon period in 1886, as he stood at the top of a hill looking out over the valley, a Chinese man who was carrying wood in his wagon came there. When he got out and bowed, he was asked what he was doing. He responded in broken English, "I holly-wood", (I am hauling wood). Eureka!!! It was on the spur of the moment when he made this decision of calling the place Hollywood. According to an estimate Whitley founded more than 140 towns in his lifetime.

16. Scarcity of metal during the Second World War led to the making of the Oscar trophy from wood.

17. 'Harry Potter and the Cursed Child' sold so well that the two seats that The Palace Theatre of London had permanently bolted open for the theatre ghosts to sit in, had to be brought in for the use of common people which they had never used.

18. Before Jeetendra began his career in Bollywood he used to supply imitation jewellery to the film industry. It was during one such meeting, that director V. Shantaram, who was making Navrang with Sandhya in the lead, convinced him to act in his film. Jeetendra was the body double of Sandhya in this 1959 movie.

19. In an interview, John Abraham revealed that, while playing the character of an invaterating smoker in the 2007 movie "No Smoking", although he had quit smoking long back, he chain smoked as many as 99 cigarettes a day and it was health damaging.

20. The digital rain of the green symbols trailing down in 'The Matrix', the code that creates the fake reality where people live, was nothing but a creative idea of a production designer, who scanned symbols from his wife's Japanese sushi recipe books, then manipulated them to create the iconic "code", and we went crazy wondering where this complicated algorithm came from!

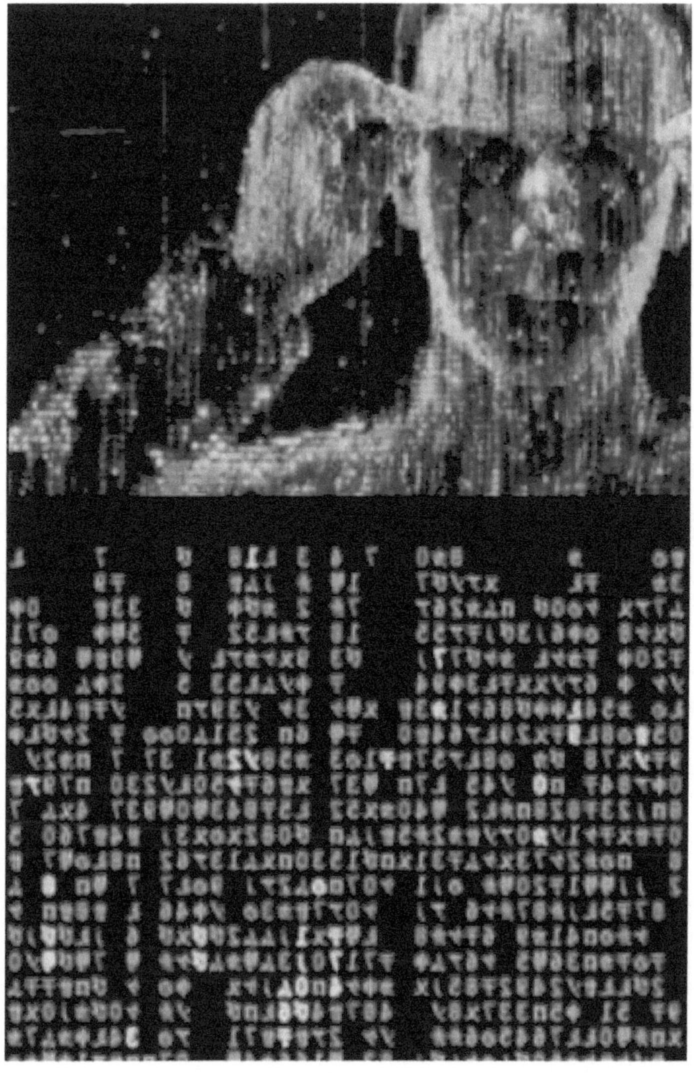

*(MATRIX: "The digital rain or the falling green code represents the activity of the virtual reality environment of the Matrix on screen. Image Credit: Steve Miller)*

21. The most profitable movie ever is the 2007 horror film Paranormal Activity, which cost about $460,000 to make and became a major box-office success, bringing a whopping 19,758 percent of investment returns (around $89 million).

22. With about 2.7 billion annual sales of movie tickets, India may top the world chart, but the tickets being low priced, it generates only a fraction of the revenue in comparison to what Hollywood earns.

23. During the construction of Walt Disney World, Disney decided to create its own city to bypass the local laws.

24. The most popular ballet in the world is Pyotr Ilyich Tchaikovsky's The Nutcracker for which he composed the music and thus turned it into the world's greatest Christmas ballet. It was first performed in 1892 at St. Petersburg's Mariinsky Theatre in Russia.

25. Armageddon, a 1998 Sci-Fi drama, is shown to the management trainees at NASA, under their management program, primarily to spot errors in the movie. Some 868 have been pointed out so far.

26. While shooting for the 1957 Hindi movie 'Nau Do Gyrah', (9-2-11) in the Chambal region of MP India, which was infamous for the dacoits in those days, film actor Dev Anand along with the other crew members was resting. At night, to everybody's shock, a fully armed dacoit stood at Dev Anand's doorstep. He had come to take Dev Anand's autograph.

27. Kamal Amrohi, known more as the husband of Meena Kumari, was said to be a perfectionist. While directing Razia Sultan, he was to create a scene of a Royal Feast, and even though it was supposed to be a couple of minutes' scene in the movie, the precisionist in him ensured that he would get the 'real stuff'. It is said that 45 goats, 251 fish and 455 chickens were cooked for the scene. Interestingly, on the editing table the director snipped off the scene because it did not appeal to him.

28. Arnold Schwarzenegger was paid $15 million for his role in 'Terminator 2', which averaged out to $21,429 per word.

29. The most curtain calls ever for a ballet was 89, after Rudolf Nureyev and Margot Fonteyn performed their 1964 'Swan Lake' in Vienna.

30. The first person to have more than a hundred million followers on Twitter is American singer, actress, and television personality, Katy Perry.

31. Parinda, a 1989 Bollywood movie is believed to be the inspiration for the majority of the underworld slangs used in Mumbai today.

32. One of Walt Disney's first art jobs was drawing cartoons for a local barber in exchange for haircuts.

33. Robert Downey Jr. used a unique way of protesting for not having enough time to relax. He actually peed in jars and left them lying around the set of "Zodiac", thus registering his dissent.

34. American author Lyman Frank Baum, best known for his children's books, particularly The Wonderful Wizard of Oz and its sequels, named Oz after a filing cabinet that was kept in his office. One cabinet was labelled - A to N and the other was labelled- O to Z. It's from here that he got inspired.

35. Taylor Swift has a framed picture of the infamous moment of Kanye West interrupting her at the 2009 MTV Video Music Awards, in her living room. It's captioned, "Life is full of little interruptions". This ugly episode which started in 2009 hasn't died yet.

36. It was a visit to Jallianwala Bagh, which impacted Director Shoojit Sircar so much that he spent the next 20 years visiting libraries, reading books, collecting documents and even meeting and interviewing the massacre survivors. Equipped with enough material he made Sardar Udham, which was released in 2021, and won him both, rave reviews and awards.

37. While shooting for Schindler's List, Anna Biedrzycka-Sheppard, the costume designer, needed costumes for about 20,000 extras in the movie. She took out an advertisement seeking clothes in fashion during the 1930s and 40s. There were hundreds of Polish people in poor financial condition, who willingly sold their family's clothes they still had. Sheppard got Oscar nominations for costume designing for the film.

38. Since a lion's roar isn't as intimidating as that of a tiger, movie makers usually use a tiger's roar and not a lion's, to make it more impactful.

39. For the movie Fight Club, Brad Pitt and Edward Norton actually learnt to make Soap.

40. Dharmendra received a remuneration of Rs. 51 in 1960 for his debut film "'Dil Bhi Tera Hum Bhi Tere".

41. In the movie 'Slumdog Millionaire', Jamal is shown to jump on a pile of dump. It was actually a mix of chocolate and peanut butter made to look like a refuse heap.

42. According to a report, Netflix's share of downstream traffic for the first six months of 2019 was 12.9%. During this period, Netflix garnered 0.6%. more traffic than Google.

43. Shooting commercial films takes hours, that's why the foods shown in the films are usually synthetic ones and not the real. For instance the ice-cream seen in TV commercials is actually mashed potatoes and the milk is created with white glue.

44. "It, Chapter Two", a 2019 American supernatural horror film in which Jessica Chastain is shown in a kiddie pool of blood. To make the scene look real, a record 19 thousand litres of fake blood (the most for any movie ever) was used to shoot that iconic bathroom scene.

45. The Conqueror, a 1956 movie, was made near a nuclear test site in Utah desert. After being assured that it was safe, about 220 cast and crew shot for the film and the makers even shipped into Hollywood some 60 tons of sand for the reshoot purposes. A little over a decade later 91 of them developed some type of cancer, of whom 46 died, including John Wayne, the lead actor and popular icon of Hollywood's Golden Age. While giving an interview to the People magazine in 1980, a university director of radiological health said, "In a group this size, you'd expect only 30-some cancers to develop. With 91, I think the tie-in to their exposure on the set would hold up even in a court of law".

46. The fourth film in the Pirates of the Caribbean franchise 'Pirates of the Caribbean: On Stranger Tides', is the most expensive film ever made. Despite the general feeling that the movie was an "overindulgent mess that stretched the narrative", it did well on a financial level and became yet another film in the series to cross the $1 billion box office mark and went on to become the fourth highest-grosser of 2011.

47. The 1975 Bollywood blockbusters 'Sholay' and 'Deewar' were shot at the same time. Amitabh Bachhan, who was in the lead in both the movies, used to shoot for Sholay during the daytime and Deewar at night.

48. In 'Candyman', Tony Todd's character had to fill his mouth with real bees and was stung several times during the shoot, though painful, it didn't damage him much. That became possible only because the bees were specifically bred for the movie. It was ensured that the bees were only twelve hours old, and although looked like an adult, didn't have a powerful stinger.

49. The Bollywood blockbuster 'Zindagi Na Milegi Dobara' is said to be the only movie in the world which brought an unprecedented hike of 65% to Spain's tourism business, after its release. In order to create the La Tomatina festival scenes in the movie, some 16 tonnes of tomatoes were flown in from Portugal to Spain, because tomatoes were not in season then.

50. This might sound crazy but Donald duck comics got banned in Finland because he doesn't wear pants.

51. In 1958 Kishore Kumar made two movies- 'Chalti Ka Naam Gaadi' (Hindi) and 'Lookochuri' (Bengali), in the hope that they would flop. It is said that he wanted to show losses in his income. To his dismay both movies went on to become huge commercial successes.

52. Ever heard an actor refusing the lead role in a movie on a flimsy ground such as a dislike for a certain smell? In 1973, Raj Kumar was offered to play the lead role in Zanjeer, but he refused on the grounds that he couldn't stand the smell of Director Prakash Mehra's hair oil. The role went to Amitabh Bachhan and the rest is history.

53. James Cameron, the director of the 1997 epic romance Titanic, deserves to be lauded, besides other accomplishments, for the precision with which he has handled the 'duration' of the disaster. In that context the 195 minutes movie can be divided into two parts- one that comprises the present day scenes, the credits at the beginning and towards the end, the other is the exact time that Titanic took to sink, which is 160 minutes. Even the collision with the iceberg which reportedly lasted 37 seconds, has a similar time coverage in the movie.

54. Walt Disney, a high school dropout, was fired by a newspaper editor because, "he lacked imagination and had no good ideas."

55. Jingle All the Way, a 1996 Christmas comedy film, starring Arnold Schwarzenegger and Sinbad, the two rival fathers who are desperate to get a toy 'Turbo-Man', for their sons, a last-minute shopping spree on Christmas Eve, was inspired by real-life Christmas toy sell-outs of the Cabbage Patch Kids. It was in the 1983 Christmas season that saw parents literally camping out at stores to make sure they got the dolls. Such was the madness to get the Cabbage Patch Kids, that shoppers got into unimaginable physical fights, store mobbing, trampling and in the process hurting many. Just two years after its release, Murray Hill Publishing sued 20th Century Fox for $150,000, for stealing the film's idea from a high school teacher Brian Webster entitled 'Could This Be Christmas?' In 2004, not finding any merit in the case, the original verdict itself was quashed by the court.

56. Once Sean Connery single handedly beat 4 men in a night club while Michael Caine held his coat. Also in another incident, famous gangster Johnny Stompanato stormed onto a movie set in the UK and pointed a gun at actor Sean Connery due to jealousy involved in Stompanato's affair with Lana Turner, only to have Connery take the gun from him and force him out of the movie set.

57. The character in TITANIC who drinks from a flask and rides the ship down into the ocean with Jack and Rose is based on a real person who did just that. He survived and thanked the alcohol.

58. Richard Torres, the Peruvian actor married a tree in Santo Domingo. Bizarre, though it may seem, it made perfect sense, particularly when the intent was environment protection. Richard wanted to draw attention towards the problem of illegal logging in the Dominican Republic.

59. It was in 1933 when the exiled Russian Prince Felix Yusupov sued MGM over the biopic, Rasputin and the Empress, for inaccurate portrayal of his wife Irina. The English court awarded her $127,373 and an out-of-court settlement with MGM reportedly got them $250,000. It's since mandatory for movies and serials to give the disclaimer: "This is a work of fiction. Any similarity to actual persons, living or dead, or actual events, is purely coincidental."

60. David Holmes, who had done the stunt doubles for Daniel Radcliffe in every "Harry Potter " movie, was left paralyzed neck down, after he met with an accident during a broomstick flying scene in his last one. To pay for his medical bills, Radcliffe organized a celebrity charity auction which helped Holmes to get on his own feet. He now runs a company with a couple of his quadriplegic friends.

61. In the 1930s it was common for foreign language films to use the same set and shoot the film, instead go for a dubbing later. 'Dracula', a 1931 movie, was shot both in English as well as Spanish. While the English version didn't do good business, the Spanish one, which was shot during the night time, using the same script and the set, not only wrapped up in about half the time but even did fairly well at the box office.

62. Wayne Anthony Allwine was an American voice actor, sound effects editor and foley artist, best remembered as the 3rd official voice of Mickey Mouse, which he held for 32 years. During one such project in the 90s he fell in love with Russi Taylor, a voice over artist for Minnie Mouse and the couple got married in 1991. Taylor had started as the original voice of Minnie Mouse in 1986, and continued for 33 years until her death in 2019. In 2008, both the husband and wife were honoured with Disney Legends Awards.

63. Nestlé provided 1,850 real chocolate bars for Charlie And The Chocolate Factory.

64. The 2013 Hollywood release 'Dallas Buyers Club', was made on a shoestring budget of $5 million. Shot in 25 days, with hand held camera, no customary lighting set-ups and a meagre $250 for make up, went on to win three Oscars in 2014, which included one for Makeup and Hairstyling.

65. 'Home Alone' starring Macaulay Culkin, is the highest grossing comedy film of all time.

66. Aradhana, a 1969 Bollywood movie with Rajesh Khanna and Sharmila Tagore as its lead pair, was the first Hindi movie to run successfully for more than 100 days with four shows a day in non-Hindi speaking North-Eastern states of India.

67. Bollywood movie Kaala Patthar (1979) was inspired by a real coal mine disaster known as Chasnala Mining Disaster that happened on 27th December 1975 near Dhanbad, Jharkhand and killed 372 miners.

68. American actress Jennifer Lawrence, has a tattoo on her hand that reads "H20". It's to remind her to drink water.

69. Scrubs, an American sitcom that aired between 2001-2010, is one of the most realistically picturized medical dramas ever made. It even received a perfect score of 10 by IGN.

70. Frozen 2 is the highest-grossing animated film of all time with a $1.325 billion collection at the global box office.

71. In 1979, Dolly Parton entered a Dolly Parton Lookalike Contest in Phoenix and well - lost it ! She lost it to a drag queen.

72. A man by the name of Juan Catalan got arrested for a murder at the time when Larry David's acclaimed series 'Curb Your Enthusiasm' was being filmed at Dodger stadium. Miraculously their camera caught Juan, proving his alibi true. Thus the HBO comedy saved an innocent man from being falsely accused.

73. The world's first animated feature film was made in Argentina. It was a political satire called El Apóstol made up of 58,000 drawings and had a running time of 70 minutes.

74. Kulbhushan Pandit known to film buffs by his screen name Raj Kumar was born in Loralai, Balochistan, into a Kashmiri Pandit family in 1926. Well educated, Kumar became a sub inspector under Bombay Police, when he moved here in the 1940s. He married an Anglo-Indian air hostess named Jennifer, whom he had met on a flight. He debuted with the film Rangeeli in 1952 and went on to become a legend.

75. "The Great Dictator", a satirical comedy drama, was one of the most famous Charlie Chaplin's movies, directed and produced entirely with his own money. Since Chaplin's film advanced a stirring condemnation of Hitler, Mussolini, fascism and antisemitism, Hollywood stayed away from involving itself with this lest it should enter into any controversy and lose the money too.

76. According to one estimate, Japan contributes to about sixty percent of the world's animated films and television shows, popularly known as Anime. It's in such a high demand globally that it's viewership has spread across 65 countries, making it an extremely successful industry, so much so that the tiny country has around 130 voice-acting schools, training the artists today.

77. In a gap of two years, Waheeda Rahman played a mother and the love interest in two movies opposite Amitabh Bachhan. She romances Sr. Bachhan in the 1976 'Adalat' and dons the role of his mother in the 1978 release "Trishul'.

78. Talking of playing mothers, Sridevi who was 13, played 26 year old Rajinikanth's stepmother in 1976 Tamil film 'Moondru Mudichu'.

79. Netflix made special socks known as 'Netflix Socks', that could detect when a user fell asleep and pause the show/movie so that they don't miss out on anything when they wake up. The socks came with a sew-in electronic device that detects the wearer's pulse.

80. The personal Star on the Walk of Fame is a 'paid for' recognition. You have to pay around $30,000 in order to have it installed there.

81. The longest television series of all time is an anime currently running over 7000 episodes. Initially published in Hasegawa's, a Japanese local paper, as a comic strip Sazae-san in 1946, was adapted in animation for television in 1969. This Guinness World Record holding series has now been adapted into many radio shows and theatrical plays.

82. Kim Kardashian has a 'glam' clause in her will. According to which if she is ever in a position where she is unable to get herself ready, or communicate with someone or is unconscious, it's got to be ensured that her hair, nails, and makeup are all perfect, before she is brought in public view.

83. When she was growing up, Eva Mendes wanted to be a nun. Until then she didn't know that -nuns don't make money. She changed her mind the instant she found out the actual job of the nuns.

84. William Shakespeare is the most filmed author ever in any language.

85. Three American Presidents have won Grammy under the 'Best Spoken Word Album' category. Introduced in 1959 for the first time, it is awarded for spoken words such as in audiobooks or documentaries' narrations. The three Presidents are Jimmy Carter, who won it three times, followed by Bill Clinton and Barack Obama, both of whom are two times winners of the award.

86. Steven Spielberg, who had declared : "I'm committed to Holocaust education", and strengthening the cause of social Justice, refused to accept any fees for Schindler's List. It would be like "blood money", he said, any profits that the movie made, should be returned to the Jewish community.

87. When directing "Elizabeth: The Golden Age!", director Shekhar Kapur had to create a scene of Elizabeth's arrival at St. Paul's Cathedral while its construction was still on. Incidentally, there was some actual renovation work going on when he came to shoot. Instead of hiring extras to play the role of the construction workers, he got the site workers to wear the period costumes and hold in their hands the 16th century tools to cut stones that were being installed in the cathedral. So when you watch the construction work going on in the movie, it's the real stonemasons.

88. In 2017 archeologists found a 300- pound Sphinx head near the Californian coast. Excavations revealed that this was actually a buried movie-set of the silent era, "The Ten Commandments". The director of this 1933 movie felt that the artefacts including 21 Sphinx replicas were too expensive to be given to anyone (other movie makers). He considered it cheaper to bury the entire thing. Interestingly despite being inside the earth for 94 years, most of these excavated stuff were found in good condition.

89. During the early years of the Academy Awards, the press would be provided with the names of the winners in advance with the condition that the results wouldn't be revealed before 11 pm. In 1940, The Los Angeles Times broke the news of 'Gone With the Wind' winning ten Oscars, even before the statue was handed out at the award ceremony. The incident led to a rule change that stands today.

90. "All The President's Men", a 1976 film in which Bob Woodward (Robert Redford) and Carl Bernstein (Dustin Hoffman), the two reporters from The Washington Post investigate the Watergate scandal, involving the administration of the US President Richard Nixon. To give it a realistic feel, the production company Wildwood Enterprises-spent thousands of dollars to create the most authentic newsroom set- from true-to-life filing cabinet labels to the waste papers on the news desks, just everything. In fact the trash was shipped from the actual WaPo office to Hollywood to create the authentic environment. In 2010, the Library of Congress selected the film for preservation in the United States National Film Registry for being "culturally, historically, and/ or aesthetically significant."

91. While directing "Interstellar" (2014), Christopher Nolan wanted a cornfield scene. Instead of looking for one, he decided to grow one of his own. Since his 2013 production "Man of Steel" had been a box office success so funds weren't an issue. Nolan grew corn in five hundred acres, shot the movie Interstellar in the fields then sold the crop making a huge profit from the corn crop.

92. Stephen King, the most successful horror writer, whose works have been adapted into films, TV shows, miniseries and comic books, ghost wrote for himself. Of the 64 novels, he wrote 7 under the pseudonym Richard Bachman. For the unsuspecting world 'they' were 2 different bestselling authors. King had created a comprehensive background for Bachman. Bachman lived in New Hampshire with his wife Claudia. They were still mourning their young son, who had died in an accident. He kept himself busy by writing at night and working on his dairy farm during the daytime. He had undergone a brain surgery recently, hence couldn't make a public appearance. To make all this look authentic, King even put a picture of his agent's insurance broker as the 'author' of the novels. Thus Bachman's cover stayed on until blown by a bookstore clerk Steve Brown, whose suspicion and a little sleuthing undid Bachman. King later in his typical sombre manner announced that Bachman had "died of cancer of the pseudonym". His reason for creating this alter ego, was majorly to see if he was really a talented writer or was he riding on the success of the critically acclaimed movie 'Carrie', that was an adaptation of his novel.

93. What we know as 'The Hollywood' in Los Angeles, was originally spelled out as "Hollywoodland". In 1923 real estate agent Harry Chandler had put this sign up to attract potential home buyers. Initially meant to stay for 18 months the 'HOLLYWOODLAND' sign, had cost him $21,000 to raise it. In 1949, the 'Land' was removed to read just 'HOLLYWOOD' as it stands today. From 1995 onwards, the Hollywood Sign Trust is looking into its maintenance work.

94. The world's first television commercial was for Bulova Watches, with a voiceover "America runs on Bulova time". Transmitted on July 1, 1941, before the beginning of a baseball game in New York, this 10 second long advertisement had cost just $9. The first commercial on the Indian television came out some 37 years later in 1978 for Gwalior Suitings and within next five years the first colour ad that of Bombay Dyeing got televised. The beginnings of the telecasting commercials may have been dirt cheap, today the industry generates tens of billions in a year.

95. The Incredible Hulk's original colour was Grey. Due to a printing error the grey got green. Stan Lee was impressed and the green stayed.

96. Flappy Bird, a mobile game developed by Vietnamese video game artist and programmer Dong Nguyen was released in May 2013 but was removed from both iOS App Store and Google Play on February 10 2014. In such a short span of 9 months, it got downloaded 50 million times, making an earning of $50,000 a day from in-app advertisements as well as sales. Despite it becoming a sleeper hit, Nguyen withdrew the App, claiming that he felt guilty over what he considered to be the game's addictive nature and over usage.

97. As per their depiction the Disney Princesses can be classified into three eras, namely : The Golden, the Renaissance and the Modern. While the Golden includes Cinderella, Snow White and Aurora, in the Renaissance era we were introduced to Ariel, Belle, Jasmine, and Mulan. The Modern Era has Tiana, Rapunzel, Merida, Anna, Elsa, and Moana.

98. The first film made in Hollywood was "In Old California" in 1910. This silent Western was directed by D. W. Griffith. India had its first full length feature film in 1913- "Raja Harishchandra", a silent film, directed and produced by the legendary Dadasaheb Phalke, also known as the Father of Indian Cinema. The Indian film industry today, generates around 2000 films every year as against Hollywood which produces just about 800 films per year.

99. Unlike the Hollywood celebrities, Neil Armstrong and the Apollo XI crew have Moons on the Hollywood Walk of Fame instead of a Star.

100. The creators of three immensely popular American animated series of the 90s were all roommates in their college. Filipino American Van Partible, who created Johnny Bravo, shared room initially with Craig McCracken maker of "The Powerpuff Girls", Paul Rudish, a designer on that series and Genndy Tartakovsky, a Russian American, creator of "Dexter's Laboratory" and "Star Wars: Clone Wars". So much Creativity in One Room!!!

# Innovations

*If I had asked the public what they wanted, they would have said a faster horse.   - Henry Ford*

1.  The Japanese created a special device called a bite-scan - that measures the chewing strokes. It analyses your eating habits- from how much one eats to how quickly.

2.  Alphonse Bertillon, a French criminologist is credited for pioneering the mug shot in 1879. Tired of the criminals escaping, he came up with a new method to track them down. He got every suspect's head, middle finger, left foot, and forearm measured. The police would file the measurements on cards along with photographs. Thus the data of every suspect or a criminal got recorded.

3.  In 1928, Alexander Fleming left a Petri dish in his lab. On returning from vacation, he saw mold growing on the dish of Staphylococcus bacteria. The mold, by producing a self-defence chemical, prevented the bacteria from growing. This was the world's first antibiotic- Penicillin. In 2017 Bonhams auctioned this mold disc for $14,597.

4.  An English chemist John Walker accidentally discovered that a stick coated with certain chemicals burst into flames when scraped against a rough surface. His invention revolutionised 'fire production', which earlier used to be a very laborious job. He sold the first "Friction Light" on 12th April 1827. Soon it gained popularity. He packaged the wooden splints 'matches' in a cardboard box and equipped it with a piece of sandpaper for striking. Since he hadn't bothered to patent it, Samuel Jones, a Londoner, copied the idea and launched his own "Lucifers" in 1829. Lucifers was an exact copy of "Friction Lights".

5.  Chocolate milk was invented by an Irishman in Jamaica in the 1680s, he then brought it back to Europe, where it was sold as medicine.

6.  Kodak developed the first digital camera in 1975, they kept it secret for fear it would hurt the film business.

*(The first digital camera.Photo : Richard Trenholm/CNET)*

7.  William Kent, a landscape architect, invented the first stroller for the third Duke of Devonshire in 1733. Since it was too much to expect the affluent parents to push a stroller themselves, Kent designed his model to be pulled by a small animal, like a goat.

8.  Microwave inventor Percy Spencer was an American physicist with no formal education and yet became one of the well known names in the field of technology. One day while building magnetrons, he noticed the candy bar in his pocket had melted down because of the electromagnetic waves in the radar set he was standing before. Instantly an idea struck him. He made a metal box using microwaves to heat food. As per the company's policy, Spencer received no royalties but a one-time $2 gratuity. Raytheon, his company, got its patent on October 8, 1945, with the name Radarange. During his career Spencer received as many as 300 patents.

9.  British scientist Dr. William Brownrigg is credited with creating the first artificial mineral water, by adding health giving minerals and carbon dioxide for fizziness.

10. Before the invention of tubes and bottles for paint, it used to be stored in pig bladders. The bladder would be sealed with a string after filling it with paint. It would be pricked to get the paint out but this would often break open. The 19th century American painter John G. Rand is credited with the invention of paint tubes made out of tin which had screw caps.

11. His abhorrence for rich and non spicy foods, which he believed stimulated 'abnormal excitement', led John Harvey Kellogg along with his brother to invent cornflakes- just the right kind of healthy, "ready-to-eat anti-masturbatory morning meal". Kellogg wrote some arbitrarily extreme methods preventing masturbation advocating women to apply "pure carbolic acid" to their private parts and all young boys be circumcised as a "remedy". In fact, he's said to be one of the main driving forces behind routine infant circumcision in the 1890s in the US .

*("Ready-to-eat anti-masturbatory morning meal by Kellogs)*

12. Google Images was literally created when Jennifer Lopez stepped out on the Grammy red carpet in that infamous jungle print Versace dress in 2000. People went crazy searching for her green outfit, leading to Google adding an image function to its search engine.

13. In 1965, a patent was filed by George and Charlotte Blonsky, a couple
from New York City for an 'Apparatus for Facilitating the Birth of a Child
by Centrifugal Force'. This birthing apparatus was a table to which the
pregnant woman would be strapped down and rotated at high speed until
the baby was flung out due to the centrifugal force. Thankfully the device
never made it into general use.

14. Broccoli is a human creation. It's the result of years and years of selective
breeding between wild cabbage plants. The earliest varieties are believed
to have been cultivated in the Mediterranean region during the Roman
Empire in the 6th century BCE.

15. The history of the creation of YouTube is interesting. When Jawed Karim,
one of the creators of YouTube got upset at missing Janet Jackson's
infamous wardrobe malfunction at 2004 Super Bowl, and couldn't find its
clip online, decided to combat this. He along with two of his friends Steve
Chen and Chad Hurley began working on a site where people could upload
their own content, which ended up being what we know today as YouTube.

16. The famous German chocolate cake has nothing to do with Germany. It
was in fact invented in Texas by an American named Sam German in
1852, when he created the formula for a mild dark baking chocolate bar
for Baker's Chocolate Company, which was subsequently named Baker's
German's Sweet.

17. No! The French have nothing to do with the French toast. As a matter of
fact the French toast was invented even before France came into existence.
The first known recorded recipe for French toast comes from Rome around
300 CE. Apicius, the Roman author included its recipe in his cookbook
titled "Cooking and Dining in Imperial Rome". Since it makes use of stale
bread it's called "lost bread", in many countries. The French themselves
had been calling it "Roman Bread". Actually it was the Americans who
started referring to this dish as "French Toast" because it was a hit with the
French immigrants, who popularised it all around.

18. American hosiery businessman LaMarcus Thompson despised the Americans' attraction for hedonistic places so he set out to straighten up, what he believed to be one of the most immoral places- Coney Island in New York. He opened America's first roller coaster called 'Gravity Switchback Railway' in 1884. Known as the Father of the American Roller Coaster", he definitely did succeed in giving not just the New Yorkers but to the world, some good, clean fun with plenty of adventure, and more importantly- away from seedier pastimes.

*(Gravity Switchback Railways: Photo: www.westland.net)*

19. Winner of the Kenneth Hudson Award for Europe's most innovative museum in 2011, the 'Museum of Broken Relationships', was founded by Croatian artists Olinka Vistica and Drazen Grubisic, who had broken up after their four-year relationship. In 2006 they got together to set up a museum of the leftover personal items. They collected similarly left behind articles from friends and acquaintances from their break-ups. The overwhelming response made them put the collection on a public display in Glyptotheque Zagreb the same year. The Museum is not just collecting 'stuff', but engages with people and encourages all kinds of discourses including the fragility of human relationships and the circumstances surrounding the stories shared by the visitors. Celebrity lawyer John B. Quinn, got so impressed with the idea that in 2016, he teamed up with the duo and set up a similar museum in an area of a thousand square metres in Hollywood.

20. Founded by Captain Dick Stevenson in 1973, 'Sourtoe Cocktail' has become a popular drink in Canada's Yukon province. You are served a drink of your choice garnished with a mummified human toe. An estimated 100,000 people from across the world have tasted it. There's an interesting story behind its establishment. Louie Liken, a miner and rum runner, who had his frostbitten appendage amputated, preserved it in a jar of alcohol in his cabin for memories. Half a century later, a local captain was cleaning the cabin when he found this jar. He brought it down to Sourdough Saloon and started plunking it into the drinks as a challenge. Began as fun, soon it became a strong club and the rest is history. The hotel gets 'toe' donations and as of now they have about 10 in rotation.

*(Sourtoe Cocktail. Image:Atlas Obscura/Jimmy Emerson/Flickr)*

21. Funded partially by the Swedish Innovation Authority Vinnova, 'Museum of Failure' was founded in 2017 by Dr. Samuel West. It showcases the innovative projects, products and services that failed. The idea is to encourage people and organisations to learn about the critical role of failure in innovation and how one can improve upon the directions of their efforts. The museum has around 159 items on display. Some major ones are : Apple, Google Glass, N.Gage, lobotomy instruments, Harley-Davidson Cologne, Kodak DC-40, Sony, Betamax, Lego Fiber Optics and many more.

22. Chimichanga means "thingamajig", in Spanish. It's considered to be Mexican food but Chimichangas actually originated from Tucson, Arizona. The name was coined in the 1950s by a cook who was trying not to curse in front of kids.

23. Sam Panopoulos, a Greek-born Canadian is credited with inventing the first Hawaiian pizza at the Satellite Restaurant in Ontario, Canada in 1962. Panopoulos took his inspiration from the Chinese cuisines, which are known for mixing sweet and savoury flavours. The use of pineapple, cheese, ham and bacon toppings on pizza may not have impressed the Canadians initially, but today Hawaiian Pizza has become a go-for-it dish globally, so much so that in 2014 the TIME magazine placed it on top in the list of "The 13 Most Influential Pizzas of All Time". Panopoulos called the pizza after the brand name of the Hawaiian canned pineapple he would use in those days.

24. The history of Caesar Salad goes back to 4th July 1924. Caesar Cardini, an Italian Mexican who lived in San Diego but had a restaurant Caesar's in Tijuana, had to cook dinner for some friends that evening. He had to make do with whatever was available in his kitchen at that time, he tossed everything together and created what we know as Caesar Salad. The dish has become so popular that there is even an annual festival in the Mexican city of Tijuana every June in honour of Caesar Salad.

25. There's an interesting history behind the rise of the first Vegetarian movement in America. Reverend Sylvester Graham, a Presbyterian minister, who was part of the 19th-century temperance movement, believed sexual desires were sinful and could cause physical ailments such as epilepsy and spinal disease. And only a simple vegetable diet could control stimulation of all kinds, including the prevention of masturbation. It was this concept of a meat and fat free fibrous diet, that a dull, sugarless, and unsifted flour biscuit, called Graham Crackers got created. Since this was also the period of cholera pandemic (1829- 1851), Graham's products - Graham flour, Graham crackers, and Graham bread immediately found an acceptance among the Americans and are still widely popular. His followers began to be called Grahamites, the harbingers of the first vegetarian movement.

26. Air Conditioning was originally invented in 1902 to dry printing ink, but it became popular after its installation in a movie theatre in New York two decades later.

27. Lieutenant Neville Francis Fitzgerald Chamberlain, a 19 year old British Army officer from the 11th Devonshire Regiment, which was stationed in Jubbulpore (Jabalpur, MP, India), in 1875, created the game of snooker. He did so by throwing in a few coloured balls to the existing Black Pool game, which was played with 1 black and 15 red balls and called it Snooker. 'Snooker' was a slang-word, used back in the Royal Military Academy at Woolwich for the rookie cadets. Chamberlain reasoned that anybody who plays this new version of the pool game will be a novice- a rookie - a snooker! He formulated rules that combined black pool and pyramids. It was John Roberts, the then British Billiards Champion who was visiting India in 1885, learnt snooker rules from Chamberlain and introduced it to the English, back home. Today this cue- sport is a very popular elitist game played across the globe.

28. Fortune cookies, often served as desserts in Chinese restaurants, are called so because these cookies come with a "fortune", an aphorism, or a vague prophecy, written on a piece of paper, inserted in them. Its origins had been hotly debated. While some believe it to be inspired by 14th century Chinese rebels, who sent messages hidden inside the traditional Chinese moon cakes against the Mongol invaders. Others believe it to have Japanese roots. The traditional tsujiura senbei (paper fortunes stuffed rice cakes) was made at the Hyotan Yama Inari shrine in the 19th century. The 1983, San Francisco's Court of Historical Review verdict in favour of Makoto Hagiwara, a Japanese confectioner who claimed to have created it in 1914 in San Francisco, put to rest any further debate.

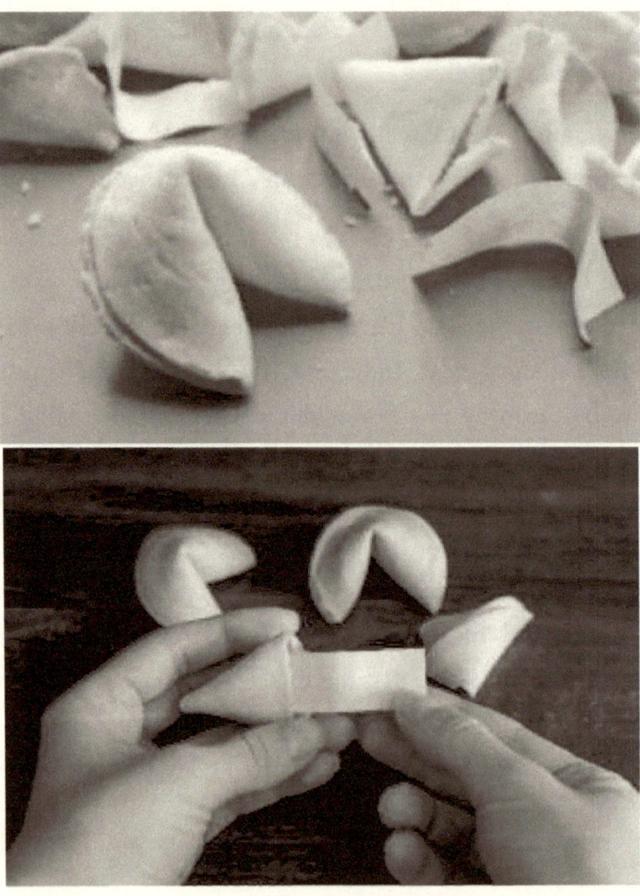

*(Fortune Cookies, with paper strips predicting future:Getty Images)*

29. Your dentist may frown upon your consuming sugary stuff but it was an American dentist who is credited with inventing the first cotton candy machine. Known in India as "Dadi Maa ke baal", candy floss or spun sugar has been around for centuries. William Morrison, a dentist from Tennessee and his confectioner friend John C. Wharton created the machine in 1897. It was at St. Louis World's Fair in 1904, which ran for seven months that the duo sold about 65,655 boxes of "Fairy Floss" at the cost of 25 Cents each. It was no looking back from then on.

30. Located at the Hard Rock Hotel on the island of Ibiza in Spain, "Sublimotion", is the world's most expensive restaurant. It's run by Paco Roncero, a two Michelin star chef, who uses molecular gastronomy in cooking. In 2014, Sublimotion won the award for the most innovative Food & Beverage. The restaurant charges $2,000 per person and entertains only 12 guests a night.

31. An Australian couple James and Kerry West coined the idea of fruit salad trees in the early 1990s. A fruit salad tree, also referred to as 'Fruit Cocktail Tree', bears up to eight different related fruits. In order to create a fruit salad tree, fruits within the same family are grafted. The four major types of fruit salad trees are the stone fruit, citrus, multi apple, and multi nashi. The fruit salad trees have now come out of the confines of Australia and have become global.

*(A Fruit Cocktail Tree. Photo by: https://pining.com)*

32. Nutella was a chance invention during WWII, when cocoa supplies had become scarce. Peitro Ferrero, an Italian pastry connoisseur ingeniously created Nutella by blending hazelnuts, sugar, and cocoa to form a chocolate paste.

33. The earliest methodology for fingerprint classification was developed by two Indian police officers, Sub-Inspectors Azizul Haque and Hem Chandra Bose, which led to the establishment of the world's first fingerprint bureau in Calcutta, Bengal (India), in 1897. Instead of accrediting them, it got named 'Henry's System of Fingerprint Classification', after the then Inspector General of Police Sir Edward Richard Henry. Thus fingerprinting replaced anthropometry in British India, and four years later when he got appointed Assistant Commissioner of Scotland Yard, established the first UK fingerprint bureau there and stayed until it got replaced in the early 1990s by more sophisticated modern technologies.

34. Pasta was not invented in Italy. Although Italy made the pasta dish popular with more than 200 different shapes of Italian Pasta. In all likelihood it was Marco Polo who, after his return from China, introduced it to the Italians.

35. Originally the tea was drunk in small bowls. It is believed that Robert Adam, an influential architect, suggested adding a handle to the bowl to avoid ladies burning their fingers. A much smaller saucer was used to rapidly cool a small amount of tea for easier drinking and would be sipped from the saucer itself. The saucer also prevented scorches and drips from ruining expensive tea tables. Today, we use a saucer to hold the cup securely and to rest the spoon.

36. The colour orange was named after the fruit. It was previously referred to as yellow-red. The Spanish word for orange is 'naranja' and in Old French, 'orenge' which came from Arabic 'nāranj', which in turn was adopted from the Sanskrit 'nāranga'. The English included it in their vocabulary sometime in 1300. The word's use as a colour name appeared two hundred years later, in the early 1500s. Probably by this time the fruit had become popular and its colour inspired its name too. This is how the 'yellow-red' colour became orange.

37. The phrase "As American as apple pie", may give an impression of it being a 'typical American' stuff, it isn't. Pie was invented in Medieval England and the modern apple pie with a lattice crust was created by the Dutch.

38. Dragon's Breath chilli pepper is a weapons-grade chilli, invented by Mike Smith, a hobby grower along with scientists from Nottingham University. It was initially developed for medical treatment as an anaesthetic that can numb the skin. However, it's so downright deadly that just consuming one of these could potentially cause a type of anaphylactic shock, burning your airways and closing them up.

39. Bubble wrap is an accidental invention. In 1957 Swiss inventor Marc Chavannes and Al Fielding, an engineer by profession, were trying to create a textured wallpaper, using two shower curtains together to trap air bubbles in between..and bingo.. the bubble wrap got created.

40. Chhattisgarh in India is one of the world's largest rice-producing areas. Farmers here began spraying Coke and Pepsi products instead of the usual pesticides which brought out great results. It was both economical and non-toxic. The sweet syrup attracts ants to the fields, who eat up the eggs and the larvae of insects that commonly destroy the crops.

41. The most expensive flower ever sold is a man made one. This flower, named Shenzhen Nongke Orchid, blooms only once every 4 to 5 years. It took around 8 years for this rare orchid to cultivate. In 2005, an anonymous bidder bought it at an auction for a whopping $200,000.

42. Momofuku Ando, a Japanese businessman, invented the first instant noodles (chicken ramen) in 1958. It took him a year's research which he did in the backyard of his house in Osaka. So successful was this venture, that it soon caught popularity. He established Nissin Food Products and founded the Ando Foundation and created the popular brands Top Ramen and Cup Noodles. A museum called the 'Cup Noodles Museum' in Osaka is dedicated to Ando. The focus of the museum is to highlight the importance of inventiveness through the discovery and history of instant noodles. It has a recreation of Ando's working shed where visitors can create their own cup noodles, the only place in the world that allows you such a liberty.

43. It was in 1968, Spencer Silver, a scientist, was trying to develop a super strong adhesive, but all he could manage to get was a weak adhesive that stuck but when pulled, would peel off from the surface. It was regarded as a failed experiment until another 3M scientist, Art Fry, came to him with the idea of creating a bookmark that would bond but won't damage the base. Thus were born the Post-it note. By 1980, Post-it Notes became available commercially and today they are a part of a must-have-stationery for students and office spaces alike.

44. Creation of Mountain Dew has an interesting story. Two brothers - Barney and Ally Hartman were looking for their favorite lemon-lime mixer, on learning that it wasn't available in their state Tennessee, they decided to create their own. When they tried their concoction with a dash of alcohol they felt it tasted like Moonshine. Moonshine (nickname Mountain Dew), was a traditionally made high-proof liquor, distributed illegally (bootlegged), and since it was nighttime that it would be made, it was called moonshine. The brothers decided to call their creation by the nickname - Mountain Dew, however their version was more like today's Sprite. The beverage we enjoy today is a makeover by the Tip Corporation of Marion, Virginia, to whom the Hartman brothers had sold "Mountain Dew".

45. Most early physicians in Europe had an aversion to surgery, they offered consultation and preferred academia. They considered themselves above these 'tasks', which were largely left to the barbers. These barbers, who did everything from giving haircuts to giving enema, extracting teeth, cupping and leeching to attending to wounds and amputating limbs, began to be called as barber-surgeons. In 1561, Ambroise Paré, a French barber-surgeon, who had served the kings- Henry II, Francis II, Charles IX and Henry III, published a book on surgery, making the knowledge accessible for the surgeon-barbers. Paré is regarded as one of the fathers of surgery and modern forensic pathology. He was a pioneer in surgical techniques and battlefield medicines. His contributions also include invention of several surgical instruments and reintroducing the midwifery technique of the podalic version.

46. Initially called the "health cage", the urban window baby cage was a bed in a wire cage suspended from city apartment windows. Invented by Mrs. Robert C Lafferty, it was to provide babies with fresh air and sunshine while living in crowded cities. These baby cages gained huge popularity in the 1930s, but first due to WWII and possibly due to safety concerns and the increase in urban vehicular pollution, gradually they completely vanished.

*(Health Cages:Images credit:  Mental Floss/Getty Images)*

47. In 1936, Alan Turing, a British logician and computer pioneer, invented what is now regarded as the first modern computer. He called this prototype an "a-machine (automatic machine). It was his Doctoral Advisor who coined the term 'Turing Machine'. His decoding of the encryption of German Enigma machines during WWII led to a critical turning point, saving 'millions of lives', by shortening the period of war. One of the most significant works was a paper he published in 1950, - "Can machines think?" Later known as the Turing test, it became a foundational part of AI. Two years later, he was convicted for having an 'illegal' relationship with a man and was asked to choose between jail term and hormonal treatment. He committed suicide. In 2013, Turing was posthumously pardoned. Post decriminalisation of LGBTQ, a new £50 note, with his picture went into circulation on 23rd June 2021. He was born on 23rd June 1912. Too little too late for the Father of Modern Computer Science!

48. Franz Reichelt was a French tailor, inventor, and parachuting pioneer. He
jumped to his death from the Eiffel Tower while testing a parachute suit
that he had designed.

49. John Montagu, the 4th Earl of Sandwich was a British statesman who lived
in the 1700s. His addiction to the card game was such that he would often
have his valet get him slices of bread stuffed with meat at his table so that
he didn't have to leave the game. This 'handy' and hassle free food came
to be called sandwich after his name.

50. A French aerialist Jules Leotard invented the famous ballet garment in
1859. It was to show off his physique, the ease and comfort with which he
impressed the judges. Today leotards are synonymous with gymnastics.
Léotard even inspired the 1867 song The Daring Young Man on the
Flying Trapeze, made popular by George Leybourne.

51. Though there is an ambiguity about the invention of the first teabag, in
1901 a patent was filed for a tea-leaf holder by Roberta C. Lawson and
Mary Molaren from Milwaukee. The teabag as we see is credited to
Thomas Sullivan an American coffee and tea merchant who had been
using cans to send samples of the products to his customers. When he felt
this procedure was a little expensive, he decided to use small hand-sewn
silk bags. Some of his customers dunked these bags into hot water, instead
of transferring the content in another container. Although Sullivan had no
idea how the customers would find this packaging, it turned out that many
of them loved it for its convenience, particularly by using these pouches as
tea bags. This happened in 1904, and tea bags were born. The Modern
tea bags are heat-sealed paper fibre invented by William Hermanson.

52. When King Umberto I and Queen Margherita were visiting Naples in 1889,
they decided to have a pizza instead of any fancy food. Though pizza, a poor
man's food back then, when served to the royal couple was anything but 'poor'.
Turns out, they enjoyed immensely the "pizza mozzarella,"- a pie topped with
soft white cheese, tomatoes, and basil. Soon the pizza became so popular that
it ended up being named after the Italian Queen.

53. Although Badminton's history can be traced to more than 2,000 years when it was called the game of Battledore ('bat') and shuttlecock, the modern version has its origins in the garrison town of Poona (Pune, Maharashtra, India). To amuse themselves, the British Army officers posted there used to play 'Poona', the improvised version of Battledore. They continued playing it even after their return to Britain, at the Duke of Beaufort's Gloucestershire residence called 'Badminton House'. Soon it caught on and in 1867, some rules were introduced. The sport now became 'Badminton' and a net got added to the game. The following year world's first Badminton organisation the 'New York Badminton Club' was founded. In 1877 the Bath Badminton Club developed the first written rules for the sport. By 1893, 14 affiliated clubs had formed a Badminton Association and laid down the foundation for modern Badminton by standardising the measurements of the court and the shuttlecock for both indoor & outdoor games, fixing the number of players, and listing a new set of written rules. The first International match was played between Ireland and England on 31st January 1903 in Dublin. A total of 7 games: 3 Singles (M), 2 Doubles (M) and 2 Mixed Doubles were played with 4 men and 2 women players.

*(19th century British officers playing Poona : Indian Express)*

54. Sri Lanka is the birthplace of Lipton brand of Tea. In 1890, Sir Thomas Lipton, a Scot, bought about 5,500 acres of the Dambatenne Tea Plantation in Ceylon's (Sri Lanka's) Badulla. And from here he packaged and shipped the first Lipton tea. He even introduced an innovative cable car system to make transporting leaves more efficient. His advertising slogan: "Direct from the tea gardens to the teapot", became an instant hit in the US and gradually in the world too. It's presently owned by Ekaterra.

55. In 1878, Constantine Fahlberg, a Russian chemist, when analysing the chemical compounds in coal tar at Johns Hopkins University happened to have his meal without washing his hands, when he accidentally tasted some of the chemicals he was working with and found it to be very sweet. This was anhydroorthosulphaminebenzoic acid. Working further on it, Fahlberg had discovered artificial sugar, which did not decay, mould, ferment, or be attacked by bacteria. Fahlberg gave this chemical "body" the trade name Saccharin. After he got it patented, Fahlberg started a company in Germany to manufacture saccharine, which no sooner launched than it became a roaring success.

56. The story of the Potato chips invention is quite interesting. Popular legend has it that sometime around 1853, George Crum, a chef in Saratoga Springs, New York, was so irked by a costumer's repeated demands of further slicing and longer frying of the potatoes, that Crum sliced the potatoes very thin, fried them till they were curly crisps and salted them. The crispy potato slices became an instant hit with the customer, who kept returning to relish this snack. Soon the word spread and this dish became popular by the name of Saratoga Chips.

# Record Makers

*If records refuse to be broken, shatter them. Bend the rules only if you have learned them; break the rules only if you have mastered them.*   - Mashona Dhliwayo

1.  Ashrita Furman, born in 1954, as Keith Furman in Brooklyn New York, is the Guinness world record holder of the most World Records. Furman has set more than 600 official Guinness Records and currently holds over 200 records as of now. He has been breaking records since 1979.

2.  In 1998, an original printing of Geoffrey Chaucer's book The Canterbury Tales, written between 1387 and 1400, was sold at an auction for a record $7.4 million. Written in Middle English, the book with 24 stories that run to over 17,000 lines, is regarded as Chaucer's magnum opus.

3.  Linda Wolfe (Essex) holds the Guinness Record of being the World's most married woman. She walked down the aisle twenty three times and has seven children.

4.  The world's largest pizza was prepared by Dovilio Nardi and his teammates Andrea Mannocchi, Marco Nardi, Matteo Nardi and Matteo Giannotte from NIPfood at Fiera Roma, Italy, on 13 December 2012. It had a total surface area of 1,261.65 square metres.

5.  The record of highest price ever paid for a single photograph was for a photo titled- "The Pond - Moonlight", taken by American photographer Edward Steichen in 1904. The photograph was sold for $2.9 million in an auction in New York on 14 February 2006. It is one of the earliest color photographs in existence and is very rare. Today only three copies of it are known to exist.

6.  The youngest person to climb mount Everest is Jordan Romero. The American teen was 13 years old when he reached the summit, accompanied by his father.

7.  The most densely populated island in the world is Santa Cruz del Islote near Colombia. It's the size of two soccer fields. Some five hundred people live on the island.

8.  The Guinness Book of Records holds the record for being the book most often stolen from Public Libraries.

9.  The most expensive piece of furniture is a 1726 badminton chest which is said to have belonged to the third Duke of Beaufort. Sold on December 9, 2004, it fetched an eye popping $36.7 million. The masterpiece, which features gilded statues, fleur-de-lis, coats of arms, and other designs with precious stones on its decorous drawers, took 6 years and 30 designers from Florence to create it. Presently the cabinet is at the Liechtenstein Museum.

*(Henry Scudamore's Badminton Chest:Photo:The Amazing World)*

10. In 1988 Luciano Pavarotti received 165 curtain calls and was applauded for 1 hour 7 minutes after singing the part of Nemorino in Gaetano Donizetti's L'elisir d'amore at the Deutsche Oper in Berlin.

11. Bobbie became the 'Wonder Dog' when he covered some 4,105 km all by himself to return home to Silverton, Oregon, after he was lost while his owners were visiting family in Wolcott, Indiana. A sort of record for a dog!

12. Hans and Fritz Schlumpf, well known textile mill owners in France, had built up one of the world's largest car collections in the late 1970s. They had 427 vehicles, including 120 rare Bugattis. This incredible collection is now on public display in Cite de l'Automobile museum and is perhaps the finest single assortment of 20th century motor cars in existence.

13. Robert Opie, founder and director of the Museum of Brands, London, owns the world's largest collection of British packaging and advertising material. He has spent his life meticulously documenting the evolution of various brands from Victorian times to the present day. Today he has in his collection more than 500,000 items, which he began in 1963 with the wrapper from a packet of sweets.

14. The person to perform the first recorded C-section successfully was Dr. James Barry. Barry, a military surgeon, had risen to the rank of Inspector General in charge of military hospitals, the second highest medical office in the British Army. Although born a female and named Margret Anne Bulkley, Barry (1789-1865), lived as a man in both public and private life. Barry's biological sex became known to the world, including the military colleagues, only after her post mortem examination.

15. Mary Ann Bevan, a good looking English woman developed acromegaly, a disorder marked by the overproduction of growth hormones in the pituitary glands, making her unsightly. A widow with four children to support in the past century was rather tough for a woman. Her circumstances forced her to perform as the 'Ugliest Woman In The World' in sideshows and circuses. In just two years of performing in New York she earned £20,000, which would be roughly equivalent to $1.6 million today.

16. Sir Thomas Phillips was so crazily passionate about books that he wanted to own a copy of every book ever printed. He managed to procure more than 50,000 books and 100,000 manuscripts. His eccentricity made his family plunge into heavy debts, but he deserves credit for rescuing many priceless treasures from dying. Consequently after his death in 1872, every year sales from his collection are organised for the pay off.

17. Translated in more than 683 languages as a whole and in sections in about 3000 languages, Bible is the most translated book ever.

18. Romania's parliament building in Bucharest, is believed to be the world's heaviest building. It is constructed from 700,000 tonnes of steel and bronze, 3,500 tonnes of crystal glass, one million cubic metres of marble and 900,000 cubic metres of wood.

19. Iceland may have one of the largest gun ownerships than any other country, but it has one of the lowest crime rates in the world.

20. In October 2018, a bottle of 1945 Romanée-Conti fetched an exorbitant $558,000 at Sotheby's sale in New York, earning more than 17 times its original estimate of $32,000. It smashed not just the world record for a 750ml bottle of Burgundy but also the highest for any bottle of wine ever at an auction. Soon after this at the same auction, a second bottle of the same wine got sold again at a record breaking amount of $496,000.

21. John Reznikoff, who holds the Guinness Book of World Records citation for the largest and most valuable collection of "world's pre-eminent historical hair", has hair from over a hundred celebrities ranging from Abraham Lincoln, George Washington, Einstein, Napoleon to Elvis Presley Michael Jackson, Marilyn Monroe, Beethoven, Eva Braun, John Wilkes and the likes. This might sound weird but these hair strands and locks which are like the autographs of those gone carry a hefty price. Who knows someone wanting to clone Einstein, can get the DNA from his hair!

22. The United Kingdom and Portugal hold the longest standing alliance in the world, which started in 1386.

23. A nearly black Densuke watermelon was sold for a record $6,125 in Japan in 2008. This watermelon is the speciality of the Japanese island of Hokkaido.

24. The Trans-Siberian Railway is the longest railroad in the world. One way journey takes seven days, during which time one passes through eight different time zones and crosses 3,901 bridges.

25. Miguel de Cervantes' Don Quixote, originally written in Spanish (El ingenioso hidalgo don Quixote de La Mancha) is one of the most translated books in the world. Labelled as the first modern novel and one of the greatest works ever written, it has sold more than 500 million copies so far, becoming one of the world's best- selling books of all time.

26. Nisiyama Onsen Keiunkan in Japan, is the world's oldest hotel. It was founded in CE 705 and is still functional.

27. Torre Mayor, Mexico City, is one of the sturdiest buildings on Earth. It has been designed to withstand earthquakes of as high magnitude as 8.5 on the Richter Scale. Occupants inside at the time of the 2003 earthquake did not know that a 7.6 tremor had occurred.

28. One of the most famous and the final public appearances that Marilyn Monroe made was at the gala event held to celebrate John F. Kennedy's birthday. The iconic dress that she wore to serenade "Happy Birthday" to the American President, was sold in 2016, for an exorbitant figure of $4.8 million. To this day, this remains the most expensive article of clothing ever sold.

29. Located in Russian Siberia, Yakutsk is the coldest city in the world. It experiences an average winter temperature of around -50° C. The lowest temperature ever recorded has been -64.4° C.

30. Denmark's amusement park, Dyrehavsbakken, is the oldest in the world. Located 6.2 miles north of Copenhagen, it opened in 1583 and is still functional.

31. The first ever ebook published is "The Declaration of Independence", released in 1971. Michael Stern Hart transcribed it and made it available for everyone for free, starting the famous Project Gutenberg.

32. The most expensive jewellery ever made specifically for a movie, is the necklace worn by Nicole Kidman in 'Moulin Rouge'. The $1 million Stefano Canturi platinum necklace, weighing 134 carats, was made with 1,308 diamonds.

33. Ziona Pâwl, the leader of Lalpa Kohhran Thar, a polygamy- practising Christian sect in Mizoram, India, is world record holder for being the head of the "world's largest existing family". Their 4 storey mansion with 100 rooms and their lifestyle are major tourist attractions. At the time of the record entry in 2011, he had 39 wives, 94 children, 14-daughters-in-law, 33 grandchildren and 1 great grandchild. Of his 39 wives, 22 are below 40. Ziona who died on 13 June 2021, had a roster according to which, his wives took turns to sleep with him. There were always 7-8 wives attending to his needs during the day.

*(Ziona's house/Ziona with all family members:Getty Images)*

34. The 1933 Double Eagle was a $20 U.S. coin made of gold that never went into circulation. A few of the coins were made, but most were destroyed-save for nine that were presumed stolen by U.S. mint workers. After years circulating the globe and falling into the hands of a few notable owners-including the king of Egypt-one of the coins was auctioned off at Sotheby's in 2002 for a stunning $7,590,020. That made it the most expensive coin ever sold at auction.

35. In Search of Lost Time (French : À la recherche du temps perdu), first translated into English as Remembrance of Things Past, is the longest book in the world with 9,609,000 characters.

36. British Sculptor Willard Wigan, who is a Guinness World record winner, once inhaled his own work. Wigan's works are micro-sculptures. A single sculpture can be as small as 0.005 mm and can be viewed only through a microscope. In creating his art, Wigan has to work between pulses, so as not to disturb his hands. Once he inhaled his work, which was Alice, from Alice in Wonderland, but he created it again, apparently even better than before.

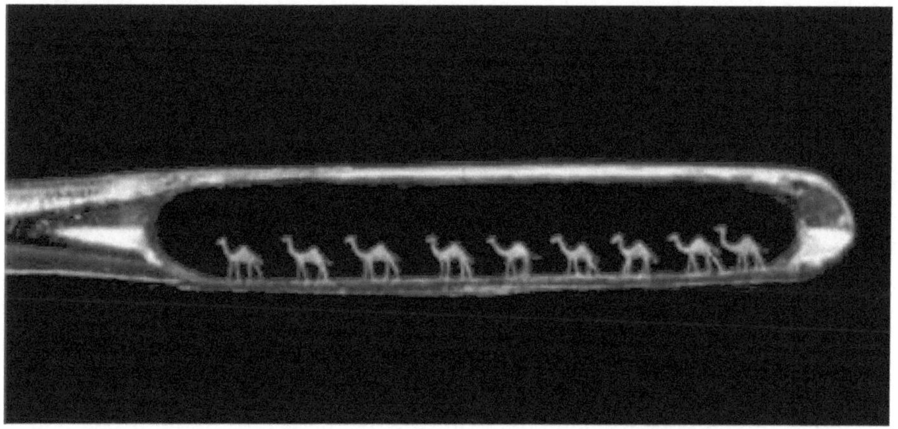

*(Photo credit: Bluethumb; 'Nine Camels' by Wigan)*

37. An Irish Pub in Namche Bazar, Nepal, located at a height of 3,450m above the sea level, en route Mt. Everest, is dubbed as the "highest and the remotest Irish pub in the world."

38. A painting attributed to Leonardo da Vinci, called "Salvator Mundi" was sold for $450.3 million at the Christie's auction in New York to Prince Badr bin Abdullah Al Saud in 2017, setting a new record for the most expensive painting ever sold at public auction. It's believed to have been commissioned in 1500.

39. The world record for the most number of non-stop push-ups, which is 10,507, was set by Japan's Minor Yoshida in October 1980.

40. The Lion King is the highest-grossing hand drawn film in history.

41. San Marino is the oldest republic on the planet and the third smallest country in Europe.

42. In 2018, to commemorate the 500th anniversary of Leonardo da Vinci's death, eighty-eight children in England set the world record for playing on one piano at the same time.

43. Istana Nurul Iman, ("The Palace of Light and Faith"), the official residence of Hassanal Bolkiah, the Sultan of Brunei's is the world's largest residential palace. It has 1788 rooms, 257 bathrooms, a 5000-capacity banquet hall, a mosque that can accommodate 1,500 people, a 110-car garage, 5 swimming pools and an air-conditioned stable with Sultan's 200 polo ponies.

44. The National Stadium in Beijing, appropriately monikered "Bird's Nest", due to its intricate lattice steel design made using 36km of unwrapped steel, is the largest steel structure in the world. Built between 2003 and 2008, it has a capacity to accommodate 80,000 people. The stadium has had a number of international sporting events, pop concerts, and pageants, apart from staging the grand Opening and Closing ceremonies of the 2008 Summer Olympics, 2022 Winter Olympics and 2022 Paralympics.

45. The 1976 release Manthan is India's first crowd funded movie, which was technically produced by 5,00,000 farmers, the largest number of individuals ever! Helmed by Shyam Benegal, Manthan was inspired by the real life experience of Dr. Kurien Verghese, 'Father of the White Revolution" in India.

46. Jankidas Mehra, who donned multiple hats, that of an actor, a production designer, writer, athlete, was also an ace cyclist. Between 1934 and 1942, this multi talented champion broke as many as eight World Records. He even hoisted India's national flag at the World Sports Congress, the first one to do so in the pre-Independence era. He founded the Cycling Federation of India.

47. Stretching across a staggering 192,000 acres of land, King Khalid Airport in Dammam, Saudi Arabia, is the world's largest airport. It houses five-passenger terminals, a Royal Terminal for VIP guests and the Saudia Royal Family, with eight aero- bridges each, a covered and uncovered parking lot for 11,600 vehicles, two parallel runways and a mosque that can accommodate 5,000 worshippers inside and an additional 5,000 in the plaza outside.

48. A Christmas card, considered to be 'the world's first Christmas card', was sold at an auction in Devizes, Wiltshire, U.K. on 24th November 2001, for $28,158, making it the most expensive Christmas card ever. It was sent by Sir Henry Cole, a Bath-born businessman, to his grandmother in 1843. There are only 12 of the original 1,000 cards still in existence. A black and white version sent to a certain Miss Marinda Cundy, London, by someone, who simply signed it J.C.J went for $5,100 in 2013.

49. Greek gymnast Dimitrios Loundras, who finished third at the 1896 Olympics, has the distinction of being the youngest ever Olympian, being 10 years and 218 days old at the time of the competition. Loundras later joined the Hellenic Navy and reached up to the rank of Rear Admiral. In 1936, he became a prefect of Lesbos Prefecture, but was recalled to active service in 1940, when Greece entered into a war with Italy. He headed the Aegean Naval Command and finally retired in 1945 as Vice Admiral.

50. The first commercial passenger flight took place in 1914 and it lasted only 23 minutes. The passenger Abram Pheil paid $400 for the plane ride. The two- Pheil and his pilot Tony Jannus, were the only people aboard the flight which flew in Florida between St. Petersburg and Tampa, where only 33.8 km of water separate the two cities.

51. PG Tips, a Tea brand based in the UK celebrated its 75th anniversary in 2005, with special packs, including a limited-edition Golden pack, and a one-off Diamond tea bag. This Diamond tea bag, which was designed by UK's jewellery brand Boodles using Makaibari Silver Tips (Imperial), took 3 months to create. This 280 high-quality diamonds encrusted tea bag fetched $15,000, in an auction, the most for a tea bag. Since there was only one tea bag, whether it was even used by its buyer or how it tasted would never be known.

52. Norman Gilbert Pritchard, a British-Indian athlete, born in Calcutta, is India's first and most decorated individual Olympian till date. Prichard set a series of national records in India- winning the Bengal province 100 yards sprint title for 7 consecutive years, the 440 yards run and the 120 yards hurdles. The gifted sprinter is also credited with the first hat- trick in an open football tournament in India in 1897. He went on to win two silver medals- in 200 metres and 200 m hurdles, at the 1900 Paris Olympics. After his return, he served as Secretary of the Indian Football Association from 1900 to 1902 and stayed here until 1905. He then moved to Britain where he lived only for a while before permanently shifting to the United States and taking acting as a career. He acted in 27 films produced by MGM studios under the screen name Norman Trevor. Although the International Olympic Committee lists Pritchard as an Indian athlete, it describes him as "controversial" because both India and Britain lay claim on his victories. Completely penniless and fighting his chronic brain disease in the last days of his life, the great athlete and actor died in California in 1929.

53. Nigel Richards, a New Zealander has distinguished himself by not just winning three different international championships of English Scrabbles but also the French-language Scrabble World Championship. Nigel doesn't speak French but he memorised the entire French Scrabble dictionary, which has 386,000 words, in nine weeks to earn this title. He has won the English World Scrabble Championship three times, the U.S. national championships five times, and the U.K. Open Scrabble tournament six times.

54. A group of eight British criminals, with an average age of 57, the oldest being 83, (probably the oldest ever age-group of criminals), were running a business of printing counterfeit currency. Caught in 2009, the gang was in possession of £5m in counterfeit currency: £4.4m worth of fake euros and £600,000 in bogus £20 notes. The Bank of England admitted that these were among the most realistic notes ever seized in the history of counterfeit haul.

55. The Book of Mormon, currently holds the tag of being the priciest antique book in the world. In September 2017, The Church of Jesus Christ of Latter-day Saints (LDS), paid $35 million to purchase it. The book is considered as the religious text of the Latter Day Saint movement. It consists of writings of ancient prophets who, according to their theology, lived on American soil between circa 600 BCE and CE 421. Considered as their central texts, it was first published in March 1830 by Joseph Smith as "The Book of Mormon: An Account Written by the Hand of Mormon upon Plates Taken from the Plates of Nephi". Although claimed as historically authentic by LDS apologists, the mainstream historians, archaeologists, and the scientific communities have found almost no evidence of their existence. Thus far some 150 million copies in 112 languages have been printed of the Mormon book.

# Food Facts

*Food for us comes from our relatives, whether they have wings or fins or roots. That is how we consider food. Food has a culture. It has a history. It has a story. It has relationships.*   - Winona LaDuke

1.  Tiny holes in the pizza bases not only stop formation of air bubbles but even prevent the dough from being soggy or limp.

2.  Eating broccoli, almonds, lima beans, cabbage, brussel sprouts and cassava, which contain a little bit of cyanide, equips your liver to deal better with other poisons.

3.  Baby mice wine', is a popular stimulant in China and Korea. And it's exactly what its name suggests - rice wine infused with dead baby mice.

4.  Pule or magareci sir is a Serbian cheese made from 60% Balkan donkey milk and 40% goat milk. Produced in Zasavica Nature Reserve, Pule is reportedly the world's most expensive cheese. It takes about 25 liters of milk to create 1 Kg of Pule cheese and this costs around $1300. There are only about 100 jennies in the landrace of Balkan donkeys that are milked, hence exorbitantly priced.

5.  Until fairly recently beer and other alcoholic beverages under 10% ABV were treated as soft drinks in Russia. Both local and international brands were available in the street kiosks, at railway stations, bus stands as well as the numerous 24-hour corner shops, just like fruit juice or mineral water is. People could guzzle it down in public places, before going to work, or swimming or driving. It was in 2013 that Beer got to be classified as an alcoholic drink in Russia.

6.  Ice Goby, are a special fish species that are consumed alive. A delicacy in Japan "Shirouo no odorigui", is usually served in a shot glass with soy sauce and you gulp it down like a shot, letting it wobble down right through the throat into your stomach.

7. So how do you know whether the egg is fresh or a rotten one? Simply put them in a pan full of water. A fresh egg will always sink to the bottom while the bad one will float.

8. Can a simple vegetarian snack delight or offend anyone to take such an extreme decision of banning it? Well Samosa, one of the most popular street foods of India is banned in Somalia because of its shape. Yes you heard it right! The 'Al-Shabaab' an Islamic outfit in Somalia, finds it offensive because it resembles the symbol of the holy trinity of Christians, hence against Islam. It was banned in the year 2011.

9. Processed cheese was invented in Switzerland by Waltz Gerber and Fritz Settler in 1911 to lengthen the shelf-life before shipping overseas.

10. If stored in a closed jar, honey does not have a shelf life and will never spoil, which is because it's very low in moisture content and very acidic, bacteria cannot survive in it. Honey is the only food that includes all the substances necessary to sustain life, including enzymes, minerals, water and vitamins.

11. Strawberries may be called berries but they aren't, instead they belong to the rose family. To quote Carnegie Museum, " A Strawberry is a multiple fruit which consists of many tiny individual fruits embedded in a fleshy receptacle".

12. Black sapote is a fruit native to Central and South America that tastes like chocolate pudding and sweet custard.

13. The world's most expensive tuna was sold in Japan for US$3.1 million, at Tokyo's fish market.

14. Hershey Bars contain 11% cacao, which is just 1% more than the minimum requirement to be called chocolate as per the FDA legal.

15. A recent study claims that chicken contains 266 percent more fat than it did 50 years ago. Now it has more fat than proteins.

16. 'Cheese' is the most stolen food in the world. If reports are to be believed, then about 4 percent of all cheese produced globally ends up stolen. There's even a black market for cheese.

17. Nutrition labels provide the information on the ingredients in a particular order. The more of the ingredient is present in the product, the higher up in the list it is placed.

18. Studies have shown that caffeine acts as a natural pesticide and produces a bitter smell to scare away insects. However, it is perfectly safe for people, but the same can't be claimed of our pets, it can be toxic to them.

19. India is the highest vegetable consuming nation and the lowest in meat consumption, which is about 3.18 kg of meat per person per year as against Australia, which is the highest meat consuming country with 121.6 Kg per person per year.

20. So as to achieve the perfect crunch level of their snacks, Frito-Lay spent $40,000 on a 'chewing' machine.

21. Popcorn was never a popular snack. It's become a staple at modern theatres because of the Great Depression and sugar rationing during World War II.

22. According to experts dark chocolate and cheese have antibacterial properties that prevent tooth decay.

23. Almond, often confused for a nut, is actually a drupe, a seed. It consists of an outer hull and a hard shell with the seed, which is not a true nut. Shelling almonds refers to removing the shell to reveal the seed.

24. Bananas, pumpkins and lemons are berries, which means they all developed from the ovary of a flower and have three layers - the skin, the flesh and the seeds. Any of the three parts can be edible or inedible.

25. The common red food dye, often used in candies, skittles, maraschino cherries, raspberry and strawberry-flavored junk food, and even lipstick, is carmine, also known as carminic acid. It is usually made from the crushed bodies of a parasitical insect called the cochineal.

26. A general misapprehension is that the British drink most tea. Actually it's the Turkish people and not the British, who do that. Turkey consumes around 3.18 kg of tea per person per year.

27. Coffee beans can help eliminate bad breath.

28. White chocolate does not contain any real chocolate. In fact this confectionery item is made of sugar, vanilla and milk products but no chocolate.

29. Carrots come in a rainbow of colors - orange, white, yellow, red, magenta, purple and black. Kern County in California produces almost 90 percent of the world's produce. Which makes California the "Carrot Capital of the World." ( The Western Hemisphere majorly grows orange carrots). That the Dutch invented the orange carrot to honour their royal family, a popular belief, is a myth. John Stolarczyk, curator of the World Carrot Museum, finds this highly unlikely to happen.

30. Although goat meat is not particularly popular in many cultures, it is the most consumed red meat in the world. Around 70% of all the red meat people consume is goat meat.

31. France produces over fifteen hundred types of Cheese.

32. One of the most exotic snacks that South Korea is famous for, is 'Beondegi', which is silkworm pupae, served both fried and boiled. Although sericulture has been practiced for 4,000 years in Korea, silkworm pupae began to be consumed only in the 1950s. It was after the Korean War, when the government there started promoting silkworm pupae as a protein source, that its consumption increased. Today it's one of the most popular delicacies in South Korea.

33. It is a common misconception that brown sugar is a healthier option. In fact brown sugar is no less refined than the white sugar. During the refining process some of the molasses that gets removed, is added back in it later, which gives it a brown hue. And even if certain beneficial minerals do remain in it, they are of such insignificant amounts that it hardly makes any difference.

34. There isn't any clear link between the intake of MSG and any of the harmful side effects attributed to it. MSG is basically sodium (regular salt) and glutamic acid (an amino acid, which is naturally present in a lot of products, such as walnuts, tomatoes, and asparagus).

35. A 2018 study into foods found Pizza to be a healthier breakfast option than most American cereals.

36. Bottled water has an expiry date, though it has nothing to do with the water itself, but rather with the bottle it's stored in. Plastic bottles eventually start releasing chemicals into the water, which makes it taste stale and off-putting.

37. Garlic may have an unpopular reputation of creating bad breath and overpowering taste, but it's one of the most nutrient-dense foods. A clove of garlic contains 0.2 grams of protein and 2% of vitamin B6. Allicin that gives garlic its pungency, is good for cholesterol and blood pressure.

38. Jam is made with fruit and jelly is with fruit juice. One is lumpy, the other smooth.

39. Cashews grow on trees in fruits called cashew apples. Cashew apples can be eaten and fermented into alcohol called feni, however the green shell of the cashew contains a toxin similar to that of poison ivy.

40. According to some studies, artificial sweeteners significantly increase the risk of dementia and Alzheimer's.

41. Japan has over 200 flavours of Kit Kats. Exclusively created for different regions of the world, cities, and seasons, the flavours can be as varied as banana, blueberry cheesecake, Oreo ice cream to baked potato, melon, cheese, wasabi, and vegetable juice.

42. Although people tend to think that Coriander and cilantro are the same things with a different name, that's not the case. Cilantro is the plant's leaves and stems, while coriander is the name of the dried seeds.

43. It's an open secret now, that in the 1960s, the sugar industry bribed U.S. scientists to make sugar seem much healthier than it really was.

44. Ranch dressing, just like sunscreen or regular white paint, contains titanium dioxide that makes it whiter. Although it has been deemed safe for consumption, titanium dioxide is linked to a few adverse side effects for health.

45. We actually lose a large percentage (20-30%) of sense of smell and taste while on a flight. It's because moving to higher altitudes results in chemical changes in our body. A decrease in our smell and taste sensitivity affect the taste whether for sweet or savory. This might explain why the in-flight meals do not appeal to our palates, as much they would otherwise.

46. The French wedding cake is unlike your usual four or five tiered cake covered with fondant, marzipan and ganache. The French have "pièce montée", or 'croquembouche' meaning "bite in the mouth", which is actually an assemblage of small French pastries called 'pâte à choux'. In the Middle Ages, it was a French custom for the guests to bring a small cake each, to the wedding, which would then be stacked on the table in a high pile. During Napoleon's time, one of France's first celebrity chefs, Antoine Carême, gave it a twist by creating a no-flour mound of orange carpels, cherries, walnuts and candied chestnuts glued together with caramel. Over the period, the custom of guests bringing in pastries phased out, only the shape of it stays on which has multiple small pastries stuck to each other in a pyramidal shape.

*(American & French Wedding Cakes: Image:Michomigato)*

47. While popcorn might be the go-to movie snack for most, for the Colombians it's dried ants which is the popular option. The Koreans prefer dried cuttlefish and the Chinese, strangely enough, go for a vegetarian preference of dried salted plums.

48. Potato skin is very rich in nutrients, including potassium, vitamin B3, iron, magnesium, phosphorus, calcium, copper, and zinc, therefore the Nutritionists always recommend eating potatoes with their skin on.

49. As per FDA standards, there's an allowance for the level of traces of bugs that could be in your food. For example, chocolate can have no more than 60 insect fragments per 100 grams and peanut butter can't have more than 30 per 100 grams.

50. Fruit-flavoured snacks such as gummy candies shine because they're coated with what is known as Carnauba, Brazil or Palm wax. It's the same stuff that is used on cars to make them shiny.

51. Cinnamon is derived from the dried bark of an evergreen tree. The name itself comes from a Greek word, which means "sweet wood" Although cinnamon is not particularly sweet by itself, it enhances the sweetness of all the other ingredients..

52. Pineapple is neither from the pine family nor is it related to apples in any way. When the early explorers saw pineapples for the first time, they thought they looked like the pine cones which is how the fruit got its name!

53. Seafoods like lobster and oyster are regarded as expensive delicacies today, but once these were considered barely worthy of human consumption. In fact, these undesirable creatures were available in such abundance that they were either used as fertilizer and fish bait by Native Americans and colonists or were fed to apprentices, slaves and the prisoners because it was cheap. With the introduction of railways and canning industries in the 1880s, these "cockroaches of the sea" caught the fancy of the colonists and their demand suddenly arose. Because of the rising demand restaurants began to serve them, recipe books began to be written and soon the seafood became fashionable.

54. Ripe cranberries are also referred to as bounce berries because they can bounce like rubber balls. This springiness is a sign of it being fresh, firm and good and it is a common ripeness test for farmers and consumers alike.

55. Limes sink while lemons float.

56. McDonald's once made bubblegum- flavoured broccoli but it didn't go well with the child testers.

57. The original oranges from Southeast Asia were a tangerine-pomelo hybrid, and they were actually green.

58. One of the most expensive delicacies of Chinese cuisine is Bird's Nest soup, which are particularly prized for their aphrodisiacs. The nest, which is built out of the bird's saliva, solidifies into a small deep dish-like structure which eventually holds two eggs. A nest requires each pair of Swiftlets to spit about 10gm of saliva to build it. When exposed to sunlight, the nest gets a golden hue, because of which it is often referred to as 'white gold'. Edible bird's nests are among the most expensive animal products consumed by humans, with nests being sold at prices up to about $3,000 per pound depending on grading.

*(Dried out nests of Swiftlets(Top); A Soup Dish of Swiftlet nest(Bottom):Delishably/South China Morning Post)*

59. Cherries, apricots, plums, pears, apples, quinces, peaches, raspberries, strawberries, and blackberries are members of the rose family, hence share a lot of similar characteristics. Just as a rose has, these fruits too, typically have flowers with five equal petals arranged around a central core and not to forget thorns, which they have in plenty. While the wild rose has five petals the cultivated ones have multiple sets of petals.

60. Fatty fish is excellent for the brain for the simple reason that it contains Omega 3. Around 60% of the human brain is fat, and about half of that is Omega 3 fatty acids, which the fish has in abundance.

61. Quinine, one of the components of tonic water, makes it glow in the dark.

62. There are approximately 70 ingredients in a McRib sandwich.

63. Even though Froot Loops come in a variety of colours, they have the same flavor.

64. Watermelon, Cucumber, Lettuce and Celery are more than 90% water and super low in calories.

65. The beef burgers available in the fast food joints or grocery stores in American and European markets, use ground beef made of a collection of muscle tissues and one burger patty may contain hundreds of different cows.

66. Wild salmon are pink because they consume a lot of shrimp, algae and krill, on the other hand the farm-raised salmon are either grey or white because of the difference in their diet. But keeping in mind the perception of people that a healthy salmon is pink, the salmon farmers add carotenoids (plant pigments) to the fish feed to get the natural hue.

67. Caffeine is more addictive than marijuana.

68. Bright blue lobsters are a rarity. The probability of their being is believed to be one in two million. The bright blue lobsters are no superior species as many believe, it's actually their genetic abnormality that causes them to produce more of a certain type of protein than the others.

69. Back in the 1800s tomato ketchup was sold as a medicine known by the name of "tomato pills" and was prescribed to people suffering with indigestion.

70. Corn, often believed to be a vegetable, like wheat, oats and rice, belongs to the grass family. These species grow much longer than grass and flower and produce grains.

71. Although lemons are tangy in taste their sugar content is higher than strawberries.

72. Artificial vanilla scent and flavoring are extracted from castoreum, the dried and macerated castor sac scent glands of adult beavers. It has been in use for both food flavorings and perfumes for decades now!

73. Oysters deteriorate really fast and have to be served expeditiously. Once they die, they are not safe for eating, which is why they are stored under regulated conditions. Chances are a nice fresh dish of oysters that you are chewing on, are still alive.

74. Pufferfish, called Fugu, is a highly prized delicacy in Japanese cuisine. However it can turn out to be fatal due to the presence of 'tetrodotoxin', a toxin that is up to 1,200 times deadlier than cyanide to humans. It's said that a pufferfish has enough poison to kill 30 people and it has no antidote. Cooking it therefore, is an art and it takes about 2 years for a Japanese chef to learn and obtain a licence to cook it properly.

*(Pufferfish/Fugu (Left) An exotic fugu dish (Right). Image Credit: Wikipedia/ Savor Japan.)*

75. A Sardinian cheese called Casu marzu is eaten with live maggots. It's created by allowing the cheese fly to lay eggs on pecorino (sheep milk) cheese. The fly lays about 500 eggs at one time. Once hatched the larvae begin to eat through the cheese. The acid from their digestive system helps cheese become soft. By the time the cheese is ready, it has thousands of these maggots. The practice of consuming it while the maggots are still alive, is based on the belief that it is aphrodisiac. Though the EU's Food Hygiene- Health regulations, have outlawed the cheese for being unsafe for consumption, it's abundantly available in the black market. While eating Casu martzu, you are supposed to keep your face shielded with one hand because, on being disturbed, the larvae can jump up to 15 centimetres. Imagine hundreds of them jumping into your face.

76. In 1987, American Airlines saved around $40,000 by just removing a single olive from each salad serving for the passengers.

77. McDonalds make an estimated $59,178,080.00 per day which is 21.6 billion a year.

78. Japan had a prohibition on eating meat of four legged animals for more than a thousand years until 1868.

79. The earliest mentions of salad eating appear around the 1st century CE with the ancient Greeks and Romans. They arranged a variety of raw vegetables and dressed with drizzling vinegar, oil and herbs, pretty much like a modern salad.

80. Before the cultivation of sugar beets and sugar cane, parsnips were used as sweeteners in Eurasia. It was introduced by the French and British colonists to the North American continent.

81. In South Africa, beware when asking for 'popcorn', you might be given roasted termites and ants.

82. This might sound crazy- about 40% of the vegetables and fruit produced in the US doesn't get sold just because it's ugly to look at. Since consumers won't buy these, supermarkets refuse to stock them.

83. According to historians, potato frying started in the late 1600s in Europe. What we know as 'French fries', have their origin in poor villagers living in Meuse Valley, Belgium. The folklore has it that the villagers who depended on small stream fishes had to fall back on the potatoes during the harsh winter months when the rivers would freeze. They would deep fry the potatoes in the same fashion as they did the fish. It was during World War I, the American soldiers who were stationed in Belgium began referring to the fries as 'French fries', because it came to them from southern Belgium, which has French as a dominant language. Gradually the world caught up with this vocabulary and the potato fries became French fries.

# What The Heck...!!!

*The Silence of the good people is more Dangerous than the Brutality of the bad people.  - Martin Luther King, Jr.*

1. In 1903, to prove that his usage of Direct Current was safer than Nikola Tesla's Alternating Current, Thomas Edison conducted an experiment in public. He used Topsy, an Asian circus elephant, offered by Luna Park in Coney Island, for this demonstration. He electrocuted her to death, and filmed it before thousands of visitors. Topsy wasn't the only victim of Edison's trials, he had recorded other animals' electrocutions as well.

2. According to former Cuban counterintelligence chief Fabián Escalate, as many as 634 attempts were made to assassinate Fidel Castro. In fact a BBC report even claims that some of the most outlandish plots to topple the Cuban leader Fidel Castro, including exploding cigars and rigged sea shell bombs' was a plan to attack his beard to make him less virile. One failed plot even involved sprinkling thallium salt on Castro's shoes during an overseas trip so his hair would fall out.

3. Albert Einstein's eyeballs are in New York City preserved in a safety deposit box. They were given to Einstein's eye doctor Henry Abrams by Thomas Harvey, the man who performed the autopsy on Einstein and had illegally taken the scientist's brain for himself.

4. A passenger who lived through the traumatic fire and sinking of a ship in 1871 faced his fears and boarded the Titanic in 1912, only to sink with the ship.

5. As many as 2.5 million people die due to consumption of alcohol every year.

6. A 15- foot beer wave that spouted out of an exploded vat of beer in London in the year 1814, killed 8 people. The incident is usually referred to as the London Beer Flood.

7. Belgian King Leopold Il, was more evil than Hitler, Stalin or Mussolini. He oversaw the deaths of 15 million innocent Congolese during his rule of Congo. After the Congo Basin became a free-trade zone, Leopold established Congo Free State in 1885. About 76 times bigger than Belgium itself, Congo was the largest plantation in the world then. The decrees he issued in 1891 and 92, stripped the native populations of their control of resources and forced them to deliver all ivory and rubber, harvested or found, to his officials, giving him the monopoly on rubber and ivory trade. Unlike the Brazil rubber, Congo rubber came from wild vines in the deep jungles. A worker needed to slash them and lather his own body with the rubber latex. After it had hardened, it would be scraped off the skin, wounding the worker's in the process. Force Publique, the Free State's military, was responsible for enforcing the rubber quotas, failing which unbelievable atrocities including death or amputation of limbs were inflicted on those who didn't toe the line.

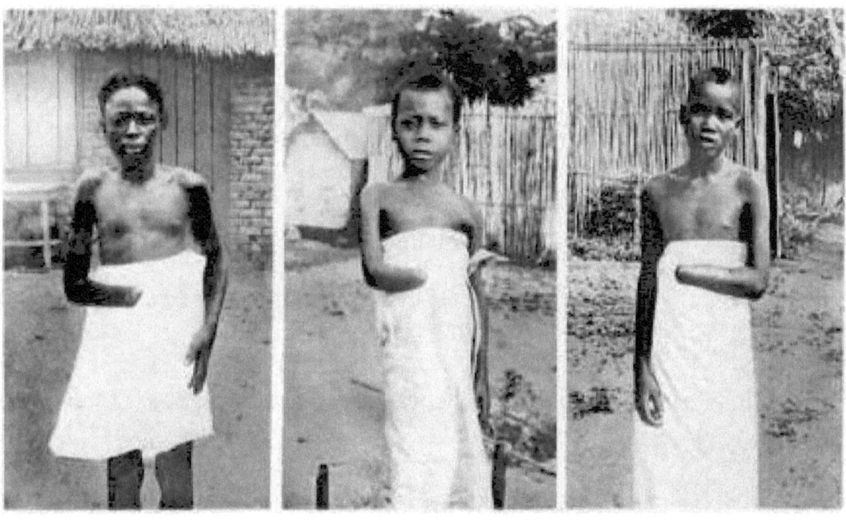

*(Congo Rubber workers, even children, who refused to work in the jungles, had their hands chopped off: Wikimedia Commons)*

8. Fiji water is the nation's largest export, yet 67.53 percent of the people who live there don't have access to clean and safe water.

9. Prostitution is legal in Canada but buying a prostitute's services, illegal.

10. In 2014, a man from Arizona stole a diamond that was worth $160,000 and traded it for $20 worth of weed.

11. According to researchers, the established Dollar- Wall Street Regime, based on the US dollar as the international currency and the centrality of international private financial markets, gives liberty to the US to control international financial affairs.

12. A gay bar in Melbourne had fought a legal battle to ban women from entering their bars. Their argument was- women made men uncomfortable. They won the case!

13. The United States de facto authorizes the practice of extraordinary rendition, meaning that a prisoner is at the mercy of the US government, because he/she could be transferred to any country for the purposes of interrogation.

14. 50,000 fake PhDs are estimated to be purchased every year in the United States, while only 40,000 PhDs are earned legitimately.

15. Until the 1980s, it was illegal for a woman to drive a car down Main Street in Waynesboro, Virginia, unless her husband was walking in front of the car waving a red flag.

16. In 2000 Walmart was sued 4,851 times, or about once every 2 hours.

17. An average American consumes the same amount of resources as 32 Kenyans in a year.

18. According to its national data, America has the highest number of serial killers in the world.

19. As much as ten percent of food consumed in Chinese restaurants is prepared from sewage. The oil is thus referred because of its extraction from sewers. Companies involved collect, filter and refine this sewage oil to such an extent that it's almost impossible to tell the difference between the regular cooking oil and this processed one. The sewage oil may be cost effective but it has a disastrous impact on the consumer's health.

20. The Canadian government had plans to build a museum for the soldiers who laid down their lives in WWI. Around 800 body parts were sent to be part of the proposed museum which never got built, instead the organs became teaching aids at McGill University before being destroyed some time in 1960.

21. Anthropodermic bibliopegy is the practice of binding books with human skin! In recent times certain collectors reportedly claimed to have books that were bound in this fashion. Such assertions are tested by Anthropodermic Book Project, a US based organization. As on date, of the 50 claims, 31 have been examined by the team and found 13 with animal skin and 18 had real human skin. One such book was an 1852 edition of Poetical Works by John Milton. It was bound using the skin of George Cudmore, who was executed in front of a thronging crowd in Exeter, Devon in March 1830 for murdering his wife. It was when his body was sent to the Hospital for dissection, that W Clifford, an Exeter bookseller was able to lay his hands on a portion of the dead man's skin, which he used in binding Milton's book. Why would one use human skin? Historical reasons vary-some 19th century doctors made them as personal keepsakes for their book collections, while some others used human skin on the State's demand either to create fear psychosis or further punish executed prisoners. Whatever, thankfully this sickness is a crime today.

22. In order to prevent women from riding bikes, the 19th century 'experts' invented a fake disease, which they called 'bicycle face', the condition was "characterised by a hard, clenched jaw and bulging eyes."

23. In 2001, Taliban, the extremist regime under Mullah Omar, demolished two 6th century gigantic statues of the Buddhas of Bamiyan, carved into the side of a cliff in Hazarajat, Afghanistan. Since idol worship is against the principles of Islam, they were blown up. International condemnation did little to restore the loss. After the blast, the destroyed site revealed caves where researchers found ancient Buddhist artefacts including the oldest known oil paintings in the world.

24. Until 1977 France used guillotine for execution.

25. In 1979, 16 year old Brenda Ann Spencer was arrested after killing two people and wounding eight children in California. When asked why she did it, her reply was "I just don't like Mondays". When Bob Geldof read the story he wrote the Boomtown Rats song "I don't Like Mondays".

26. As much as 3% of ice in Antarctica glaciers is Penguin urine.

27. In 1924, a dog named Pep, was sentenced to life in prison for killing Pennsylvania governor Gifford Pinchot's cat.

28. Lepa Radic, a 17 year old Serbian girl was hanged by Nazis in 1943 near Gardiska, for not disclosing the names of her 'accomplices'. The unrelenting young woman simply said: "You'll Know Them When They Come To Avenge Me". She had already lost her younger brother, her father and her uncle to the Kozara battle.

29. There are around 15,000 Indian restaurants in the U.K., and London alone has more restaurants serving Indian food than Mumbai or Delhi. Interestingly most of these supposedly 'Indian' owners are actually of Bangladesh and Pakistan descent. 'Indian Food' sells well.. hence India's name...Remember- All's fair in Love and War..and Business...!!!

30. During Prohibition in the United States, the federal government poisoned the industrial alcohol. By the end of Prohibition in 1933, it is estimated that around 10,000 people were killed as a result of the federal poisoning program.

31. Of the babies born annually in the United States, about forty percent are born to unmarried women.

32. Netflix's policy of 'secrecy' is so stringent that its employees are sworn to keep tight-lipped about their DVD warehouse location/s, so much so, it does not figure on the Maps and even their delivery vehicles move unmarked and sometimes undercover to obscure locations to their stockpiles.

33. Some thirty five divorce cases were filed in 2012 in British court, the video game 'Football Manager' was cited as the reason.

34. It's legal to marry a dead person in France. All one requires to do is to prove the deceased had intentions of marrying before their passing.

35. The United States is one of the biggest e-waste contributors of the world. About 220 million tons of old computers and other technological hardware get discarded there every year.

36. Germany was in crisis in the years following the end of the First World War, and it's economy began to buckle resulting in hyperinflation. In early 1922, $1 (US) equaled 160 German Marks, by November 1923, the currency depreciated to 4,200,000,000,000 Marks to one US dollar. The price of a loaf of bread rose from 160 Marks at the end of 1922 to 200,000,000,000 Marks at the end of 1923.

37. Do your eyes turn red after a swim in the pool? Well it's due to urine mixing with the pool's chemicals. Your eyes become the tellers!

38. It is illegal to carry live snails on a train in France unless they have a ticket. This is in keeping with the law that states animals weighing less than 5 kg must travel with their own ticket. In 2008 a man was fined for being in possession of live snails on the train.

39. In the UK, it is forbidden by law to wear a fake moustache to church, for that causes laughter!

40. In 2006 someone tried to sell New Zealand on eBay. The price got up to $3,000 before eBay shut it down.

41. Joanne had to take a male pen-name when she went for the publication of the Harry Potter series. Since this was deemed to be a "book for boys" the publishers feared that a female author wouldn't gel well with the boys. Hence Joanne Rowling became J K Rowling and the rest as they say is history.

42. Thomas Jefferson, the third president of the United States who had strong thoughts on anti-slavery, propagated "all men are created equal" and famously wrote that slavery was a "moral depravity", a "hideous blot", himself had more than 600 African American slaves over the course of his life. In spite of having the authority, he did not free these slaves under his own service. While 44 himself, Jefferson, had physical relations with his 14 year old slave Sally Hemings, who he had employed to take care and be a companion to his own daughter, of the same age as Sally was. Jefferson had six children with her, except for two, who Sally traded her own freedom with, others remained slaves all their living years.

43. J. Marion Sims, a 19th century American physician, hailed as the "father of modern gynaecology", made a considerable contribution with his revolutionary tools and techniques. Although revered as a medical hero in his own time, Sims has come to be known as the most controversial figure in medical history. He is criticised by the modern medical fraternity for his medical ethics, manipulating the institution of slavery and performing morally and humanely unacceptable experiments on powerless, unconsenting Black women. For instance in 1886, he experimented 30 times on a young African woman called Anarcha, without inducing anaesthesia at any of the times. A defender of his, eulogised it by calling it Sims' "perseverance". The general belief among the Europeans during those days was that Black women do not feel as much pain as the white ones did. In other words it was perfectly fine to use them as guinea pigs. He is even accused of causing deaths to the babies on whom he operated for the neonatal tetanus (trismus nascentium condition). It is said that Sims spent a few years honing his skills on black women before he started treating white women, but there he administered anaesthesia to them. Harriet A. Washington's book "Medical Apartheid", which was published in 2006 threw light on the racist practice adopted by Sims. In April 2018, during the nationwide protests over Confederate Statues, Sims' statue, which had been erected in 1894, the first ever, honouring a physician, standing across the New York Academy of Medicine, in Bryant Park was removed.

44. The most littered man-made waste item in the world is cigarette butts. Some 4.5 trillion cigarette butts are added to the global waste annually !

45. "Fox tossing" was a popular 'sport' in 16th century Europe. As the name suggests it was a fox that needed to be caught & tossed. Two people held a 23-foot-long cloth on both sides and waited for the fox to come towards them, then pulled it tight enough to send the fox plummeting in the air. The game continued until the animal hit the ground from a height and crashed its bones and then it was killed by a hunter.

46. Hitler was confident of winning the First World War and had plans to build a museum called "Museum of the Extinct Race", which he intended to dedicate to the Jewish race. The museum would have had all kinds of valuable objects that belonged to the Jews once.

47. Men accounted for more than 80% of all suicides in the US in 2021. The National Center for Health Statistics' report shows that more than 47,000 people committed suicide in a year, of which a shocking 38,025 were men.

48. Mongol invader Genghis Khan's DNA has been linked to over 16 million people living today. In 2003, a groundbreaking genetics paper reported that around 1 in every 200 men are his direct descendants. During his lifetime between 1162 and 1227, the barbaric Mongol reportedly pillaged, looted, burned houses and fields, raped thousands of women, slaughtered hundreds and thousands of men, women, children and animals.

49. Louis Armstrong "Satchmo", was made Goodwill Ambassador in the late 1950s and was sent on a concert tour around Europe and Asia. Since he never faced any trouble due to his ambassadorial status, Satchmo didn't expect to be asked to go through the customs at Idlewild Airport in New York when he landed there in 1958. He was in possession of three pounds of marijuana. He was just trying to figure out how he could evade a security check, when Vice President Richard Nixon showed up there. Nixon recognized him and on learning why he was waiting, offered to carry his suitcases himself. Satchmo for obvious reasons willingly accepted. Ironically, the father of the War on Drugs, Nixon inadvertently facilitated the smuggling of Satchmo's marijuana into the US.

50. Germany still has thousands of unexploded bombs leftover from WWII, buried across the country. About 2,000 tons of unexploded bombs are uncovered each year. A builder must have specialists certify the ground clear of any munitions, before the construction companies begin digging for a new project. In 2013, over 20,000 people were displaced when a 4,000-pound Blockbuster bomb was discovered in the western German city of Dortmund.

51. It is illegal for a woman in Liverpool to be seen topless in a public place, unless she is a clerk in a tropical fish store.

52. If you are a guy living in the U.K., relieving yourself in a public place is legal, but hold on, there's a condition to that- the guy must aim for the rear wheel of his own car and keep his right hand on the vehicle! (Seriously???)

53. During WWII, Hershey made a chocolate bar for U.S. soldiers that was meant to taste so bad, soldiers would only eat it if they were starved.

54. When tulips were introduced in Holland in the 1600s, they became a craze with people, so much so that their bulbs became as expensive as gold. This madness for the flowers is referred to as Tulip Mania or Tulipomania, the first known speculative bubble in history, resulting in the crash of the Dutch economy. In February 1637, when tulip traders realized that there were no buyers willing to pay the inflated prices- led to the bursting of the speculative bubble.

55. According to historians, there was no explorer by the name of Christopher Columbus. The actual person was the Spanish explorer Cristóbal Colón, whose name was repurposed to an anglicised version 'Christopher Columbus'. And even though the text books tell you he discovered America, he did not. Columbus made four separate trips, from 1492 on, but they all ended up on various Caribbean islands (Bahamas & Hispaniola). Though he explored the Central and Southern coasts, he never made it to North America. The first European explorer to have landed on the American coasts was Leif Erikson, a Norseman in the 10th century, which was 500 years before Columbus's imaginary discovery of the Americas. Columbus is said to have indulged in despicable atrocities against the native islanders, eliminated their population and forced conversion on the others. Columbus was No Hero!

56. In 2019, a study published in Geophysical Research Letters, it was alleged that the 1943 Bengal Famine which resulted in the death of more than 30 lakh Bengalis, was not a natural disaster but a man-made one- a policy failure on the part of the British government under PM Winston Churchill. Britain literally snatched food grains from the mouths of millions of starving Indians to flush it to British soldiers and for stockpiling for itself and Europe. In fact Churchill even went on to make a most deplorable and racist comment at his war-cabinet meeting : "I hate Indians," he reportedly had said. "They are beastly people with a beastly religion." The famine was their own fault for "breeding like rabbits." Churchill is widely loved and respected by most educated Indians, the uneducated ones have no clue about him.

*(These heart wrenching images of the starving Indians during unnaturally created Famine in Bengal by Winston Churchill government, which led to the death of more than 3 million Indians. Photo Courtesy: The Statesman/Good Morning Science/ Resurgent India/ Harper Collins India)*

57. The weird fashions in the early nineteenth century of American women included covering their hats and gowns with bird feathers - and sometimes entire bird corpses. In 1886, an American ornithologist reported sighting pieces of 40 native birds on the hats of fashionable ladies in New York City.

58. "Chainsaws', the horror-movie murder weapon of choice, was inspired from an actual 'surgical instrument', invented back in the 18th century to assist in a childbirth procedure called symphysiotomy.

59. A high profile con man in India by the name of Natwarlal repeatedly "sold" the Taj Mahal, the Red Fort, the Rashtrapati Bhavan, the Parliament House and various other famous sites to the foreigners. Although sentenced to 113 years, he managed to escape prison 9 times, last when he was 84 years old. Though uncertain, he is believed to have died in 1996, as claimed by his brother.

60. A 2016 study conducted in the UK's leading Fast Food Chains, such as Starbucks, revealed their ice to have faecal bacteria. Poor maintenance of their ice machines was one of the major reasons that the ice cubes used in these restaurants were dirtier than their toilet water.

61. With the age of exploration came to Europe the practice of putting up 'Human Zoos'. The sailors began bringing along human trophies, from the newly explored regions of the world. These 'exotic' humans, plants, animals and foreign objects were then put on display at the Royal courts and for the European crowds, who would pay for the ticket to see them. For instance from his first trip Columbus brought seven 'Arawak Indians' of the West Indies and Amerigo Vespucci got along more than 200 natives from America, who were subsequently exhibited at the public fairs in Spain. In fact between 1875 and 1930 'Völkerschauen' in Germany put up some 400 shows of 'exotic' people brought in from the continents of Africa, Asia and North and South America. However, with the invention of talkies and other means of entertainment in the later part of the 20th century, these human zoos lost their charm and finally completely shut down.

62. Nicknamed by the Russian media as "The Lord of the Mummies" and "The Perfumer", Anatoly Moskvin was a professor, a historian, a military intelligence translator who spoke 13 languages, a journalist and a "necropolyst" with expert knowledge on cemeteries. He was arrested in 2011 on the charges of grave-desecration. It was when the police raided his apartment that they were shocked to find some 26 life-sized mummified girls, ranging in age from 3 to 25, stacked away in the room. These 'human dolls' were stuffed with rags and wrapped around with nylon tights. Some of them even had music boxes inside, which produced sounds when Moskvin touched them. He even celebrated their birthdays as if they were his own children. Moskvin  confessed to visiting 752 cemeteries between 2005 and 2007. He was arrested and charged with about a dozen crimes. Moskvin is still in custody and undergoing psychiatric treatment.

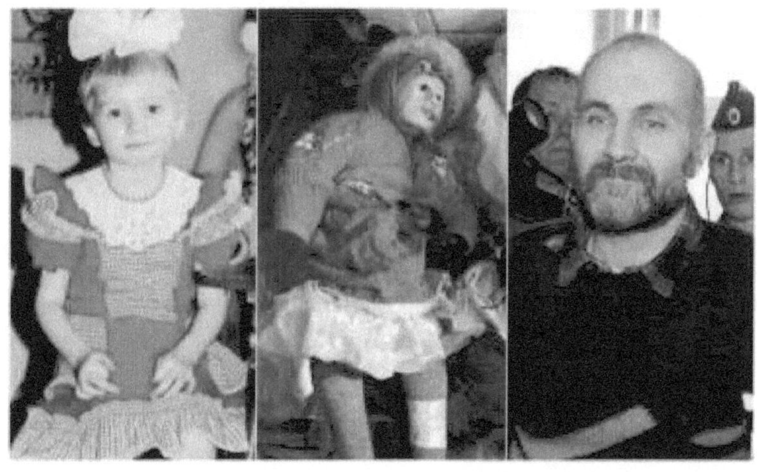

*(Though at the time of arrest 26 bodies were found in his home, Moskvin, had dug up an 150 graves before he was finally caught in 2011: Pravda)*

63. Thomas Edison, may have a staggering 1,093 patents to his name, but majority of them were not his original inventions. It is said that he stole them. For instance, the patent of the light bulb that he got in 1880, was actually invented some forty years before by a British astronomer and chemist called Warren de la Rue.

64. After the Great Fire of London' in the late 1600s, construction codes changed, requiring narrower chimneys. The new design posed serious cleaning issues. Instead of inventing new tools or equipment to deal with it, the Brits found the easy way out- use children! These children, who could be anything between 3 years to 10 years, were employed by the Master Sweep, to scramble up through chimneys, clean the inside of the flue with small hand-held brushes and if required, scrape off the harder tar deposits left by wood or log fire smoke from the chimney lining. Since these 'apprentices' were picked up from orphanages, streets, or poor families, no regulations were followed. Deplorable living conditions, hazardous work, physical injuries, and constant exposure to toxic soot, posed tremendous health risk. This, using small kids for chimney sweeping jobs could finally be banned only in the twentieth century.

65. A study published in June 2015 in a German book: "Bankerte, Besatzungskinder in Deutschland nach 1945, ("Bastards, the children of Occupation in Germany after 1945"), reveals that after the end of the World War II, the Allied Forces (Russian, American, British and French), fathered 400,000 children during their occupation of Germany. These children suffered ostracism all their life for being born illegitimate and that too from a relationship with the "enemy." Researchers conclude that the Soviet Russia's Red Army Soldiers committed no less than 2 million rapes.

66. William Tyndale was an English biblical scholar and linguist who became a leading figure in the Protestant Reformation in the years leading up to his execution. He is well known as a translator of the Bible into English, and was influenced by the works of prominent Protestant Reformers. On October 6, 1536 William Tyndale was burnt alive for translating the Bible into English.

67. Idi Amin Dada, Uganda's President (1971 -1979) was responsible for the killings of more than 500,000 people. His confession to cannibalism, ordering 4,000 disabled people to be thrown into the Nile to be torn apart by crocodiles, indulging in most atrocious savagery against those he felt enmity with, earned him the epithet : "The Butcher of Uganda "! His 6 wives and about 30 mistresses from different Ugandan ethnic groups gave him political strength. Such self conceited and arrogant was he that he gave himself the title : "His Excellency President for Life, Field Marshal Al Hadji Doctor Idi Amin, VC, DSO, MC, CBE, Lord of all the Beasts of the Earth and Fishes of the Sea, and Conqueror of the British Empire in Africa in General and Uganda in Particular". Forest Whitaker, who played this brute in the Hollywood historical drama, 'The last king of Scotland', in 2006, won him an Oscar in best performance. Amin who died in 2003 used to claim himself to be Scotland's uncrowned king, hence the film is thus named.

# Miscellany

*It Is Better To Have Useless Knowledge Than To Know Nothing.*
- Lucius Annaeus Seneca

1.  A dollar or a rupee, the Paper Currency  is a blend of 25 percent linen and 75 percent cotton mixed with a gelatin adhesive solution for strength and longevity. Its durability is tested through a host of challenges including turning in the washing machines, cement mixtures, and crumple tests. Infrared inks are used to hide secret features in the notes, which makes counterfeiting extremely difficult. Your notes can have traces of multiple things that stay on. During one of the researches in 2009 at UMass Dartmouth, it was discovered that about 90% of paper money in the US has cocaine residue on it. Imagine the number of substance users the bill passed hands through.

2.  In 1999, the founders of Google were willing to sell Google for $1 million to Excite, but were turned down. Twenty three years later, as on April 06, 2023, Google is worth $1341.15 billion.

3.  China is the biggest exporter of goods in the world, and its employment growth depends on its exports. On the other hand the US is the biggest importer of goods in the world. Therefore, by extension, China depends on the United States for its economic development.

4.  A dice's opposite sides always add up to seven.

5.  Las Vegas casinos do not have any clocks. Yup, for obvious reasons!

6.  The incredible economic growth of South Korea, referred to as the "Miracle on the Han River", happened largely because of the tax paradise the government created for chaebols (Korean conglomerates).

7.  Tablecloths were actually large napkins that the guests would use to wipe their hands and faces.

8.  Pope Benedict XVI was issued an organ donor card in 1970, but after he ascended to the papacy in 2005, the card became invalid. It's because the Pope's body doesn't belong to him anymore, instead to the universal Catholic Church, hence must be buried intact.

9.  In 1968, Sweden's Central Bank Sverige Riksbank instituted a prize in the memory of Alfred Nobel, called the Economic Sciences Prize. The first recipients of the prize were Ragnar Frisch and Jan Tinbergen in 1969, which was more than 60 years after the distribution of the first Nobel Prizes. The prize in Economic Sciences is announced along with the other Nobel Prize awardees and even presented during the Nobel Prize Award Ceremony, nonetheless it is technically Not a Nobel Prize. It is conferred by the Royal Swedish Academy of Sciences in Stockholm and not by the Nobel Foundation.

10. France has the fourth largest gold reserves of 2,436 tons, without having a single gold mine. The gold is believed to have been brought from Mali, its colony, which has 860 gold mines and produces 50 tons per year but has no gold reserves in its banks.

11. Mother's Day creation is primarily attributed to three American women - Ann Reeves Jarvis, her daughter Anna Jarvis and Julia Ward Howe. In the mid-1800s Mother Jarvis, who was an activist, organised "Mothers' Day Work Clubs" to educate mothers to fight unsanitary living conditions and high infant mortality rate. Julia Ward Howe was a famous poet and a reformer, who volunteered for the U.S. Sanitary Commission. Around 1870, she called for a "Mother's Day for Peace" and eradication of war. Anna Jarvis memorialised her mother's lifelong activism with a memorial service in 1907. The following year, on May 10, a Mother's Day service was held at the Methodist church to acknowledge all mothers. In 1914 it was declared a national holiday in the US. Disgusted with how the holiday had been commercialised, Jarvis spent the last years of her life lobbying against the holiday she had brought into being. A day, which was quite literally invented to be anti-commercialism has become exactly that.

12. The U.S. government earns money just because it has the monopolistic right to print dollars. The process is known as seigniorage, and it is the difference between the cost to produce a bill or a coin, and its actual value.

13. In December 2013, a lonely research scientist working at the United States Antarctic McMurdo Station turned to Tinder to find a date, 'just for fun'. He wasn't actually expecting to find anyone. But was astounded when he matched with a woman who was camping just a 45-minute helicopter ride away from him.

14. With 5 million vending machines Japan has the highest density in the world with one for every 24 people. While most sell various types of beverages, saké, noodles, ice creams, flowers others feature batteries, umbrellas and disposable cameras.

15. 'Drunk Baskets' were quite common in Istanbul in the 1960s. Bars hired porters to carry the drunk customers in them, particularly those who lived close by. These baskets were hung like a rucksack on the porter's shoulders and a drunk customer would squat in it to be transported to their homes. This helped in avoiding drunk brawls in the bars or the streets..

16. The country to have suffered the worst hyperinflation of all time is Hungary. In 1946, it faced a monthly inflation rate as high as 41.9 quadrillion percent and all the prices doubled every 15.3 hours.

17. After returning from his Moon Explorations, Neil Armstrong had to fill an immigration form to enter the US.

18. Nikola Tesla never married, for he felt sex disturbs a man at his work. However, he admitted to falling in love with a white dove, which he considered very special. He took care of her and even spent $2,000 on her when she felt sick.

19. Unlike their counterparts in the other parts of the world, the judges in England and Wales do not use gavels. It's used only "to alert parties in court to the entrance of the judge into the courtroom". Indian films never had a judge who didn't use a gavel and shout "Order-Order".

20. The motto on the first US coin read "Mind your business".

21. The Californian law deems it illegal to eat frogs that have died in frog-jumping contests.

22. Modern thong lingerie was introduced by Fiorello LaGuardia, the mayor of New York City.

23. Selling a haunted house without informing about it to the buyer can land you in legal soup in New York

24. At 74 litres per citizen every year, the Vatican City holds the world record for the most wine drunk per capita.

25. Since Denny's restaurants in the United States originally stayed open all day and night, their buildings were built without locks. In 1988, when they decided to close on Christmas Day, they could not lock the doors.

26. Unless you are a magician, you cannot legally have a rabbit as a pet in Queensland, Australia.

27. So what one thing is common to Google, Microsoft, HP and Apple?- They all started in the garage.

28. Iceland has an elf whisperer who inspects construction sites before anything gets built to make sure no elves are hanging around.

29. Although the Khewra Salt Mine in the Punjab region of Pakistan has the second largest salt deposits in the world, it produces 325,000 tons per annum. The mine comprises 19 stories, with 11 below the ground and stretches about 40 km into the mountain. Also known as Himalayan Pink Salt, it was a chance discovery, when Alexander's army horses were found licking the rocks in BCE 320. Before their downfall, the Mughals traded it with Central Asia. In the 19th century Hari Singh Nalwa, the Sikh Commander-in-Chief and the Raja of Jammu, Gulab Singh began sharing the management of the Salt Range, until the British took over and further developed the infrastructure. Khewra Salt Mine is a major tourist attraction earning a considerable revenue for Pakistan.

30. India has more honour roll students than America has students.

31. Swiss people can actually alter a law, all they need is 50,000 signatures of their fellow citizens.

32. A specific law mandates the Swiss parents to give gender appropriate names- a girl to have a female name and a boy, a male.

33. The University of Victoria in Canada once taught a course called "The Science of Batman."

34. In Israel, all citizens who are 18 years of age or older on election day are automatically registered to vote. In Sweden, eligible voters are automatically registered when they turn in their tax registration rolls.

35. The national anthems of Spain, Kosovo, Bosnia and Herzegovina, and San Marino have no words. Spain's national anthem: La Marcha Granadera (March of the Grenadiers), had lyrics in the past, but they are no longer used now.

36. "Operation Babylift" was one of the most astounding rescue operations in American history. A whopping 3,300 War orphaned infants and babies were rescued in just three weeks between April 3 and April 26, 1975, as the US forces were pulled out towards the end of the Vietnam War. Some 30 flights brought these orphans to settle them in safe homes across America and other countries.

37. Rabbit Hash, a tiny town of fewer than 500 people in Kentucky, has never had a human mayor. The elections take place along with the Presidential elections, now due in 2024. The town elects a canine one to the office, to represent their community, a practice that started in 1998. People from around the world can cast online votes at the fee of $1 per vote. The present mayor is Wilbur, a French bulldog, who managed to rack up more than 13,000 ballots in his favour. An amount of $22,985 was raised in the elections, which would go in welfare and maintenance work of the town. Wilbur's duties as a mayor include getting clicked with people, enjoying bones and sitting on the front porch of the general store.

38. The Pentagon has its own private island off New York.

39. Facebook had originally planned to have an 'Awesome' button, somewhere that one became the 'Like' button.

40. T-shirts were originally marketed to the unmarried men who didn't know how to sew buttons back on collared shirts.

41. The University of Pennsylvania has produced 25 billionaires, the most of any college in the world.

42. Istanbul has a vending machine that releases food and water for the city's stray dogs in exchange for recycled plastic bottles.

43. A law in Alderson, West Virginia, USA, says that "No lions shall be allowed to run wild on the streets"!

44. In Singapore, elderly pedestrians can tap their Identity Card to have more time at the pedestrian crossing.

45. Colombian police arrested Lorenzo, a parrot after it was found that he had warned the drug cartels about the police being nearby.

46. It is mandatory for the owners of monkeys in Indonesia to have an identity card with the photograph of the monkey.

47. The first online transaction ever was Stanford students buying Marijuana from MIT students.

48. In Switzerland, if you fail your driving licence test three times, you will be expected to visit a Psychologist to explain why you couldn't get through.

49. There are "retirement homes" for senior dogs in Japan so that they can receive adequate love and care during their final years.

50. A year after Steve Jobs resigned as the Chairman, the company decided to see how strong was their fan base and if their fresh launches would be taken in the same zeal as their previous Apple products. So in 1986, the tech giant launched 'The Apple Collection', a line of Apple brand -clothing, accessories, and lifestyle items. They described their clothing line as 'Train wreck', a bad idea probably, the response was lukewarm and thus had to be discontinued.

51. In the 1920s, women in several US cities organised Anti-Flirt Clubs to combat catcalling.

52. Fort Knox is home to the bigger half of the US gold reserves, and is often referred to as the world's most heavily guarded place. To gain access, one needs to know several combinations, whereas each staff member knows just one of them.

53. A year after opening Dominoes in 1961, one of the co-founders James Monaghan traded half of his shares for a second hand VW Beetle. Fast forward to thirty eight years, the other co-founder sells his shares - he does it for $1 billion.

54. In 1922 Mechanical Engineer Elis F. Stenman built a house including its furniture entirely out of 100,000 newspapers using homemade glue and apple peels. The structure still stands today in Rockport, Massachusetts and is a major tourist attraction.

*(The Paper House is run as a museum by members of the Stenman family. Image: Atlas Obscura)*

55. A post WWII study found that an alarming 37 percent of all armour unit casualties occurred when the crew member was outside of the vehicle. One among other reasons that got the soldier out of his confines was to brew tea by the roadside. Thereupon the tanks that were developed in the UK were equipped with a boiling-cooking apparatus, nominally designed for tea.

56. The people in the town of Churchill in the Canadian province of Manitoba, do not lock the doors of either their cars or their house because of polar bear attacks. Since Churchill is located in the core region of Polar Bear Alley, the polar bears walk by freely to the Hudson Bay.

57. Canadians say "sorry" so much that the government passed the Apology Act in 2009, declaring that an apology can't be used as evidence of admission of guilt.

58. San Michele Island in Venice acts purely as a cemetery to this day.

59. Cormac McCarthy used the same typewriter for more than 50 years. When it broke in 2009, its auction fetched him $250,000.

60. Stray dogs In Russia can use the metro. They can be seen hopping on and off the trains. Most of them are friends with security personnel and have learnt the stops through the tannoy announcements. Besides they control the rat population, just like the cats at the Hermitage Museum do.

61. Japan's Aokigahara forest is known as 'the perfect place to die'. It has the unfortunate distinction of being the world's second most popular place to commit suicide. The first is the Golden Gate Bridge in the US.

62. An inmate on death row in Texas requested a ridiculous meal costing hundreds of dollars. He then refused to eat saying "he wasn't hungry". After this, the tradition of allowing inmates to request their final meal was stopped.

63. Most people assume English to be the official language of the United States, which is untrue. It may be an official language of some states but the federal government does not have any official declaration on the language- English or any other.

64. The translation of Hell in the modern Bible, refers to an actual place outside Jerusalem, called "Gehenna", where it is believed they used to burn garbage and thus a fire was always burning there. Also, bodies of those deemed to have died in sin without hope of salvation (such as people who committed suicide) were thrown there to be destroyed.

65. Once a group of thieves posed as mannequins in a department store in England as it closed down for the night, then grabbed £10,000 in merchandise.

66. If someone commits suicide by jumping in front of a train in Japan, the family of the deceased will be slapped with a fine for causing damages to the Railway property.

67. In a strange coincidence, Robert Todd Lincoln, Abraham Lincoln's son, was in close proximity to three out of four presidential assassinations in the United States.

68. April 18, 1930, was such a slow news day that at 6:30 PM, the BBC's radio announcer said, "There is no news." ( Probably in those days they didn't know how to create one!)

69. The Federal Reserve Building in New York was built in the 1920s. Its gold vault rests on Manhattan's bedrock, 80 feet below street level and 50 feet below sea level. The vault contains the largest known monetary-gold reserve in the world.

70. Russian cosmonaut Yuri Gagarin, the first man in space, stroked Queen Elizabeth's leg above the knee during a state breakfast at Buckingham Palace in 1961. According to reports, she managed to keep a smile on her face as she sipped her coffee. During an interview, Gagarin explained that "he'd touched her leg in order to make sure she was real and not just an animated doll."

71. Daffodils are used as currency for King Charles, he receives one daffodil per year as rent for his lands on the Island of Scilly and off the coast of Cornwall.

72. 'Michelin Star' is a highly coveted global restaurant rating system. Although India has some of the best places in the world for food, so far no Indian restaurant has received it. Interestingly, however some Indian chefs do have the Michelin Star for their restaurants abroad: Vineet Bhatia- Zaika (London), Alfred Prasad- Tamarind (London), Vikas Khanna- Junoon (New York), Gaggan Anand- Gaggan ( Bangkok), Manjunath Mural- The song of India (Singapore), Atul Kochhar- Tamarind & Benares (London).

73. Located in New Delhi, Rashtrapati Bhawan, the official residence of the President of India is the world's largest presidential house. When initially constructed in 1929, it was known as the Viceroy's House, which was rechristened as Rashtrapati Bhawan post independence under the first President Dr. Rajendra Prasad. The H shaped building covers an area of 5 acres on a 330 acre estate. The majestic complex houses a total of 340 rooms spread over four floors, 2.5 kilometres of corridors and 190 acres of garden area.

74. Japan has the shortest national anthem in the world. It has only four lines. The title "KimiGaYo" is usually translated as "His Imperial Majesty's Reign.

75. Santa Cruz del Islote in the Archipelago of San Bernardo off the coast of Colombia is just two acres in all, but about five hundred people live on it, making it the most densely populated island in the world. Imagine so many people living on two soccer fields, that's how small it is.

76. Abraham Lincoln was a licensed bartender before becoming the President. He even partly owned 'Berry and Lincoln', a store in Illinois, which sold a variety of items that included liquor, bacon, firearms, and honey.

77. The British royal family isn't allowed to play Monopoly! The reason - it gets too competitive

78. In Iraq, booksellers just leave books outside at night unattended because "the reader does not steal and the thief does not read.

79. When Australia was being colonised, initially it had no formal police force. Although the Marines of the Royal Navy assumed the responsibility in 1788, the provisional police force proved to be insufficient. Soon a local self governing body 'Night Watch' was created. Australia having more convict residents than non criminal ones at that time, the governor there formed the law enforcement agency with twelve most well behaved convicts. Historical records indicate that the Night Watch and its extensions throughout the country, was a successful experiment at controlling and reducing crime.

80. Twitter's home button is a birdhouse. You are an egg when you join it. The logo is a bird, named after Larry T Bird, the NBA legend who used to play for Twitter co-founder Biz Stone's home-state team- the Boston Celtics. Interestingly even though he is the inspiration behind, the Basketeer doesn't have a Twitter account of his own. (Not so far, at least!)

81. The Bible was written by over 40 authors over a period of 1500 years.

82. Concerned with the demographic crisis- declining birth rate, an unequal proportion of women to men, and an alarming short lifespan of men, the government of Russia, in 2006 instituted September 12th, as the Day of Conception aka Procreation Day, and couples who then have a child on June 12th are rewarded by the regional government, with cash prizes and other such incentives.

83. A 72-page notebook, the Codex Leicester, written between 1506 and 1510 by Leonardo da Vinci, was bought by Bill Gates at Christie's on 11 November 1994 for a humongous $3.8 million. Vinci's manuscript is a collection of his scientific writings containing sketches, diagrams and illustrations of the link between art and science. Gates got its pages scanned into digital image files. Of which some were made into screensaver and wallpaper files on a CD-ROM as part of a Microsoft Plus. The physical pages of the book have been individually mounted in glass panes, which are exhibited around the world every year.

84. Shopping online isn't without risks, is what the first ever item sold on eBay tells. In 1995 Mark Fraser ordered a laser pointer for $14.83 and he received a damaged piece, apparently fully aware of what he was going to get, from Pierre Omidyar, eBay's founder.

85. Although Denmark might seem like a tiny country, the Kingdom of Denmark, which includes Denmark, Greenland and the Faroe Islands, has a territory of 2,210,579 square km, making it the second largest in Europe after Russia.

86. Africa couldn't develop as it should have due to adverse economic conditions such as the free- market policies imposed on the continent by the developed countries via the so-called Structural Adjustment Programs of the World Bank and the IMF.

87. Holland is actually just the name of one of the provinces in The Netherlands, not the name of the whole country.

88. Blaine High School in Minnesota won hearts when they published the pictures of 2 'four-legged' staff members in their Yearbook's Faculty pages. These two special members are Dakota, a certified therapy dog, and Caramel, a service dog, who work with their educator owners at the high school. While Vicky Camacho, Dakota's owner is a para educator in the special education department, Rebecca Thomas, who owns service dog Caramel, teaches American Sign Language. The dogs are immensely popular with the staff and students alike.

89. Besides being a black belt in judo, the Russian President Vladimir Pitin can speak fluent Russian, German and English- all these he had learnt when he served in the KGB as an intelligence officer. While studying in Moscow, he used the pseudonym Platov.

90. Ethiopia follows a 13 month calendar, which is similar to the Julian calendar. The western world used to follow the Julian colander before the introduction of the Gregorian calendar. In that sense, the country is almost 8 years behind the Western calendar. The most interesting differences are the yearly holidays - unlike the rest of the world, Ethiopia celebrates New Years on September 11th and Christmas on January 7th.

91. The legal status where a French couple lives together, and even may have children without marrying each other, is officially called the period of Concubinage. According to Cambridge Dictionary, a concubine is a woman who, in some societies, lives and has sex with a man she is not married to, and has a lower social rank than his wife or wives.

92. US President Ronald Reagan was a dedicated lifeguard in his youth and saved 78 people from drowning. The last one was a 7 year old girl, who he rescued when he was the governor of California. As a lifeguard at Lowell Park in Dixon, once he retrieved a set of false teeth of an elderly swimmer. The gratified man gave young Reagan $10 for his efforts. In an interview Reagan reminiscently mentioned, "That was the first time I was ever paid for doing anything".

93. Liechtenstein, world's sixth smallest nation and a microstate principality, has no military. Due to financial issues, it had abolished the Army soon after the Austro-Prussian War in 1866. Its National Police, which has 125 employees, maintains both internal law and order as well as a paramilitary force. The country has one of the world's lowest crime rates. It has just one prison which holds only a few inmates, and those with sentences over two years are transferred to Austrian jurisdiction. It maintains a trilateral treaty with Austria and Switzerland. Once known as a billionaire tax haven, the principality of Liechtenstein enjoys one of the highest GDP per person in the world. With granting voting rights to women on 1st July 1984, Liechtenstein became the last European country to do so.

94. According to the New York Post King Charles is very particular about certain things, one of them is his shoelaces. He has a special valet, whose job is to iron the shoelaces of every pair of shoes he owns. When travelling, his own toilet seat and Kleenex Velvet toilet paper travel with him.

95. In 2011 the Saudi Arabian government detained an Israeli vulture, a gryphon, alleging animal espionage. The GPS tag it wore belonged to the University of Tel Aviv, which was studying the movement patterns of this endangered species. A similar detention was done by Iran in 2007, when they detained 14 squirrels accused of spying. Allegedly, the squirrels were equipped with some sort of radio device attached to their bodies for eavesdropping.

96. Established in 1976, the Alaska Permanent Fund Corporation is a state owned organization which pays each Alaskan a guaranteed income-dividends out of oil revenues. It was designed to be an investment where at least 25% of the oil money would be put for future generations, who may not have oil as a resource.

97. Juliane Koepcke, a German-Peruvian mammalogist specialising in bats, was seventeen in 1971, when her aeroplane was struck by lightning. She was the sole survivor of the 98 co-passengers, including her mother. She got sucked out of the plane and while still strapped to her seat, she hurtled uncontrollably towards the earth, 3,000 metres below her, at a speed of 45 metres per second. The training given by her zoologist-scientist parents helped her survive 11 days in the Amazon Jungles. Her horrific ordeal there included: bracing heavy rains, swimming through a river-stream for days with a broken collarbone, an eye injury, concussion, suffering severe insect bites and an infestation of maggots in her wounded arm, all this before she got rescued by local fishermen.( An unbelievably strong person!)

98. A Swiss law allows Euthanasia. Anyone seeking death must have a genuine reason to end their life. They can demand an assisted voluntary death. A doctor can assist only until a drug needs to be provided, it has to be consumed by the person himself.

99. Queen Elizabeth II apparently used her handbag to send secret signals to her staff. For instance when she needed help to get out of a conversation with someone or she needed something urgently, it would come 'handy'.

100. Principality of Monaco has the world's highest GDP and the lowest poverty rate. It has the highest number of millionaires and billionaires per capita in the world. Practically every third person who lives in Monaco is a millionaire.

101. The US Library of Congress saved every single public tweet sent out since Twitter's inception in 2006, which is about half a billion tweets a day. In 2017, the Congress decided to "preserve" tweets only "on a selective basis". The reasons put forth were a tremendous rise in the number of Twitter users, increase of character limit from 140 to 280 and the tweets no longer limited to mere texts. Since the library receives only text and not images, videos or linked content, it began to face difficulties in archiving them, hence the restricted chronicling. The Library of Congress, which was created on April 24, 1800, serves as the unofficial library of the United States, as well as Congress' official research centre.

102. The cats at the Hermitage Museum in St. Petersburg, Russia are valued as the guardians of the museum. It's they who keep the rodents away from destroying the invaluable pieces of art. The museum has a "Press Secretary to the Cats". The entire staff including the cats are paid as employees and not just the human staff but the cats too have their own personal passports with their photos.

103. Pastel colours in baby clothing were introduced in the mid-19th century. Although both boys and girls wore a wide array of pastels, it was sometime at the beginning of the 20th century, kids' stores began with "sex-appropriate" colours- Pink for boys and Blue for girls. Pink was believed to be "a more decided and stronger colour, more suitable for the boy, while blue, which is more delicate and dainty, is prettier for the girl." By the 1940s, the baby boomers had swapped the colours to what we see today. However, owing to the Women's Liberation Movement in the 60s and 70s this stereotypical gender-specific colours took a dip. By the 1980s colour codes came back in fashion and are going to stay, because of commercial successes- the Blue for boys and Pink for girls is no more restricted to clothing alone, it's in everything a child uses and even in adult men and women products, the colour code has made inroads.

104. Since 2015, the Swedish blood donors not only get a "Thank You" texted to them but are even notified when their 'blood' is being transfused into someone else.

105. The Ig Nobel Prize, instituted in 1991 by Marc Abrahams, are satiric prizes awarded annually since its inception. The word 'Ig Nobel' (not Noble), is a play on the word Noble. It celebrates ten frivolous achievements in scientific research, with an aim to "honour achievements that first make people laugh, and then make them think..", for discoveries "that cannot, or should not, be reproduced". The categories that IgNobel prizes cover are almost similar to that of Nobel, namely Peace, Literature, Physics, Chemistry, and Physiology or Medicine. In addition it awards Public Health, Engineering, Biology, and Interdisciplinary Research as well.

106. With negative decibels of '-9.4 dBA', the anechoic chamber at Orfield Laboratories in Minnesota is the quietest place in the world. So quiet, that "you become the sound" - your heart beats, lungs and stomach sounds can be heard loudly. According to the lab founder Steven Orfield, the longest time, a person sat inside the chamber was 45 minutes, so unbearable is the soundless sound, it literally disorients you. The chamber is meant for various purposes- from companies testing the sound intensity of their products to psychological experiments to NASA sending their astronauts to help them adapt to the silence of space to psychological experiments and many more.

107. In 2005, the Second place in the Powerball lottery was won by as many as 110 people. Interestingly all these winners had bought their tickets after reading their predictions in the Fortune Cookies. Had it even been 4-5 winners, it would still have been normal but this was bizarre. So an investigation was conducted to see if there was some kind of foul play, none was found- it all came clean.

108. With just 82 soldiers, Monaco's army is the smallest in the world. Its military orchestra, however, has 85 musicians. In its history Monaco's army has been put on alert only once. It was in 1962, when the French President threatened to cut off Monaco's electricity and water if Prince Rainier III did not impose an income tax on Monaco's residents.

109. Paro International Airport, the only international airport of Bhutan, is among the world's most dangerous airports. Surrounded by as high as 18,000 ft Himalayan peaks and a very narrow runaway which is only 7,431ft long and is visible only moments before landing, the pilots take off and land manually only by daylight. There are just 8 pilots qualified to fly from this airport.

110. Liechtenstein, a microstate principality, is the sixth smallest nation in the world. Due to financial issues, it had to abolish the Army soon after the Austro-Prussian War in 1866. It has a total of 125 employees who manage both - the Internal Law & Order and Paramilitary Force. The country has one of the world's lowest crime rates. It has just one prison which holds only a few inmates, and those with sentences over two years are transferred to Austrian jurisdiction. It maintains a trilateral treaty with Austria and Switzerland. Once known as a billionaire's tax haven, the principality of Liechtenstein enjoys one of the highest GDP per person in the world. It was the only European nation which had not granted voting rights to its women and which it did on 1st July 1984.

# Acknowledgment

The author is grateful to the following magazines, newspapers, books, websites, journals, encyclopaedias, writers and museums from where the pieces of factual information were sourced.


1. Amusing Planet
2. Australian Geographic
3. bbc.com
4. BG Badminton
5. Britannica
6. Bullenwächter/Deutsches Apothekenmuseum Heidelberg
7. cnet.com
8. Flickr/"Victorian Photographic Portraits of People"
9. face2faceafrica.com
10. fifa.com
11. George Cruikshank
12. Getty Images
13. guinnessworldrecords.com
14. historicalphotos.com
15. History Channel
16. History Today
17. Independent Record
18. Lewis Hine
19. Literary Hub
20. Paul Dominique
21. pbs.org
22. Philippoteaux
23. Pinterest
24. Punch Magazine
25. Merriam-Webster.com
26. Metropolitan Museum of Art
27. nasa.gov
28. natgeokids.com
29. National Geographic
30. Natural History Museum
31. nature.com
32. NewScientist
33. nibblepop.com
34. npr.org
35. Reddit
36. Royal Museum Greenwich
37. Science World
38. Scoopwhoop.com
39. Smithsonian Magazine
40. SSPL
41. Swarajya Magazine
42. The Economic Times
43. The Indian Express
44. The New York Times
45. Thomas Rowlandson
46. Time
47. Victoria and Albert Museum
48. Washington Post
49. Wellcome Library
50. Wikimedia commons
51. Wikipedia
52. WorldAtlas
53. worldhistory.org
54. www.chinahighlights.com
55. visitcalifornia.com